CONTENTS

ACKNOWLEDGMENTS

Without the assistance of the following people, this book might not have been written. Or if it had been written, it might not have been published. Or if it had been written and published, it almost certainly wouldn't have been as coherent. So thanks to: my editor, Maureen O'Neal; and my agent, Liza Dawson. Rebecca Cohen of Vanguard and Steve Murphy of Morningstar helped with some facts.

The following is a list of people who contributed nothing whatsoever to this book. They're acknowledged here (in no particular order) because they were nice to me at one time or another, and I figure immortalizing them here is a cheap way to say thanks. Many of them are also the kind of people to whom this book is dedicated. Plus, who knows? Maybe they'll buy a copy simply to win drinks by betting friends that their names are in the Library of Congress. If you've been nice to me and I didn't mention you, cut me some slack—the '70s were a rough decade. Catch you next time.

James Withers, John and Leslie Guerin, Andrew Greene, Roy

Brown, Anne Perry, Fred and Jayne Shaffer, Manuel Gadea, Chris Tindall, Martin Fleischhauer, Rob and Cheryl Coggins, Frauke and Olaf Haus, Monty Gary, Harold Wilke and Marilyn, Fabio and Kita, Chuck and Stephanie, Ann Alexander, Sue Davis, Angela Puckett, Sharon Barnes, Lee Karsh, Ron and Cheryl, Brad Davis, Jessica and Jamie, Emma Barnes, Lois and Dee Arnold, Corbett and Lucy Clark, Bob Stoner, Greg Wager, Christina Spillane, Paula and Rob Wethy, Joe and Christina Sabo, Mary Blair, Tracy Cohen, Helen Barnes, Alec Plosky, Wendy Hutsko, Allan and Jan, Deanna and Kim Onisko, Jeff and Gretchen, Frank and Dolly, Scott and Sabine, David Lotz, Mike Gianakas, Craig and Robin, Benny and Shira Levy, Dave and Terri, Bruce and Tonya, David and Kathy, Sandy Blevins, Wolfgang and Jennifer, Ed Messick, Frank and Anna, Ross and Marcie Simmons, Petey Mazara, Jan and Sally, Jean Landry, David and Sarah, John and Tracy, Karen Turner and son Jason, Jeff and Sonya, Joe and Shelly, Ralph and Rosie, Michael Leftwich, Robert Swain, Scott and Veronica, Shari Ford, Darlene Sanders, Marshall and Clara, Bill Sawyer, Jacques and Lise, Jeff and Danielle, Lucien Campolo, Marie Warfel, Mike Nunn, Rick and Katy, Bill and Marsha, Steffan, Albert and Cara, Adolpho and Paige, Little Alan, Big Alan, Pat and Sabrina, Max and Ali, Julian and Samantha, Luciana, Roberto, Carla, Janice Boyle, Steve and Julie Graham, Tom and Sandy, Michelle and Teresa, Bob and Gene, Norm and Betty Germani, Jeff and Heidi Glaza, Karen Emanuel and Jesse, Louise Mazara, Judy, Candace and Marty Bush, Daphne Lawson, Neal and Carrie, Kiki and Rick, Jennifer and Jose, Sara Forsgren, Fred Ertz, Ray Depa, and Marcy Richardson.

MONEY MADE SIMPLE

MONEY MADE SIMPLE

How to Flawlessly Control Your Finances in Minutes a Year

Stacy Johnson

BALLANTINE BOOKS
NEW YORK

This book is a guide to managing your money and achieving your financial goals. It is not a guarantee; all investment decisions have inherent risks. Internet addresses and links are subject to change.

A Ballantine Book
Published by The Random House Publishing Group

www.ballantinebooks.com

Library of Congress Catalog Control Number: 2003099658

ISBN 0-345-45565-7

Manufactured in the United States of America

Cover photo by Steve Lyons at Lyons Photography
Text design by Mary A. Wirth

First Edition: February 2004

2 4 6 8 9 7 5 3 1

This book is dedicated to people
who advance human evolution by
deliberately coloring outside the lines.
That especially includes my proofreader,
inspiration, comic relief, lover, and wife,
Gina Germani. As to the rest of you . . .
you know who you are.

MONEY MADE SIMPLE

INTRODUCTION

> The entire essence of America is the hope to first make money—then make money with money—then make lots of money with lots of money.
>
> —Paul Erdman

As a member of the media, I'm continually annoyed by words and phrases journalists often use. For example, consider the oft-used phrase "rushed to a local hospital," as in "the critically injured victims were rushed to a local hospital." Why is a reporter telling me that critically injured people were rushed to the hospital? Do ambulance drivers normally stop for coffee when transporting critically injured people? Do they sometimes go to nonlocal hospitals?

What about the word "expert"?

Turn on the news tonight, and odds are good you'll see some story with an on-camera quote from someone labeled on screen as an "expert" on this, that, or the other. For example, maybe you'll see a "terrorism expert." But what makes this person a terrorism expert? Did he write a book on the subject? Was he a terrorist for twenty years? Is he one now? Until we know more, the title alone doesn't make it so, whether it's on TV or not.

All this is leading up to why I get to write personal finance books for Ballantine. The reason, of course, is because I'm a money expert.

But since this isn't the evening news, I hereby present the credentials that allow me to make that claim.

I became a CPA in 1981. I've also earned licenses for real estate, life insurance, stocks, commodities, options principal, and securities supervisor. I also have a motorcycle license, a fishing license, and I have a marriage license around here somewhere.

In terms of experience, I spent three years as an auditor (I slept through most of them) followed by eleven years as a stockbroker. (To this day, I still feel the compelling need to call strangers at dinnertime and try to sell them something.) For about the last twelve years, I've been self-employed as a TV news guy. I host an ongoing consumer/personal finance news series called *Money Talks*, currently airing on about ninety stations nationwide. So far, I've written and produced close to two thousand money-related news stories.

I don't know if these credentials qualify me as an expert, but hopefully they're enough to give you some level of confidence in what I'm about to tell you, which is how to manage your financial life in little chunks of time—like during the commercial breaks of your favorite show—even with zero financial education or experience.

It's understandable that you'd want to dispatch your financial chores with the greatest possible speed, since dealing with dough is right up there with art films and C-SPAN on the adrenaline scale. But speed isn't necessarily the most important thing you're about to learn.

If you're like most people, you already spend very little time managing your money. I read a survey a couple of years ago that said the average American worker spends less than ten minutes a year thinking about how to invest his 401(k) assets. And be honest: How much time do you really spend every year thinking about your insurance policies, your overall investment mix, or your estate plan? Most of us are already fast at financial chores because we ignore them entirely. We're like deer in the headlights. We don't know what we should be doing, so we freeze, stand there, and hope like hell we're not about to get run over.

When I used to practice pitching with my dad in the backyard, he'd always say, "You've got to get good before you get fast." Great advice, Pop. Understanding what it is you're doing and why you're doing it is integral to doing it quickly. In fact, understanding what we're doing is what ultimately allows us to achieve speed. So what we're going to do together is first learn to throw strikes. Then we'll figure out how to throw them at ninety miles an hour.

This book will deliver what it promises: total money management skills in the fastest possible time, with the least possible effort, and with no advance knowledge required. Nonetheless, from this point forward, please don't believe catchy phrases that promise immediate gratification, because they're probably just eyewash designed to sell something. Statements like "Wealth Without Risk!" or "Lose 30 Pounds in 30 Days!" or "Create a New Credit History!" are nearly always more sizzle than steak. In fact, here's my first piece of advice: Don't ever believe anything that ends with an exclamation point! And the more explanation points you see, the less you should believe it!!!

We're all brainwashed from cradle to grave with the idea that managing money requires professional expertise, great care, monster knowledge, continual vigilance, and tons of time. This isn't true, nor has it ever been. In fact, I'm going to be laying out a nearly diametrically opposed hypothesis: that paying too much attention to things like investing is often detrimental to your financial health. But wait! If managing money were really simple, the library wouldn't be full of phone-book-sized volumes about it, the yellow pages wouldn't be full of financial advisers, and there wouldn't be cable channels, radio stations, and magazines that devote 100 percent of their time to it.

It would certainly be logical to assume that the mere presence of all these institutions is solid evidence of their need to exist. But consider another possibility. That some institutions exist simply because they line people's pockets. Stockbrokerage firms. Banks. *Money Magazine*. CNBC. A legion of financial authors. In fact, nobody would benefit financially if managing money were quick and easy. Except you, that is. And maybe that's why the myth that money management is complex and time-consuming has been kept alive.

If you want to hop in the car and drive to the store, what do you do? You open your car door, stick in the key, crank up the car, and off you go. But what if I told you that before you could drive your car, you had to know everything about cars—everything from the fundamentals of the internal combustion engine to every make and model ever manufactured. You needed to be able to name every part of your car, understand exactly what part it played in the mix, and be able to fix anything that could possibly go wrong. Think you'd still drive? Probably not . . . too much hassle. But since you'd still need to get around, what would you do? If you could afford one, you'd hire a chauffer to take you. Someone who was certified to drive. Someone who had passed an exam proving that, at least at the moment he took the test, he knew every single thing there was to know about cars. And since very few of us have the time to devote to knowing something in such intricate detail, there would be quite a demand for chauffeurs. (Actually, they'd almost certainly be labeled with something conveying far more status than "chauffeur" . . . probably "transportation consultant" or "automotive adviser.") There would be an entire industry centered on providing people who know everything to people who don't. And this industry would make a ton of money, because we can't make the most of our lives without figuring a way to get from A to B.

Of course, this is an absurd scenario. Because while we are required to demonstrate basic proficiency in operating cars in order to get a driver's license, we're certainly not required to know how to fix them, or name every make and model. This kind of information isn't necessary to get us from A to B, so we don't have to know it. If we were required to know everything about cars in order to drive one, we probably wouldn't be buying them. Which would really bum out those who make money selling them. People selling cars want the experience of driving to be easy. They want everyone to qualify. Because the easier it is, the more cars they sell. They're not in the business of selling information; they're in the business of selling steel.

The financial services industry, on the other hand, isn't in the business of selling steel. It's in the business of selling information. And if you need only minimal information to get from A to B in your financial life, it doesn't have anything to sell.

Does the mere existence of an institution really prove it's necessary?

About 150 years ago, a virtual blink of an eye historically speaking, it was common knowledge in many parts of the world that if your skin happened to be any shade of brown, then your primary value was as a beast of burden. I'm talking about the institution called slavery.

Growing stuff used to require a lot of manual labor. Which was okay if you had twenty acres and a hardy family, but a big bummer if you had twenty thousand acres and family members who liked to keep their fingernails clean. And then, as now, the best price to pay for labor is nothing. So rich guys got together and came up with a simple concept. Decide that people with brown skin are animals. Develop logical arguments why this is so, and develop an institution around these arguments. Now you're set to find people with brown skin, kidnap them, and force them to work for you without pay, all with the approval and protection of the government. Of course, slavery goes back thousands of years, but whether you're talking about Egyptian pharaohs or Virginia planters, the bottom line is still greed. In the case of slavery, the desire for free labor outweighed what should have been common sense. Someone, normally someone rich, benefits. . . . This is how lies are born and institutionalized. And while institutions like this one may look completely absurd in the rearview mirror, slavery was regarded by many to be perfectly logical and respectable in its day.

So if the idea of effectively managing your money all by yourself in practically no time seems to fly in the face of modern common knowledge, remember that a book published in 1830 called *Brown Skinned People Are Equal* might have sounded silly, too. But that doesn't make either idea less true.

Both these theories—racial superiority and the idea that managing money is complicated—may have been fostered and maintained at least partially because they put money in people's pockets. We know who benefited from slavery: a tiny but influential portion of the population. (Most people back then had twenty acres, not twenty thousand, and very few people, percentage-wise, owned slaves.) But who benefits by keeping the complexity-of-money myth alive?

There are hundreds of companies that make billions of dollars providing financial advice to people like you. It's certainly in the best interest of these companies for you to believe that managing money is complicated. And these companies keep you believing by using the same tactics slave owners did. They say it, they develop logical arguments why it's so, they promote their arguments using every means available, and they use influence with people in Washington to keep the status quo. Next thing you know, it's common knowledge. And because entire industries are now in place in support of this common knowledge, it behooves all these people not to rock the boat.

And by the way, since I'm also selling financial advice, the advisory industry includes people like me: people who do television news stories about managing money and people who write books about managing money. While researching this book, I've had the opportunity to review the books of lots of other authors. And almost without fail, these books simply restate definitions and strategies that have already been written down. In other words, the most common formula for writing a personal finance book (and I suspect many other categories of nonfiction) is apparently to collect a bunch of other people's books and reword what's there. Personal finance books can appear impressively long since there are so many terms and possible investments to define and discuss. And when the author du jour is finished rewording what's already been written, he's prepared to hit the lecture circuit, since he's now an "expert" on matters financial. Then he's positioned to write subsequent, even longer books.

While this may be a great way to make a living, it's not what I choose to do with my life. I've written one book on getting out of debt, and I know from the e-mail I've subsequently received that it's helped a lot of people do exactly that. (It's called *Life or Debt*, and if there's a God in heaven, it's still out there at your favorite bookstore, as well as www.lifeordebt.org.) I'm now writing one book on managing money, and I hope it, too, opens some eyes. Perhaps I'll update either or both from time to time, but my goal here is to say everything that needs to be said. Not by restating what other people have already written, or introducing every possible complex financial management concept. Just the opposite. My angle on this topic is to paint in broad strokes. To give you a foundation in logic that will prepare you to manage your money quickly and easily. If you need to find some intricate, detailed advice on some specific investment applicable to your 401(k), I'll tell you where to find it on the Internet, but I'm not going to waste your time or mine by explaining minutia just to increase my word count.

My theory, for what it's worth, is that like slavery, the days of highly paid financial advice are numbered. Because no lie lasts forever, no matter how many people benefit or how influential they are. No matter how many people tell you that dark brown people are inferior to peach-colored people, sooner or later you'll see with your own eyes that it ain't so. Likewise, no matter how many informed people tell you that money is complicated, and you need a hired gun to deal with it, sooner or later (sooner, since you're reading this book) you'll see that it ain't so.

Before you move into the whys and wherefores, I want to take a few minutes to give you another reason not to believe the money management lie. That reason is that many of the people who are making loads of money providing financial advice are much more interested in their bottom lines than yours. In other words, while these guys should be happy to accept your money in exchange for advice you don't really need, that's not good enough. They want to take your money and sometimes give you bad advice. Why? So they can make even more money.

1

A Tale of Two Pities

Finance is the art of passing currency from
hand to hand until it finally disappears.
—ROBERT W. SARNOFF

In this chapter, I'm going to pluck a few items from recent news, pretty much at random, that should serve to convince you that it's really not safe to trust anyone else to help you with your money, no matter how well known or trusted the names may be.

If you do nothing more than watch national news on TV, you may know that Wall Street has not been acting in your best interests for some time now. Recent examples? Two of the most respected names in the financial services industry: Merrill Lynch and Salomon Smith Barney. But before I begin, I want to make something clear. I'm not telling you this because these examples are the exception. I'm telling you this because these examples are the rule. Always have been, always will be.

Let's talk about Merrill Lynch first.

In terms of number of retail investment advisers, Merrill Lynch is one of the largest financial services firms in the world. And even when the stock market is lousy, it still makes a ton of money. According to its Web site, www.ml.com, Merrill's profits for a recent three-month period (a period when stocks stunk) were $693 million.[1] Its chairman, David Komansky, was paid $16 million in 2001 while the stock market fell 7 percent that year.[2] Of course, there's no law against making money. That's the backbone of capitalism. But let's consider how some of it was made.

To fully understand this story, you'll have to learn some basics of financial advisory firms like Merrill Lynch. These firms make money several different ways. One way is to collect commissions from little guys like you and me when we buy investments. We could go to places that charge a lot less in commissions to buy investments, but we're willing to pay extra to "full service" firms like Merrill Lynch because we believe that in exchange for paying them more than necessary, we'll get something we couldn't get at cheaper places: unbiased, expert advice. The process of exchanging our hard-earned money for their objective advice is part of the business known as "retail brokerage." But there's another completely different way financial advisory firms make money. They collect huge fees from big companies when these companies raise money by selling stocks and bonds to the public. This business is called "investment banking."

If you're a company that wants to raise money by selling stock to the public, a firm like Merrill is a great place to go. That's because it has so many investment advisers who will help the stock get sold. For example, say you've got a great idea for a new Web site: www.givemethedough.com. But as you put your idea on paper, it turns out that developing your new Web site will cost $50 million, and you've only got 150 bucks in the bank. Where will you find the other $49,999,850? One of the big investment banks that you find on Wall Street: places like Merrill Lynch, Goldman Sachs, et al. But since this is a hypothetical situation, let's use a hypothetical investment house: Dewey, Cheatem and Howe. You visit its investment banking division and explain your slight cash shortfall. If your idea seems reasonable, the folks there might just offer to take

[1] http://www.ml.com/about/press_release/10162002-1_3q_earnings_pr.htm, ending September 27, 2002.

[2] http://www.aflcio.org/cgi-bin/aflcio.pl?tkr=MER&pg=1.

your company public by selling stock. They help you issue five and a half million shares of stock and sell them for $10 each. (Notice that although you needed only $50 million, Dewey raised $55 million for you . . . that's because it's charging you $5 million for its assistance.)

But how will Dewey sell millions of shares of your stock to the public when nobody outside your immediate family knows you're alive? Simple. Its thousands of retail brokers—the advisers paid to give small investors objective advice—will do the selling. This they do by calling their many clients and advising them to buy your stock.

But there's still something missing. Retail investment advisers are sales experts, but they're rarely investment experts. They don't have nearly enough training to examine your business plan, projections, and market analysis and reach a conclusion as to the value of your stock. That's where a research analyst comes in. Even before the investment bankers are putting together the paperwork pertaining to your initial public offering, Dewey's analysts are studying your business plan and profit projections. If they like what they see, they advise the investment banking people to do the deal, then they write a research report that says your stock will go up and should be bought. In fact, because these reports can have lots of big words and numbers in them, the analysts will even make the process simple by boiling down their opinion into a one- or two-word rating. For example, they'll assign it a "buy" rating. Or hopefully even "aggressive buy." Then they'll send that report and that investment rating to all their retail brokers, who in turn wave it in front of their retail clients and thereby convince them that www.givemethedough.com is going to the moon.

In a perfect world, this is a great system because everybody wins. You raise $50 million, Dewey makes a $5 million investment banking fee, retail investment advisers earn commissions by selling stock in givemethedough.com, and small investors own a stock that goes to the moon, just like they were promised. But this isn't a perfect world. What happens if Dewey's analysts look at your business plan and decide that your idea is stupid and will never fly? If they put out a negative report on givemethedough.com, retail advisers won't recommend the stock, it won't get sold, you won't raise the money you need, and, most important, Dewey won't earn a $5 million investment banking fee. So it's obvious why there would be pressure for analysts, who are supposed to be totally truthful and objective, to help everyone out (except you, of course) by saying good things about bad ideas. And this pressure doesn't happen just the first time a company goes public. You'd think that once you've raised $50 million, you'd never need more, right? Wrong. A lot of companies find that their initial cost projections were low, or maybe they forgot they needed a heated swimming pool in the CEO's office. So there may come a time when givemethedough.com raises more money with what are called secondary stock offerings, or maybe by selling bonds. Since Dewey wants this business, too, its interests will be best served by keeping your investment rating favorable. After all, would you pay the company five million bucks for a secondary offering if it had your stock rated as a "sell"? Not likely.

It should be patently obvious from this simple explanation that any firm that cares about its customers—or its future, for that matter—should never allow an analyst to compromise his objectivity in favor of potential investment banking fees. Because if an analyst lies to small investors to earn the firm a fee, wouldn't that be a fraud? (Here's *Webster's* definition of "fraud": "intentional perversion of truth in order to induce another to part with something of value." This precisely describes the process of lying to small investors to fatten corporate coffers.) Just as important, while allowing your analysts to commit fraud might result in short-term gain in the form of investment banking fees, it will cause long-term pain because when the recommended stocks go into the toilet, investors won't trust your company anymore and you'll be toast. Therefore, if you were an executive focused on either your company or your customers, you'd have a system in place to deal with the possibility of this obvious potential problem. And most companies do. If, on the other hand, you were focused on short-term profits and didn't really give a damn whether your customers would ultimately lose money, you'd ignore these policies and allow this conflict of interest to fester, or even foster it by flat out paying your analysts to not say things that might hurt your investment banking business, and say other things that help it. You might, for example, give them bonuses based on the amount of investment banking business they helped bring to the firm.

In any case, if you were a top executive with one of these firms, since this possible conflict of interest is so obvious, the one thing you could never do is pretend that you didn't know it existed. Or, if you had policies in place to address this conflict of interest, pretend you didn't know they were being violated.

Now let's step out of the classroom and into the real world. Obviously, I invented "Dewey, Cheatem and Howe" and wrote the hypothetical above to make a point about potential pitfalls that are part and parcel of paid financial advice. When it comes to what happened at Merrill Lynch, I don't know anything more than you do, since my information comes from the same sources—newspaper and other press accounts, as well as Merrill's own statements and the State Attorney General's office. So let's take a look at what our credible sources tell us. In May 2002, Merrill Lynch agreed to make civil payments totaling $100 million to settle a complaint that some of its analysts hadn't been objective when recommending some stocks to retail investors. (Interestingly, however, none of this $100 million went to the retail investors. New York State took about half, and the rest will flow to the coffers of the other forty-nine states.[3]) The reason New York State is getting Merrill to write such a huge check is that it did an investigation and uncovered a bunch of e-mails written by various Merrill analysts suggesting that their objectivity had been compromised. To be more specific, the analysts wrote e-mails among themselves admitting that certain stocks were losers while maintaining "buy" ratings on them for small investors. Here's the press release from the New York State Attorney General's office concerning the settlement, issued April 8, 2002. I added the bold print, and the part in parentheses following the word **"NOTE."**

[3] http://www.oag.state.ny.us/press/2002/apr/apr08b_02.html.

Merrill Lynch Stock Rating System Found Biased by Undisclosed Conflicts of Interest

State Attorney General Eliot Spitzer today announced a court order requiring immediate reforms in investment counseling by one of the nation's oldest and largest securities firms.

The court action against Merrill Lynch was the result of an investigation by Spitzer that concluded that the firm's **supposedly independent and objective investment advice was tainted and biased by the desire to aid Merrill Lynch's investment banking business.**

Spitzer cites dramatic evidence that the firm's stock ratings were biased and distorted in an attempt to secure and maintain lucrative contracts for investment banking services. As a result, **the firm often disseminated misleading information that helped its corporate clients but harmed individual investors.**

"This was a shocking betrayal of trust by one of Wall Street's most trusted names," Spitzer said. "The case must be a catalyst for reform throughout the **entire industry.**"

Spitzer's office uncovered a major breakdown in the supposed separation between the banking and research divisions at Merrill Lynch. In fact, **analysts at Merrill Lynch helped recruit new investment banking clients and were paid to do so. The public, however, was led to believe that research analysts were independent,** and that the firm's rating system would assist them in making critical investment decisions.

As part of a quid pro quo between the firm and its investment banking clients, Merrill Lynch analysts **skewed stock ratings, giving favorable coverage to preferred clients, even when those stocks were dubious investments.**

This problem and other conflicts of interest are revealed by internal e-mail communications obtained during the investigation by the Attorney General's office.

These communications show analysts privately disparaging companies while publicly recommending their stocks. For example, one analyst made highly disparaging remarks about the management of an internet company and **called the company's stock "a piece of junk," yet gave the company, which was a major investment banking client, the firm's highest stock rating.**

The communications show analysts complaining about **pressure from Merrill Lynch's investment banking division.** For example, a senior analyst writes: **"the whole idea that we are independent of (the) banking (division) is a big lie."**

A senior manager stated: "We are off base in how we rate stocks and how much we bend over backwards to accommodate banking." But nothing was done to remedy this fundamental problem.

The communications show that the problems at Merrill Lynch went far beyond a single analyst or research unit. For example, the head of the equity division wrote to analysts: "We are once again surveying your contribution to investment banking . . . please provide complete details on your involvement . . . **paying particular attention to the degree your research played a role in originating. . . . <banking business.>"**

[**NOTE**: On November 2, 2000, Henry Blodget, Merrill's head of Internet research, responded to this request with a note that said that his group had participated in fifty-two investment banking transactions that netted Merrill Lynch $112 million in fees. Shortly thereafter, his pay package was dramatically increased. In 1999, he earned $3 million. In 2000, Merrill paid him $12 million.[4]]

And most importantly, the communications show how individual investors were harmed. A research analyst complained about giving a buy rating to a poor investment: **"I don't think it is the right thing to do. John and Mary Smith are losing their retirement because we don't want a client's CEO to be mad at us."**

The court order obtained by Spitzer requires Merrill Lynch to now make disclosures to investors about its relationship with investment banking clients and provide more context for its stock ratings.

Spitzer described the court order as a preliminary step designed to protect investors while the investigation continues. He said his office has issued subpoenas to other securities firms. The nearly year long investigation is being handled by the Attorney General's Investment Protection Bureau, under the direction of Assistant Attorney General Eric Dinallo.

There you have it. One of Wall Street's oldest, biggest, and most prestigious firms getting nailed for selling out its clients. But as they say on late-night TV commercials, "Wait! There's more!" Because what's nearly as enlightening is the way Merrill attempted to whitewash what it had done in its own press release regarding the same incident. Before you read this one, I'd like you to consider something. How in the world could any key executive in any finan-

[4] http://www.oag.state.ny.us/press/2002/apr/MerrillL.pdf, page 21.

cial services firm not have known about this potential conflict between analysts and the firm's investment banking business? I find it almost impossible to imagine. After all . . . I explained it conceptually to you in about five hundred words . . . how complex can it be? And if you noticed the fact that head Internet analyst Henry Blodget's pay went from $3 to $12 million, apparently based on helping close investment banking business, do you think that senior management didn't know anything? They were signing the paychecks. I think it's fair to assume they knew why there were so many zeros on them.

Okay, now here's what Merrill had to say in its press release.[5] This one was much longer, so I eliminated some of it. And because it had more spin than a gyroscope, I also bolded some stuff and added some notes. You can tell what's mine because it's in italics and brackets. (And by the way, in case you think I'm only presenting the parts that support my argument, I heartily encourage you to read the whole thing. Here's the link: http://www.ml.com/about/press_release/05212002-1_ag_agreement_pr.htm).

Merrill Lynch Announces Agreement with New York State Attorney General Sets New Industry Standard for Policies to Protect Independence and Integrity of Research

[Look at this headline! You'd think they just found the cure for cancer. This is like Charles Manson issuing a press release saying he'd reached an agreement with prosecutors to explore prison conditions.]

NEW YORK, May 21—Merrill Lynch today announced an agreement with the New York State Attorney General under which it will enact significant new policies to **further** insulate securities research analysts from any real or perceived undue influence from its investment banking division. *[Further insulate? According to the attorney general, in at least some cases it had less insulation than a plastic bag.]*

The agreement settles all aspects of the Attorney General's inquiry pertaining to Merrill Lynch and all present and former employees. The

[5] http://www.ml.com/about/press_release/05212002-1_ag_agreement_pr.htm.

inquiry centered on Merrill Lynch's Internet sector securities research from 1999 to 2001. *[The company is implying that this stuff affected only one small part of its business during a brief period of time. Was the problem deeper? We'll never know, because it paid $100 million to stop the pain.]*

The settlement represents neither evidence nor admission of wrongdoing or liability. *[It didn't do anything wrong? While it's hard to isolate one sentence as the most insulting to our intelligence, this one has my vote. It's obviously there as an attempt to avoid civil suits from small investors ... and I'll bet it doesn't work.]* It provides for Merrill Lynch to make a civil payment of $48 million to New York State, and an additional $52 million to settle the matter with all other states—with both payments contingent on acceptance of the agreement by all states.

"**Because our many employees work day after day to place our clients' interests first,** resolution of this matter is very important to us. Today's result will ultimately benefit all investors and the capital markets," said David H. Komansky, chairman and CEO, and Stan O'Neal, president and COO. *[Here we have two odd things. (1) If Merrill's employees had been placing their clients' interests first, this press release, as well as checks totaling $100 million, wouldn't have been written. (2) Komansky and O'Neal are apparently talking simultaneously and saying the exact same words. How'd they do that?]*

"**Our objective from the start has been to reinforce investor confidence in the way securities analysts conduct their research and make investment recommendations.** *[Your objective from the start of what? Kinda missed the mark, didn't you?]* The actions we are taking will ensure that analysts are compensated only for activities intended to benefit investors. **We believe this establishes a new industry standard** for independence and objectivity of research," they said. *[What Merrill is apparently saying here is that it wasn't the only one abusing investors. Absolutely true: It wasn't.]*

"**Merrill Lynch has always had policies and procedures in place to protect the integrity of our research analysts.** *[Actually, this is technically true. It looks like they just chose to ignore the policies and procedures.]* Our good faith negotiations with the Attorney General have resulted in further actions to strengthen the firewalls between research and investment banking, and also enhance disclosure of the multiple relationships that a company like Merrill Lynch has with clients who issue securities as well as those who invest in them," Messrs. Komansky and O'Neal said.

Among the changes Merrill Lynch will implement:

- A complete separation of the evaluation and determination of research analyst compensation from the investment banking business, to be achieved through a number of new policies. **Research analysts will**

be compensated for only those activities and services intended to benefit Merrill Lynch's investor clients. *[So apparently in the past, at least by implication, analysts were paid to do things not intended to benefit investors.]*

- Creation of a new Research Recommendations Committee (RRC) to review all initiations of and changes to stock ratings for objectivity, integrity and a rigorous analytical framework. The RRC will be composed of representatives of private client and institutional sales management, research management and research strategists, and headed by an individual who will be paid primarily based on the performance of research recommendations for investors.
- Appointment of a compliance monitor who, for a period of one year, will ensure compliance with the agreement. *[Cool. What happens after the year is up?]*
- **A new system to monitor electronic communications** between investment bankers and equity research analysts. *[In other words, let's make sure the attorney general doesn't see any more embarrassing e-mails!]*

As previously agreed with the Attorney General, Merrill Lynch equity research reports will contain added disclosure, including:

- **Whether Merrill Lynch has received or is entitled to receive from the covered company compensation** over the past 12 months from publicly announced equity underwriting and merger and acquisition transactions. *[In other words, until now you could've had monster conflicts of interest and not disclosed them?]*
- Specific disclosure on a percentage basis of the distribution of strong buy, buy, neutral and reduce/sell recommendations for stocks in a number of different categories.

Messrs. Komansky and O'Neal noted that the company was "pleased to put this matter behind us in a way that seriously addresses investor concerns. We believe strongly in the integrity of our research, which has served investors well for many decades. At the same time we have apologized for any unprofessional behavior.

"Looking ahead, we intend to vigorously implement these new policies and reassert our traditional position as a valued source of information for investors," they said. *[I'd love to have these guys come to a party sometime at my house and watch them talk simultaneously like this ... quite a trick!]*

Under terms of the settlement, Merrill Lynch also issued the following statement.

Merrill Lynch Statement

Merrill Lynch would like to take this opportunity, as part of the agreement reached with New York State Attorney General Eliot Spitzer and other states, to publicly apologize to our clients, shareholders and employees for the inappropriate communications brought to light by the New York State Attorney General's investigation. We sincerely regret that there were instances in which certain of our Internet sector research analysts expressed views that at certain points may have appeared inconsistent with Merrill Lynch's published recommendations. *[Appeared? The views didn't appear inconsistent ... they were inconsistent.]*

We view this situation as a very serious matter and have informed our research department personnel that **such communications, some of which violated internal policies, failed to meet the high standards that are our tradition and will not be tolerated.** *[Classic buck passing. Translation: It wasn't our fault! It was all those nasty analysts!]*

As a result we have taken steps to guard against such instances in the future. In addition, we are taking steps to **reinforce** the firewalls *[maybe "reinforce" isn't quite the right word here—seems like the existing structures weren't even flame retardant, let alone fireproof]* that separate our research department from investment banking. The agreement we have reached with the State Attorney General is designed to accomplish these objectives.

Through the adoption of new policies, intensified oversight, and strengthened enforcement of existing ones, we pledge to provide investors with research that sets a new industry standard for independence.

I could write an entire book on this one Merrill Lynch betrayal of public trust, but it's not our topic, and it's time to move on. If you like reading, however, here's the link to the New York State Attorney General's report that led up the $100 million apology: http://www.oag.state.ny.us/press/2002/apr/MerrillL.pdf.

And this really is interesting reading. In fact, it would be downright amusing if it weren't for the fact that so many innocent people were harmed.

Now let's see what else happened in 2002: Let's talk about Salomon Smith Barney, another big financial advisory firm like Merrill Lynch. It's owned by Citigroup, the huge international financial conglomerate that also owns Citibank and, until recently, Travelers

Insurance. In a recent three-month period, Citigroup earned a little shy of $4 billion.[6] Yes, you read correctly . . . that's what it earned in three months. The head of Citigroup is Sanford Weill, and he took home about $30 million in 2001.[7] So Sandy brings home major bacon at Citigroup, but he's not the only one. Take Jack Grubman, for example. Jack was an analyst with Salomon Smith Barney until he voluntarily resigned in August 2002. During the years preceding his resignation, rumor has it that he was making about $20 million a year.[8] And when he left, he got a nice sendoff: a check for $30 million. This should sound a bit odd since, unlike Sandy, Jack wasn't a big boss at Citigroup. He worked as an analyst for one of many Citigroup subsidiaries, Salomon Smith Barney. Keep in mind that a research analyst is basically a glorified accountant whose job is to pore over financial statements, otherwise scope things out, then write a report telling simple folks like you and me whether we should put some of our life savings into the company in question. Since he was getting paid about $10,000 an hour (assuming a forty-hour work week), and especially since he got another thirty mil when he left, he obviously must have been a really great analyst, right?

WorldCom was one of the companies that Jack Grubman thought you and I should buy. But on this one, as well as several other telecom stocks, he not only missed the boat, he missed the marina. From January 1999 to June 2002, WorldCom stock plummeted from $71 a share to less than $1. But it wasn't until June 2002, with the stock at 91 cents, that Jack Grubman finally lowered his rating on the stock to "underperform." I won't bother figuring out exactly how much cash people just like you and me lost had we been following this guy's advice, but it was enough to sink a battleship.

Of course, everyone's entitled to be stupid now and then, even guys who make ten grand an hour. And maybe that's all we have

[6] http://www.citigroup.com/citigroup/press/021015a.htm, period ending September 30, 2002.

[7] http://www.aflcio.org/cgi-bin/aflcio.pl?tkr=C&pg=1.

[8] http://www.thestreet.com/pf/markets/matthewgoldstein/10038108.html.

here. But consider that Salomon earned boatloads of investment banking revenue by participating in billions of dollars' worth of bond sales for WorldCom. Consider that in September 2002, the National Association of Securities Dealers fined Citigroup $5 million for "misleading stock research" arising from research treatment Grubman gave to another telecom company and investment banking client, Winstar.[9] Like WorldCom, Grubman recommended buying this stock all the way up until just a few weeks before it filed for bankruptcy. And between February 1999 and July 2001, Salomon helped Winstar raise more than $5.6 billion, and earned $24 million doing it. And lest you forget, raising money means selling securities. Securities that could have been, and probably were, largely bought by people like you and me and now are suitable only for lining the bottom of a birdcage.

In December 2002, Salomon Smith Barney was one of a group of Wall Street firms to reach a settlement with regulators over asserted conflicts of interest.[10] The total settlement was $1.4 billion, and Salomon's share was $300 million.

By the way, when you read about guys like Jack Grubman and Henry Blodget, you come away with the feeling that these guys are more victim than criminal. Their primary sin was working in a system that was perfectly willing to step on little people to line the pockets of big people. By most accounts that I've read, these guys are supersmart and probably deserved a lot of the recognition they once received. But there was a system, and it appears that the system compromised them by changing the rules and pressuring them to play along. For example, remember the memo that Blodget received, the one mentioned in the New York attorney general's press release? Here's the complete memo, lifted from the report:[11]

[9] http://www.forbes.com/newswire/2002/09/23/rtr728961.html.

[10] Like Merrill Lynch's settlement, as well as those of other firms you'll soon learn about, those settlements were reached without the firms admittting to wrongdoing. I only hope that if you or I were ever dragged before Eliot Spitzer, we'd have the same opportunity.

[11] http://www.oag.state.ny.us/press/2002/apr/MerrillL.pdf, page 20.

> DEEPAK RAJ, *then co-head of global equity research, to all equity analysts:*
>
> We are once again surveying your contributions to investment banking during the year. . . . Please provide complete details on your involvement in the transaction, paying particular attention to the degree that your research coverage played a role in origination, execution and follow-up. Please note, as well, your involvement in advisory work on mergers or acquisitions, especially where your coverage played a role in securing the assignment and your follow-up marketing to clients. Please indicate where your research coverage was pivotal in securing participation in high yield offering.

As head of the Internet research group, Henry Blodget was probably responsible for not only his bonus, which would be apparently based as much on being a good salesman as on being a good analyst, but also for the bonuses of the rest of his team. If so, you have to ask yourself what he was supposed to do. Withhold money from the people who worked for him? Risk not being a "team player"? In retrospect, yes. He should have done the right thing. But as a former cog in this wheel myself, albeit a much smaller one, I can understand the pressure Blodget was under. It's just too bad that the people who caused all this to happen, the people running the firm, will undoubtedly be able to distance themselves from the disgrace that Blodget is now enduring.

It's the bosses and the system that left Grubman and Blodget holding the bag. Grubman and Blodget will end up in the hall of shame, but Weill and Komansky's names will be conspicuous by their absence on the evening news.

Now that I've spanked two of Wall Street's biggest and most prestigious firms, let me add that Salomon Smith Barney and Merrill Lynch may be two firms that forgot small investors were paying the bills, but they certainly weren't the only ones. In December 2002, ten of the biggest firms on Wall Street reached a global settlement with the New York Stock Exchange (NYSE), the National Association of Securities Dealers (NASD), the Securities and Exchange Commission (SEC), the New York State Attorney

General (NYAD), and the North American Securities Administrators Association (NASAA). In this settlement, these firms agreed to pay a fine and establish restitution funds relating to charges that investment banking interests exerted an undue influence on securities recommendations. They also agreed to put up money to pay for independent research, and contribute to investor education. Here are the firms that took part in the settlement and the amounts each agreed to pay. These numbers are all expressed in millions.

Company	Penalty	To Establish Independent Research	To Provide Investment Education
Bear Stearns	50	25	5
Credit Suisse First Boston	150	50	None
Deutsche Bank	50	25	5
Goldman Sachs	50	50	10
J. P. Morgan Chase	50	25	5
Lehman Brothers	50	25	5
Merrill Lynch	100	75	25
Morgan Stanley	50	75	None
Salomon Smith Barney	300	75	25
UBS Warburg	50	25	5
Total	**900**	**450**	**85**

In the press release announcing the settlement, here's what NASAA president Chris Bruenn had to say: "This agreement represents the dawn of a new day on Wall Street. Our goal and the goal of this agreement are simple: investors, not investment banking fees, come first."[12]

So what does all this mean to you? If you think that a momentary lapse occurred and was immediately corrected by ever-vigilant regulators or corporate titans, think again. I don't know exactly how long the conflict addressed by this settlement has been around, but it's certainly existed since I became a securities sales-

[12] http://www.oag.state.ny.us/press/2002/dec/dec20b_02.html.

man, and that was twenty years ago. In fact, I wrote an article on it for the Money Talks Web site in 1998. This type of behavior is old hat, and despite what CEOs and attorneys general may say to the media about everything changing, trust me: Past is prologue. History would suggest that something very similar will happen again, and legions of small investors will again be left holding the bag. How do I know? Your library is full of books, many written by former employees of major Wall Street companies, about how financial services firms have buried small investors in more ways than you can count. Read *Serpent on the Rock*. It's about how Prudential burned investors in limited partnerships back in the 1980s. Read *Barbarians at the Gate*. It describes the shenanigans and egos that surrounded one of the biggest takeovers in corporate history: RJR Nabisco. Remember Ivan Boesky, Dennis Levine, Michael Milken, or Martin Siegel? They were notorious figures from the 1980s who abused securities laws for their own profits, leaving investors, and ultimately taxpayers, with the bill. You can read about them in *Den of Thieves*. There are lots of well-written books that describe the despicable treatment that small investors have received at the hands of Wall Street powerhouses for many, many years. In fact, I challenge you to find any profession where more former employees have left behind lucrative careers, throwing up their hands, shaking their heads, and writing books to warn an unsuspecting public. All disgruntled former employees? Maybe . . . but I wouldn't be betting my life savings on it.

It's my nature to be overly cynical, so perhaps I'm wrong and things will change from here on out. But I don't think so, and if you'll allow me to wax philosophic for a moment, I'll tell you why.

In places of power, like Washington and New York, you're likely to run into people who are arrogant, people who believe that the rules don't apply to them. To put it simply, they think they're better than you. And the higher up the power ladder you go, the more likely you'll find this kind of arrogance. When you're paid a lot of money and thousands of people hang on your every word, it's hard to avoid becoming arrogant. A guy who's getting paid $30 million every year is making as much as six hundred people getting paid

$75,000 each. Now, you may have never considered that, but let me assure you, he has. Can you really blame him for thinking he's more important than you? Money and power breed arrogance, and arrogance breeds environments where people screw up in major ways and end up writing apologies that don't apologize. That's why we have news stories about presidents who deny having sex with people they had sex with, CEOs overseeing questionable accounting, and brokerage firms hiring spin doctors to write press releases like the one you just read. And for that matter, people who think it's their divine right to own other people. This is just the way it is. Not in all cases, mind you. Certainly there are lots of people in the world who don the mantle of leadership and wear it well. But destructive arrogance happens often enough that you should certainly feel wary when it's time to trust people who make six hundred times more than you do.

But here's the good news. If you're feeling a bit queasy about trusting the advice you're paying for when it comes to managing your savings, that's okay. Because you don't need any of these people. They're only trying to convince you that you need them to keep the cash rolling in. You're about to learn everything you need to know to manage your savings all by yourself—and measure the amount of time it takes in minutes, not hours. Plus, you'll know why you're doing what you're doing, so you'll achieve extra comfort and confidence too. What a deal!

2

Understanding Investments, Once and for All

Money isn't everything—but it's a long way ahead of what comes next.

—EDMUND STOCKDALE

Why Do Investments Appear So Complicated?

There are about a million different investments out there to choose from, so the sheer number of them is certainly enough to make your eyes glaze over. And understanding these things requires learning an entirely new vocabulary, because when you're examining investments, it won't be long before you encounter vernacular specific to the investment world. You know, terms like "accretion," "moving average," "amortization," "average weighted maturity," and other words too numerous, and way too boring, to mention. But before your eyes glaze over at the thought of sifting through all this hoo-ha, realize that 99 percent of investments aren't really unique alternatives. They're merely the result of repackaging an existing investment, or otherwise adding a new twist to an old story. Why would anyone want to repackage or otherwise disguise an investment? One reason I already gave you . . . so you'll hire help. But another reason is more fundamental . . . it's done in the hope that a new, improved version of an old idea will spark new, improved sales of an old investment.

Go to the laundry aisle in the grocery store. You'll see dozens of boxes of different detergents, most of which will be labeled as either "New!" "Improved!" or the ever-popular, "New and Improved!!" But no matter what you call it, how you package it, or how many exclamation points you print on the box, when it's all said and done these boxes and bottles are filled with nothing more than soap, same as they've always been.

Investments are no different. At first blush it may appear that all these mutual funds, unit trusts, REITs, options, futures, partnerships, and what have you are unique, thus requiring encyclopedic knowledge to understand the technicalities. But more often than not what you're looking at is just an old investment in a new box. Once you know the fundamentals, you need only identify the bell, whistle, or exclamation point that differentiates one from another.

What Are They Really All About?

If you've got a chart showing your family tree, you'll notice at the top there are only two people. One man, one woman: the nucleus of your family. Beneath them are layers of descendants portrayed in ever-widening rows as the family bears fruit and multiplies. All of the human beings portrayed here are unique individuals, but they can also fit into one of two categories: They're either men or women. (While in many families there are some who don't immediately fall into either category, under closer scrutiny, they normally will.)

Now imagine another family tree, but made up of investments instead of people. At the top we have the investments who begat all others: a stock and a bond. Like man and woman, each has certain physical characteristics that make them immediately distinguishable from one another. And also like man and woman, their differences are more than skin deep. Were these two investments people instead of paper, the stock might look like Mae West: sexy and dangerous. Big reward (wink, wink), but kinda scary, too. Not the investment you'd want to take home to Mom. The bond, on the other hand, looks like the farmer holding the pitchfork in the Grant Wood painting *American Gothic*. In other words, rock steady and boring as hell. The kind of investment only a mother would love. Stocks are sexy because they represent owning a business, which is one of the least conservative things you can do with money. Bonds, on the other hand, represent loaning—one of the most conservative things you can do with money. Stockholders are concerned with the return *on* their money. Bondholders are concerned with the return *of* their money. Stocks are all about taking risk. Bonds are all about reducing risk. Stocks offer unlimited upside potential: This is how people hope to *get* rich. Bonds offer limited downside potential: This is how people try to *stay* rich. Stocks pay off by becoming worth more over time. Bonds pay off by paying interest over time, then returning your original investment.

Like man and woman, Mae West and simple farmer, neither stock nor bond is preferable to the other . . . rather, they serve different needs and therefore complement each other. Sometimes you need to walk on the wild side; you need the growth offered by stocks. Other times you need to curl up in your pajamas with some cocoa; you clamor for the safety and certainty found only in bonds.

When you started this book, you (hopefully) knew the difference between men and women. Whenever you see human beings, you put them into one of these categories so quickly and naturally—it's automatic. Well, start working toward the same goal with investments. When you see an investment from now on, attempt to immediately categorize it into an owner investment or a loaner investment. It's not hard because, like men and women, the differences are obvious once you know what to look for. For example, an ownership investment doesn't normally have an ending date. (When you buy a stock it never "comes due." The only way to turn it into cash again is to sell it to someone else.) Loaner investments, on the other hand, nearly always have a due date. (A certificate of deposit, for example, comes due in six months, one year, five years, what have you.) Another telling distinction is the reward. Ownership investments rarely promise a specific return. When you buy a stock, there's no guarantee that you'll make any certain return; your reward is up in the air. Loanership investments, on the other hand, nearly always promise a specific reward. A six-month certificate of deposit pays 2 percent interest. There's your reward, pathetically stated in black and white. A third clear distinction between ownership and loanership investments is the promise that you'll get your money back. When you buy a stock, despite what the salesman says, nobody really knows what will happen. It may go up, it may go down, it may go to zero. No promises. But when you buy that certificate of deposit, the bank promises you that you'll see your money again. It guarantees it. In fact, even if it totally screws up and loses your money, it still can offer a guarantee because Uncle Sam will pay you back through the Federal Deposit Insurance Corporation. So loanership investments will always include or imply: (1) a promise to repay; (2) by a certain date; (3) with a stated return, normally expressed as an interest rate. An ownership investment sacrifices all of these things in exchange for the hope of a bigger reward. Wink, wink.

Now think about all the places you have your money right now. Which are loanership investments and which are ownership investments? Got a checking account? It's a loanership investment. True, it doesn't pay interest, but it does promise you your money back whenever you want it. It doesn't promise ownership-type rewards, that's for sure. Got a money market account? Another loanership investment. Got a stock mutual fund? Obviously an ownership-type investment. Got a U.S. Savings Bond? Loanership. What about your house, or maybe a piece of rental real estate you own? Ownership. Lend money for your sister's mortgage? Loanership.

The reason it's important to distinguish between ownership and loanership investments is that having too much in either category is dangerous. Too many ownership investments and you could potentially lose too much. Too many loanership investments and you might not make enough. Young people, particularly men, tend to gamble too much by becoming too heavily weighted in ownership stuff. Older people, particularly women, tend to become too heavily weighted in loanership stuff because they're afraid of risk. And while avoiding risk is obviously smart, too much risk avoidance will result in not enough return. For example, historically loanership investments haven't done a good job of keeping pace with inflation. So while you keep your money, that money loses its purchasing power over time, leaving you impoverished. Balance is the key, and recognizing whether you're buying ownership or loanership is step one.

Now you can tell the difference between investment Mae Wests and Gothic farmers. That's more than most people know, at least investment-wise.

If all this talk about ownership and loanership investments has you eager to learn the specific nuances of various types of stocks and bonds, then you need to do two things: (1) Get a life because the one you have now is too boring. (2) Read some other people's books. The library is full of cumbersome tomes that delve into more excruciating minutiae than you'll ever need to know or be able to remember for more than fifteen minutes. This isn't that kind of book. This book is about doing things fast as well as doing them right, and you don't need to know all that much detail for either purpose. But you do need to know a little more before you're in a position to pick and choose, so let's get specific and talk about stocks and bonds.

3

The Only Chapter of a Book About Investing in Stocks You'll Ever See Whose Title Is Longer than the Information It Gives

Don't ever try to pick individual stocks. It's hard, it's expensive, it's time-consuming, and it's totally unnecessary.

4

Buying Stocks the Right Way: Mutual Funds

When money talks, nobody notices
what grammar it uses.
—ANONYMOUS

If you haven't been tempted to buy and sell individual stocks, it's probably only because you've never had the savings set aside to even think about it. Otherwise, you've probably pictured yourself working from home, wearing cutoffs, and sitting in front of your computer. There you sit studying squiggly lines, fingers on the pulse of the market, buying, selling, and making a fortune like Gordon Gecko from the movie *Wall Street*. About six o'clock, the spouse walks in from the regular grind. "How was your day, babe," you ask. "Same stuff, different day," he replies, the despair evident in his voice. "How about yours?" "Had a decent day," you reply. "Made $7,000 on a cross-market arbitrage deal about nine-thirty this morning. Worked on my tan in the afternoon . . . been watching *Jerry Springer, Too Hot for TV* since then."

Okay, you've had your fantasy (or was that mine?). Now it's time to wake up. You're not going to get rich trading stocks.

I used to live in Cincinnati, Ohio, where I considered myself a pretty successful guy. Relative to my friends, I lived in a nice house, drove a nice car, and had a lot of money to spend. Now, however, I live in Fort Lauderdale, Florida. While I still consider myself a successful guy, it's a lot harder for me to cough up sufficient evidence to prove it. Because relative to many of my new Florida friends, I live in a cardboard box, drive a heap, and have so little money I can't pay attention.

Let's talk about my richest acquaintance. We'll call him Chuck, because that's his name. Chuck has at least three houses (that I know of), two planes (one's a jet), and I don't know how many boats, but one of them is 110 feet long. His waterfront house here in Fort Lauderdale certainly qualifies as a mansion: I'd guess twenty thousand square feet, but it's probably bigger. He has a lot more toys, too, but you get the picture: Chuck's a rich guy. And how did he get that way? With stocks! But not by trading them. He built a successful business and sold part of his company in a stock offering. (See chapter 1.) Now he hangs out, parties like a rock star, and flies his pals around so they can party with him. (Hint, hint, Chuck.)

While Chuck may be my most successful acquaintance, he's certainly not the only rich guy I know. Marco also has a waterfront mansion and a 110-foot yacht. Dan drives a Ferrari. Another guy I know, Marcus (not to be confused with Marco), has fourteen cars ranging from Lamborghinis to Hummers.

What do all these guys have in common? Well, let's see. They're all nice people, they're all smart people, they're all younger than fifty, they're all single (although, astoundingly, none is lacking companionship), they're all self-employed, and the point most salient to this chapter: None made his fortune by trading stocks. In fact, I've met many rich people over the years and I've never met even one who made his fortune trading stocks. I have met some who made a lot of money by owning stocks over long periods of time, but not by poring over public information, sitting in front of their computers, and trading like mad. Mind you, I'm not saying there's no such thing as people who have done this; I'm just saying that I've never met a person who had access only to public information and subsequently made a quick fortune by short-term stock trading.

The people I've personally met who made the most short-term

money from the stock market are salespeople who call themselves investment advisers, successfully convince people like Chuck to trade stocks, and make a fortune in commissions.

So if you can't get wealthy by buying and selling individual stocks, why should you do it? You shouldn't. You should, however, invest in the stock market as a whole, especially over long periods of time. And the reason for this is very simple. Because over long periods of time the stock market pays twice as much as commonly available alternative investments. And here's the best part: You don't need to know your butt from your elbow, and it won't take more than a few minutes a year.

I could just tell you exactly what to do, and I will in a few minutes. But because this is a book and not a brochure, let me give you at least a little background into what's going on with this type of investment. Specifically, why the stock market appears so complicated, what stocks are all about, why you should use stocks as part of your savings strategy, how you should buy them, and how much of your money belongs there.

Why You Should Use Stocks As Part of Your Investment Strategy

As I've already said, because they pay more than other readily available types of investments. How much more? About twice as much. Over the last hundred years or so, risk-free, long-term bonds have averaged about 5 percent per year. The stocks of big companies have averaged about 10 percent. The stocks of small companies have averaged about 11 percent. And since when it comes to money more is better, investing in stocks makes sense.

How Should You Buy Stocks?

You should buy stocks within mutual funds. What's a mutual fund? It isn't an investment. It's a form of investment. A mutual fund is simply a giant pool of professionally managed money. It could be a pool of stocks: a stock fund. It could be a pool of bonds: a bond fund. Or it could have both stocks and bonds: a balanced fund. The appeal of mutual funds is threefold.

First, a mutual fund allows you to spread the inherent risk of stock investing by diversifying among a bunch of stocks instead of investing in just a few. For example, say you want to own one hundred shares of Microsoft. First you'll have to scrape up five grand. Okay. You have the money and you buy it. The next day, Microsoft issues a press release saying that its software doesn't actually work at all; Bill Gates was just kidding. You're toast. But if you put that same five grand into a mutual fund, you're buying slivers of one hundred different stocks. The sliver that went into Microsoft is still toast, but you also own a sliver of Apple, which has now doubled. You're fine. When it comes to investing in other people's businesses, spreading your money around is a good idea. (Need more proof? Do a Web search for the word "Enron.")

The second reason you choose mutual funds is that they keep track of a lot of the paperwork for you. Since we're trying to manage our money in as little time as possible, we really don't want to continually be getting a bunch of statements, trade confirmations, dividend checks, proxies, and tax forms in the mail. Because all this paper has to be stared at for long periods of time before we can figure out what the hell it's trying to say. And since it looks official, we tend to put it in a file even though it's a virtual certainty that we'll never glance at it again. And if by some freak accident we actually do want to look at it again, we won't find it. So if a mutual fund is going to keep track of some of this stuff for us . . . more power to it.

The third reason you want to use a mutual fund is that it comes complete with an expert (or more likely a team of experts) to buy and sell stocks. Now you can watch *Oprah* and let someone who knows what he's doing figure out which stocks to buy.

Since mutual funds offer all these advantages over stocks, you'd wonder why anyone would want to buy individual stocks at all. I honestly believe that the primary reason is a compelling need to feel like Gordon Gecko. But he might also want to avoid the fees that accompany mutual funds. That's right: There are no free lunches being served on Wall Street.

Let's bring all these issues, good and bad, into focus by looking at a real mutual fund. I'm going to pick one pretty much at random, and all the information I'm going to give you I took from the Internet.[13] The fund we're going to look at is the John Hancock Large Cap Equity A Fund. Don't let all those words baffle you . . . let's quickly go over them. "Large cap" refers to large capitalization. Capitalization describes the combined total of all the money everyone's invested. So "large capitalization" merely tells us that the fund buys big companies like General Motors rather than smaller, lesser-known ones. "Equity" is just another name for stock. (Equity is basically synonymous with ownership.) The "A" refers to the fee you pay to buy the fund . . . more on that in a minute.

As of October 2002, this fund had $740 million invested in it. The minimum to join in is only $1,000. This fund is ancient, having cranked up in 1949. There are five guys picking the investments. Over the last ten years (through October 28, 2002), the fund has returned an average of 7.99 percent per year.

So here we have a fund that's been around a long time with a big management team. But now comes the question: What's all this going to cost?

Mutual funds have several ways of charging for their services, many of which you'd probably never know about because they're not always apparent. Let's use this fund to illustrate them.

The first money you'll part with is the fee to buy into the fund. This fee is known as the "load," which is an appropriate term for a commission. The person receiving this commission is an investment adviser. (In other words, a salesperson who calls himself a stockbroker, financial planner, investment adviser . . . whatever.) And that commission can be painful. This fund, for instance, charges 5 percent when you invest in it. So if you invest ten grand, you're starting off $500 behind. In other words, you're actually not investing $10,000, you're only investing $9,500. Which means that you've got to earn a little more than 5 percent on your $9,500 just to get back to square one.

What have we learned here? That commissions are not your

[13] http://quicktake.morningstar.com/Fund/NutsAndBolts.asp?Country=USA&Symbol=TAGRX&qttab=fees#anchor1.

friend. Shares in mutual funds that charge upfront commissions, like this John Hancock fund, are called "Class A." This may be because for the people selling them, they are indeed the tops in their class. But as bad as upfront fees are, at least they're a once-only event. All the other charges we're about to explore are perpetual.

We've seen how our salesperson (oops, I mean investment adviser) gets paid. But what about our superexperienced management team? They need to eat, too, right? Well, this John Hancock fund charges 0.62 percent as a management fee. This isn't money you'll ever know you're paying unless you look at the fine print (it's in a document known as a prospectus), because that's about the only place you'll find it. The management fee is taken out of your earnings before you see your results. For example, if the fund actually went up by 8 percent one year, your statement would reflect a gain of 7.38 percent. Well, at least it would if that were the only fee reducing your return. It isn't.

Further examination of fees reveals another annual expense that's always mystified me: the 12b-1 fee. This fund charges 0.25 percent. What the heck is a 12b-1 fee? It's a fee the fund imposes to help it offset the cost of promoting, marketing, and distributing its product. In other words, the old investors are paying to attract new investors. Although I have no idea how this particular fund spends its marketing money, a 12b-1 fee could theoretically include anything from the cost of that glossy brochure you received to a golf outing for top fund salespeople. In any case, why is it charging you every year so more people will hear about your fund? Search me. I guess because it can. Perhaps that's a question better addressed to the Securities and Exchange Commission.

Our last expense is called "other." It's 0.355 percent. I don't know what "other expenses" refers to, and honestly I really don't care enough to find out. Perhaps it's for the record keeping the fund does or the trading commissions it pays. Whatever . . . why quibble over a couple of million bucks a year? (To be more precise, 0.35 percent of $740 million is $2,627,000.)

Now we've reached our total annual fees: management, 12b-1, and other. Collectively, these fees are known as the expense ratio.

For this particular fund, they total 1.23 percent.[14] This is the amount that will be skimmed off the top every year before you see your results. Not much, right? Wrong. The prospectus goes on to provide some examples of what these expenses represent when translated back into dollars and cents. For example, say you put $10,000 into Class A shares, paid the 5 percent commission, the fund earned 5 percent, and you reinvested all your dividends and profits. After one year, you'll have paid a total $619. After ten years, you'll have paid $1,914. That's a lot to pay on what was originally a $10,000 investment.

By the way, as I mentioned, I really kind of picked this fund at random. I didn't pick it because it had the highest fees. In fact, its fees are lower than average. According to mutual fund watchdog company Morningstar, the average stock mutual fund in the United States charges annual expenses totaling 1.45 percent[15]—So this fund has lower fees than average.

I know the math is boring, but I needed to illustrate how mutual funds make money so you'll be better situated to select funds—not to mention appreciate the one I'm going to suggest.

As I mentioned when I began talking about mutual funds, this method of owning investments offers diversification and professional management, and these features come at a price. So while we love funds, we hate fees, and our goal is to reduce them as much as possible, so we keep more of our money. In this vein, let's see if we can eliminate, or at least reduce, the price we pay for management.

What if I told you that these high-priced investment management teams rarely beat the overall market? Shocker, huh? It should be, especially considering how much these people get paid. But as it turns out, if you could find a way to just buy the overall market and leave it alone, in most cases you'd do better over time. For example, consider the Standard & Poor's 500 index, known more often as the S&P 500. The S&P 500 is a basket of five hun-

[14] This is the total for Class A shares. There are, however, other classes: Class B and C, both of which have different fee structures.

[15] Per conversation with Steven Murphy at Morningstar on October 28, 2002.

dred big-company stocks that are assumed to be widely owned. The purpose of this index is to serve as a proxy for the overall market. In other words, while what we call "the market" is actually made up of the stocks of thousands of public companies, you can pretty much tell what it's doing by looking at an index such as the S&P 500 or the Dow Jones Industrial Average (an index made up of only thirty stocks).

If past is prologue, you'll make more money by simply buying and holding the five hundred companies represented by the S&P 500 than you would turning your money over to a team of professional stock pickers.

According to Charles Ellis's book *Winning the Loser's Game*,[16] over a fifty-year period only 5 percent of professionally managed mutual funds outperformed an unmanaged index like the S&P 500. So why would you pay extra for management when odds are that over the long term it won't make you any money?

The fact that professional stock pickers rarely beat the market bolsters the argument that there's no reason to trust "professionals" with your money. Think about it. Mutual fund companies, as well as firms like Merrill Lynch, Salomon, and the rest, spend hundreds of millions of dollars every year in advertising essentially to tell you that they're much smarter than you. But if they are, where's the proof?

Now let's talk about a different type of mutual fund. One that allows you to pool your money with other investors, thus achieving the diversification so important to mutual funds, but does so without the added expense of commissions, 12b-1 marketing fees, and high management fees. Let's explore no-load index funds.

A load, as I explained, refers to a commission. And there are many mutual fund companies that don't charge one because they bypass salespeople and deal directly with investors. Let's look at another real-life example.

The Vanguard 500 Index Fund is a mutual fund whose purpose is to mimic what would happen if you bought the five hundred

[16] *Winning the Loser's Game,* figure 14-4, page 105.

stocks in the S&P 500. In other words, the managers of this fund aren't sitting around scratching their heads trying to decide what to buy or when to sell. They already have a list of five hundred stocks to buy. Their only job is to buy them, then replace them on those rare occasions when S&P decides to change its index by dropping one company and adding another. All the information I'm about to provide on this fund I also took directly from the Internet.[17] The Vanguard 500 Index Fund hasn't been around nearly as long as the John Hancock fund—only since 1976. But its return is better. For the ten-year period ending September 30, 2002, the Vanguard fund has returned an average of 8.92 percent every year, compared to John Hancock's return of 7.99 percent. The Vanguard 500 Index has around $60 billion in it, and the minimum to join the party is $3,000. There's no commission to buy in, so all your money gets invested. There's no 12b-1 fee, because apparently Vanguard doesn't feel the need to charge you to reimburse its marketing expenses. There are other fees, however. Until you've got ten grand invested, you'll have to pay $2.50 every three months, or $10 a year, as an account custodial fee. And despite the fact that the manager of the fund doesn't have to do much in terms of stock selection, there's still a management fee: 0.16 percent. Finally, here again we have the mysterious "other" fee: In this case, it's 0.02 percent. So your total expense ratio is 0.18 percent. (Nothing to sneeze at from Vanguard's point of view. It's raking in more than $100 million every year in fees on this fund alone.) Still, you don't have to be Einstein to understand that 0.18 percent is a lot less than 1.23 percent. This could be one reason why the unmanaged Vanguard 500 Index Fund is making its investors more money. Another reason could be that John Hancock's experienced management team isn't all that hot. But when it's said and done, it doesn't really matter. The point is that you can spend less money in fees with an index fund, and you can make more money doing it. Just as important, an unmanaged fund means having less to worry about. Rather than fretting over how sharp your stock pickers are,

[17] www.vanguard.com.

you simply decide what portion of your savings belongs in stocks, put it in this fund (or one like it), and you're off to the races.

So now we've taken the complex world of stock investing and made it simple. To summarize: You invest in stocks because they pay more than most alternatives. You invest in mutual funds because they help you diversify. You invest in index mutual funds because they do as well as other types of stock mutual funds—and cost less to own. And as Forrest Gump might say, "That's all I'm going to say about that." What else do you need to know?

5

Bonds

A bank is a place where they lend you an
umbrella in fair weather and ask for it
back when it begins to rain.

—Robert Frost

Like stocks, bonds are available individually or in mutual funds. Also like stocks, I'm going to recommend that you buy your bonds with mutual funds, and I'm going to suggest a specific bond mutual fund for you. But you'll still need to know a bit more about them before you're ready to move ahead.

As you now know, bonds are about safety and interest. They're a place to keep our money safe, and/or a place to keep money when we need interest checks in the mail. If you're working and your income is adequate, you may not need that extra income just yet. So for now you'll be buying bonds primarily for their safety. But when you retire and your salary is history, you'll be buying bonds not just for safety, but also to supplement your Social Security or other retirement income you'll (hopefully) be getting. So when will an investor look for bonds or other loaner investments? When he doesn't want to expose his money to the risk of ownership investments, when he needs regular interest checks to pay the bills, or both.

Now let's put bonds in categories by seeing who's trying to sell you bonds, then looking at the safety, interest, and tax advantages of different types.

People who borrow money by selling bonds are called bond issuers, and they fall into three rough categories: private companies, local government, and the federal government. If you lend to a company, you're about to invest in corporate bonds. Lend to a state or local government, and you're investing in municipal bonds. Lend to Uncle Sam, and you're buying Treasury bonds.

When you consider safety, you can't beat Uncle Sam. That's because the federal government can print money whenever it feels the urge, so theoretically it'll always be able to pay its debts no matter how many $600 toilet seats it buys. If you're buying a corporate bond, on the other hand, the financial smarts of the company is the main thing, because if the company doesn't manage its finances well, it won't have the money to repay you. Local government bonds—those issued by a state, county, or city—fall somewhere between corporate and federal government bonds on the safety scale. Sometimes these bonds are backed by the taxing authority of the local government that issues them, making them very safe. Other times the repayment of these bonds could depend on the money brought in from some specific project, like a toll road or a stadium, making them a bit iffier.

So if safety were our only concern, the choice would be easy. We'd want to go where the money's minted: Treasury bonds. Next we'd choose local government, since in many cases it can repay debts by raising taxes. And bringing up the rear would be corporate bonds. Since every company manages its money differently, to determine the safety of a corporate bond we'd have to scrutinize the company's books. An onerous task, especially since their financial condition can change at the drop of a hat. Fortunately, however, we're spared this burden because there are people who are happy to do the detail work for us. They work at places called rating services. Two of the best known are Standard & Poor's and Moody's. Their job is to pore over the books of basically every company and municipality that issues bonds and render a final verdict on each one in the form of a grade. So bonds end up stamped with grades, kind of like eggs. AAA is best, then AA, A, BBB, BB, and so on, on down to C. Any bond that earns one of the highest four categories of rating—AAA down to BBB—is called investment grade. Bonds with ratings below investment grade are often called junk bonds. (So what would you call a company's bonds if they were AAA rated, but the company's business was junkyards? I guess investment-grade junk bonds.) In any case, pretty much all bonds are rated by one or more ratings services except federal government (Treasury) bonds. As I've explained, since Uncle Sam prints money, his bonds are automatically considered risk-free: no rating needed.

As you might imagine, the more risk you're willing to take, the more reward you're going to make. So generally speaking, you're going to be getting less interest on Treasury bonds than you are on local government bonds, which in turn will pay less than corporate bonds. And AAA corporate bonds will pay a lot less than junk-grade corporate bonds. So as with many things in life, you get what you pay for. In this case, you gain safety by giving up income.

But here's something else we need to look at . . . the taxes we'll have to pay on the interest we'll be getting.

Did you know that you've got people eyeing your wallet every time you make money? Not just your spouse and kids. I'm talking about Uncle Sam and his local cronies. Every time you get a check, the federal government wants a cut. Depending on how much money you make, the feds will expect to get from 10 to 38 cents of every dollar—and this includes interest earnings from bonds. In addition, depending on where you live, your state, city, and/or county government may also demand a piece of the action. So don't turn around too fast; there are a bunch of people back there reaching for your wallet.

Want to send some of these tax collectors packing? It's possible, because a long time ago these government guys got together and made a deal regarding taxes. Simply put, if you invest in bonds issued by the federal government, you don't have to pay state or local taxes on the interest. If you buy a bond issued by any state or local government, you generally don't have to pay federal taxes on the interest. And if that bond is issued by your resident state, you may not have to pay state or local taxes, either. All this tax forgiveness flying back and forth between federal and state tax collectors is what's known as reciprocity: You don't tax investors who buy our bonds, and we'll reciprocate by not taxing investors who buy yours. If, however, you buy a bond that's issued by a corporation, no reciprocity: You have to pay everybody. This absence of tax forgiveness is what's known as a bummer.

Now we're going to bring all this tax stuff home with an example, which is going to require a little math. So take a deep breath and focus. Don't worry, it's just a paragraph or two.

Say you live in Cincinnati, Ohio, file a joint return, and your taxable income is around fifty grand. A quick glimpse at various tax tables (as if there were such a thing) reveals that you're in the 27 percent federal tax bracket, 5 percent state tax bracket, and 2 percent local tax bracket. This tells us that when you earn a dollar of interest, you're going to pay a total of 34 cents to tax collectors: 27 cents goes to Washington, 5 cents goes to Columbus, and 2 cents goes to Cincinnati. Now let's assume we're out scouting for bonds and find three likely candidates. One is a corporate bond, issued by Procter & Gamble. One is a Treasury bond, issued by Uncle Sam; one is a City of Cincinnati municipal bond, issued to pay for a new stadium. The Treasury bond is, of course, considered risk-free, and the other two bonds are AAA rated. All three pay 10 percent interest. Which should we buy? To find out, we have to figure out the after-tax return of each.

Before we start, let's review the rules:

- Corporate bonds are taxed by both state and federal governments.
- Federal bonds are free from state tax.
- State and local bonds are free from federal tax.
- State and local bonds purchased by local residents are normally totally tax-free.

Now let's see what's happening with our three bonds.

If we earn $1 of interest from the Procter & Gamble bond,

everybody has their mitts out: We pay a total of 34 cents to federal, state, and local tax collectors, leaving us with 66 cents. So our bond that paid 10 percent before taxes only pays 6.6 percent after taxes. Now look at the Treasury bond. We have to pay federal taxes of 27 percent, so when we earn $1, we only keep 73 cents. But at least we don't have to pay state or local taxes. So on this bond, our after-tax interest is 7.3 percent. Now let's look at the City of Cincinnati stadium bond. We get to keep the whole 10 percent, because here we pay no taxes: federal, state, or local.

On the surface, these bonds seem very similar since they're all safe and all pay 10 percent interest. But hold them up to the tax tables and we see that they're not alike at all. The City of Cincinnati municipal bond puts more money in our pocket by far.

If you're not catatonic from all this computing, maybe you'd like to learn the formula so you can amaze your friends and family by magically computing the after-tax return on any interest-bearing investment. Here's all you do: Subtract your tax bracket from 100 and multiply the result by the interest rate you're looking at. Like so . . .

Total federal, state, and local tax bracket: 35%
100% minus 35% = 65%
65% times interest rate = after-tax interest rate

Got it? If this sank in, you now know more than the vast majority of investors and maybe some investment advisers, too. Sad, but true.

Perhaps you're thinking at this point, "Why bother figuring out this tax stuff at all? Since I know that practically any municipal bond is federally tax exempt, and municipal bonds issued within my home state are state and locally tax-free to boot, I'll just buy those. Problem solved." Ah, if only life were so easy. The problem is that you're not the only one who knows these tax facts. Your city, county, and state have accountants who know this stuff, too. So what do they do? They lower the interest accordingly to negate the advantage you'd otherwise have. Likewise, the feds know that you won't be paying state or local taxes on their interest payments, so they lower the interest they pay. Remember our conversation about the safety of bonds? The higher the safety, the lower the interest? Same principle here. The more tax advantages you receive, the less interest you receive. (This, by the way, is the entire reason that reciprocity exists in the first place. So the various issuers of government debt can pay less interest. Which, in turn, allows them to borrow more money.)

Now you pretty much know the ropes when it comes to bondage. But there's still another loose end or two to tie up. For example, the longer you lend your money, the higher the rate you'll lock in. To illustrate, say you're going to lend me a box of fifties. (I'll give you my address later.) I'll agree to pay you interest. (How does 0.5 percent sound?) But we've still got to decide on one other thing: when I'm going to pay you back. (How about January 2080?) Same with bonds. A bond comes with all this stuff spelled out. The amount (most bonds are sold in $1,000 increments), the interest rate (sometimes called the coupon), and when the bond comes due (known as the maturity date). If you're going to lend me money (not the smartest move you've ever made), you'd want a higher interest rate if you were going to lend it to me for a longer period of time. Why? Because when you give me your money, you no longer have the use of it. Which means you can't take advantage of a better offer should one come along. So the longer you agree to part with your money, the higher the interest rate you'd demand.

We can see this concept in action whenever we lend money. When you put your money into a savings account, you can leave it there for ten minutes if you want. And what do savings accounts pay? Squat. If you put your money into a six-month certificate of deposit, the money is tied up for six months, but you get a higher rate. Choose a five-year certificate of deposit, and the rate will be higher still. Bottom line? The longer you'll agree to leave your money with someone, the more interest you'll get. This isn't always the case, but it's a decent rule of thumb.

A couple more fine points and we'll stop with the theory and rejoin real life. As I've explained, the longer you're willing to tie your money up, the better rate you'll often get. But what happens if you agree to tie your money up for years, but then decide you need it in months? If you've invested in a certificate of deposit from a bank, getting your money back entails a penalty. The fee for breaking the deal is typically six months' worth of the interest you've earned. In the case of a bond, there's no interest penalty. You can merely sell your bond on the open market. Depending on the bond in question, there is an active market for used bonds. The market with the most volume is the U.S. Treasury market, but there is some action to be had with municipal and corporate bonds as well. So converting your long-term bond back into short-term cash isn't that difficult. Converting it into the same amount of money as you invested, however, might be.

Since bonds come with a fixed rate of interest, determining their market value isn't rocket science. All you need to know is what interest rates are on similar bonds at the time you want to sell. Let's use an example. Say that a couple of years ago, we put $1,000 into a ten-year Treasury bond with a 5 percent interest rate. When we bought it, we obviously thought that we'd be able to leave that money alone for ten years, but since then we've discovered that we like Harleys more than we like bonds and would rather have one of those instead. So it's time to sell our bond. How much will we get? Well, our bond now has eight years until its maturity date, so we check the newspaper and see what Treasuries with eight years left until maturity are currently paying. Turns out that interest rates have gone up since we bought our bond. Eight-year Treasuries are now paying 10 percent. Hmm . . . why would anyone buy our 5 percent bond when he can buy one elsewhere that pays 10 percent? He wouldn't, unless we lower the price. Remember that we put $1,000 into our bond, and it pays 5 percent, which means it pays $50 a year. The $50 a year can't change . . . that's etched in concrete . . . well, in ink at least. But what can change is the price we're willing to take for our bond. For example, suppose we sell our bond for $500. Since it pays $50 a year, that would give it a return of 10 percent (50 ÷ 500 = 10%). So if we really want to cash out, we'd have to consider taking $500. Actually less, since the broker who's going to find the buyer for us wants to get paid, too. This is not a pleasant prospect . . . getting only $500 for a $1,000 investment. But that's life. When you want to sell, you take what you can get. Our only consolation is that buying Harley accessories will soon make losing $500 in the bond market seem like chickenfeed.

In our example, we took a huge hit when we sold our bond, but we could just as easily have made a profit by cashing out early. If we'd locked in a 10 percent interest rate and rates had fallen to 5 percent instead of the other way around, we'd have been able to sell our bond for twice what we paid for it.

So here we learn two additional nuances about bonds. First, they can be sold on the open market prior to the date they come due. Second, bond prices in the open market will move in the opposite direction from interest rates. Imagine a seesaw. On one seat are bond prices; on the other, interest rates. If rates are going up, bond prices are going down. If rates are going down, bond prices are rising. So as it turns out, despite the fact that bonds are normally bought for safety and income, our boring farmer could have a little Mae West in him after all. Because it's possible to gamble with bonds. If interest rates are high and you think they could be falling soon, you could benefit by buying bonds now and selling them at a profit later. Just as with stocks, blackjack, or craps, all you have to do to win is be either right or lucky.

Whew . . . now we know a lot about bonds. But are we any closer to feeling comfortable with them? If anything, bonds may seem more confusing than ever about now. True, we've learned that bonds are basically nothing more than an IOU, complete with an interest rate and due date. But we've also learned that quality is important; there are lots of issuers to consider; income taxes play a huge role in determining what kind of bond to buy; and market interest rates can have an impact on what our bonds are worth if we decide to sell early. This is where Wall Street would like us to stand aside, write them a check, and let them take care of all this complex stuff for us. No thank you.

Just as with stocks, there are mutual funds that will do all the work for us. They pick the bonds, they do the paperwork, they send us our interest if we need it or reinvest it if we don't. For example, the Vanguard Intermediate-Term Bond Index Fund.

As I write this,[18] this fund has $3 billion in it, and that $3 billion is about half invested in U.S. Treasury–related bonds and the other half in corporate bonds. The average quality of the bonds is AA, so this is pretty safe stuff. In terms of interest, the fund is earning a little less than 5 percent (4.88 percent, to be exact). The vast majority of the bonds in the portfolio (more than 95 percent) will mature between five and ten years from now. This doesn't mean that your money has to be invested for that long . . . as you know, you can sell bonds anytime you want, and that includes selling shares of your bond mutual fund. But as you also know, bonds can fluctuate in value, which means that if interest rates go up, this fund can go down in value, and you can lose money. Today the price of the fund is $10.45 per share; over the last year, this price has been as high as $10.70 and as low as $10.05. Not huge price swings, but price swings nonetheless. So this isn't a place that we'd put money that we needed day after tomorrow. It's a place we'd put long-term money when we've had our fill of stocks but still want to earn as much as safely possible.

As with all mutual funds, this particular one charges money for the services it provides. The expense ratio is 0.21 percent, and if we don't keep at least $2,500 in the fund, we'll also have to pay a $10 annual maintenance fee. But we don't pay a commission when we buy or sell, and we don't pay a 12b-1 fee either. So we're giving up 0.21 percent of interest in exchange for diversification, professional management, and record keeping.

Now maybe you're asking, "Hey, what about those tax-free bonds you talked about?" Good question. After all, when it comes to taxes, less is always more. But as I explained when I talked about tax-free bonds, the advantage is offset by lower interest rates. For example, Vanguard has an intermediate-term tax-free

[18] http://flagship5.vanguard.com/VGApp/hnw/FundsByFundType, November 5, 2002.

municipal bond fund as well. But its tax-free interest rate is only 3.37 percent. Remember the formula we used before to convert taxable return to after-tax return? Let's use it here:

Return on taxable fund: 4.88%
Federal tax bracket: 30%
100%–30% = 70%
70% x 4.88 = 3.47%
After-tax return of Intermediate-Term Bond Index Fund: 3.47%
After-tax return of Intermediate-Term Tax-Exempt Fund: 3.37%

See how this works? Because the tax-free fund pays less, it doesn't do us any real good to choose it. In fact, we're earning a little less by trying. So let Uncle Sam have his pound of flesh . . . we'll keep our lives simple and just stick with the taxable version.

Before we leave this section, I'm going to suggest an alternative to a bond mutual fund: U.S. Savings Bonds. It's my second choice, but the simplicity, tax advantages, and low cost make these something worth considering.

U.S. Savings Bonds

Series EE and/or Series I bonds could work in place of or in addition to an intermediate-term bond fund for the income-and-safety part of our investment mix. Savings bonds offer competitive interest rates, state and local income tax exemption, and in some instances even tax deferral. They're also available direct from the Treasury Department; can be purchased online with a credit card twenty-four hours a day, seven days a week (earn frequent flier miles while you save!); have no upfront charges and no ongoing management fees; and are available in increments as low as $25. In addition, because they're obligations of Uncle Sam, they're considered risk-free. All in all, pretty good stuff.

What dissuaded me from making savings bonds our primary bond investment was trying to balance all of their advantages against the time-consuming collection of paper that results in periodically investing in them—not to mention having to learn the intricacies of the various types of bonds available. I've done several news stories on savings bonds over the years, and every time I prepare for one I find myself relearning the details relating to each type of bond. Since I never have to relearn how intermediate-term bond funds work, I surmised those would be the simpler, and therefore least time-consuming alternative. But if you'd like to check out savings bonds and make your own decision, I heartily encourage you to do so. You can find out everything there is to know by logging onto www.savingsbonds.gov. In the meantime, here's the skinny on the most popular bonds.

SERIES I BONDS

The "I" stands for "inflation," and these bonds' claim to fame is the fact that they not only come with a fixed rate of interest, but also serve up an inflation "kicker" designed to ensure that you stay ahead of inflation no matter how much it heats up. The bonds are issued every April and November. As an example, the most recent batch of bonds issued as I write this came with an interest rate of 1.6 percent. I know . . . chickenfeed. But that's before the inflation kicker, which adds another 2.46 percent (the inflation rate according to the consumer price index for the preceding six-month period). So the total interest is 1.6 percent plus 2.46 percent, or 4.08 percent. About the same rate as the best five-year certificate of deposit, albeit a bit lower than our intermediate-term bond mutual fund. The 1.6 percent is locked in and written in stone. The inflation kicker is reset every six months. So if inflation goes up, so does your interest.

I bonds stop paying interest after thirty years, so this can be considered their maturity date. You have to hold them for at least one year, and if you bail during Years 2 through 5, you'll have to pay a three-month interest penalty. But after five years, you're free to dump them anytime and there's no risk of selling them at a loss. (Of course, you can't sell them at a profit, either. You're simply going to get your original investment along with the interest you've got coming.) Again, once you've bought a bond, the rate doesn't change, but the inflation kicker is adjusted every six months. The interest isn't paid till you cash in the bond, which is cool because you don't have to pay taxes on the interest until then, either. And there are no state or local taxes to pay ever. Series I bonds come in denominations of $50, $75, $100, $200, $500, $1,000, $5,000, and $10,000. Uncle Sam won't allow you to invest more than $30,000 per year.

SERIES EE BONDS

Don't ask what "EE" stands for: I haven't the slightest idea. But a lot of the same stuff applies to Series EE as to I bonds. They stop paying interest after thirty years; you have to hold them for at least one year; there's a three-month interest penalty if you cash out in Years 2 through 5; and there's no penalty after five years. Also like I bonds, the interest changes every six months. No inflation kicker here, though: These pay 90 percent of whatever interest five-year Treasury bonds have been averaging over the preceding six months. For example, as I write this the most recent interest rate is 3.25 percent. You don't have to pay any taxes on the interest until you cash them in, and then you still get to skip paying the state and local folks.

Both Series I and Series EE bonds give you a choice as to when you pay taxes. As I said, you can defer the bill until the bonds are cashed in, but if you feel like it you can also choose to pay the taxes on the interest every year rather than wait till the end. Why would you want to? Well, maybe you're in a lower tax bracket now than you will be when the bonds mature. Or maybe you have more write-offs now that can be used to offset the interest income than you will the year you cash them in. Generally, however, I'd want to defer the taxes as long as possible. This tax-deferral bonus is one reason these bonds warrant mention here.

Unlike Series I bonds, EEs are issued at half their ultimate face value. They come in the same denominations as I bonds: $50, $75, $100, $200, $500, $1,000, $5,000, and $10,000. But you're only putting up half the money: $25, $37.50, $50, $100, $250, $500, $2,500, or $5,000. This can be a good thing when you're on a budget. Plus, Uncle Sam guarantees that they'll reach their face value in twenty years, no matter how low interest rates are during the period that you own them. As with I bonds, you're only allowed to purchase $30,000 face value during any given calendar year. But this means investing only $15,000, since this is what buys you $30,000 of face value.

SERIES HH BONDS

Don't you just love the alphabet soup offered by Uncle Sam's bond offerings? Well, we're only going to cover one more: the HH bond. And we're not going to spend much time on it, either, because these bonds are not that great a deal.

You've noted that both Series EE and I bonds don't pay current income: The interest is deferred until the bond is cashed. HH bonds, on the other hand, pay interest every six months—money that can be either sent to your mailbox or deposited directly into your checking or savings account. So on the day retirement planning ends and retirement begins, these bonds will start producing cash. And therein lies the problem.

As I write this, HH bonds pay only 1.5 percent interest. Rates on new HH bonds change every six months, same as with I and EE bonds. But unlike I and EEs, the rates on existing HH bonds are reset only every ten years. In other words, as I write this, any HH bond you buy today will pay a paltry 1.5 percent for at least the next ten years. Maybe when new bonds are issued (in May and November), deals will be better. But in the meantime, wanna lock up 1.5 percent for ten years? I certainly don't.

You can't buy HH bonds with cash. Instead, you trade in your old I or EE bonds for the HH variety. This you might consider in two situations: first, if thirty years have gone by and your Is and/or EEs have matured. Because after thirty years, these bonds no longer earn interest. By trading them for HHs, you're now earning interest again (albeit a paltry amount) and you can continue to defer the interest you've earned in your old EEs and Is for up to thirty more years, the length of time you can leave your dough in HH bonds. In other words, trading your old bonds for new HH bonds isn't a taxable event.

The second scenario where you'd consider trading your EEs or Is for HHs is when you need to start getting checks in the mail and want to defer the tax bill on all the interest you've built up. It's too bad that the interest is so lousy on HHs. Maybe it won't be by the time you read this.

For now, there's no reason to consider HH bonds, because they pay practically nothing and you've got to use EE and I bonds to buy them anyway. I just wanted you to know that they exist. But EEs and Is might be worth considering.

What would make these savings bonds a better alternative than the previously mentioned intermediate-term bond fund? The higher your tax bracket, the more valuable the tax deferral option becomes. If you live in a place with high state or local taxes, this could also be a factor. (Keep in mind, however, that our intermediate-term bond fund will also offer this advantage to the extent that it invests in federal government obligations.) Finally, if time isn't of the essence—that is, if you don't mind the extra work required keeping track of lots of different bond purchases—then maybe savings bonds could work for you.

Now we've talked about stocks, we've talked about bonds, and we understand the basics of each. And instead of having the thousands of investment products you had to consider when you began this book, you now have three. One for stocks, two for bonds. But there's still one more you'll need. Happily, however, this one you're probably already familiar with.

As you've seen, stocks return a lot more than bonds over time. And this is only fair, because they're riskier than bonds. Bonds have less risk than stocks, but they still have some risk, especially if you have to cash out sooner than you expected. We still need an investment that has no risk. This is where we'll keep our money that we may need tomorrow, next month, or next year. For this money, we'll use a money market fund.

A money market fund is a loaner investment. It's basically a bond mutual fund, but the bonds in it are very, very short-term and very, very safe. This mutual fund's price per share is always a buck, and you can take your money out anytime you'd like. In fact, these funds normally even allow you to write checks on them. Of course, there's a cost for this safety and convenience, and if you've been paying attention at all, you already know what it is. They don't pay much in the way of interest.

As I write this, Vanguard's Prime Money Market Fund is paying around 1.5 percent. Not much. But this doesn't matter because we need a place to keep our safe money, money that we might need at the drop of a hat. And there's another reason that keeping money in a money market fund is a good idea.

Remember that when interest rates rise, bond prices sink. So if interest rates go up, the share price of our intermediate-term bond fund could go down. It's a paper loss . . . in other words, if we don't cash in our shares we won't actually lose money. And unless interest rates go up a ton, the shares of our fund won't go down a ton. That's because it's an intermediate-term fund. (Long-term bond fund prices would go down more, and short-term bond fund prices would go down less.) Still, if rates go up, our smiles will fade when we open our statement. But what will happen to our money market fund when interest rates go up? Good things. It will simply pay more interest. So the extra interest that we're making in our money market fund will help at least partially offset the paper losses that we're seeing in our bond fund. That's known in the investment world as hedging.

Money market funds are available in two forms. One I just described: a money market mutual fund. The other is a bank money market fund. Bank money markets offer FDIC insurance, which means they're safer than noninsured mutual fund money markets. And if they paid the same interest, that would make them a better choice. But if there's one thing you've learned by now, it's that there's no free lunch. Hence bank money markets more often than not will pay a bit less than mutual fund money markets. Whether the insurance is worth the difference in interest depends on how allergic you are to even the tiniest bit of risk and how big the interest difference is. But there's also something to be said for having everything on one statement—stock account, bond account, and money market account—especially since the objective of this book isn't just to make you into a manager of your money; it's to make you a speedy manager of your money.

A side note before we continue: I realize that I've recommended Vanguard at every opportunity while discussing investments. I don't work for Vanguard, have no association with the firm whatsoever, and will receive no compensation for recommending its funds. The reason I've recommended its funds is that it operates the lowest-cost fund family among big mutual fund groups. But that doesn't mean that if you choose to go with another fund family, or none at all for that matter, I'll come over to your house and chop off your foot with a dull ax. I'm not writing all this as a commercial for Vanguard or anyone else. Not to beat a dead horse, but I'm writing all this so you'll understand the following:

- It behooves people who rake in billions of dollars in exchange for financial advice to keep the world of investing complex and mystifying.
- The world of investing is neither complex nor mystifying.
- Whether you have $500, $50,000, or $500,000, you only need three investments: a stock fund, preferably an index fund; a bond fund, preferably of the intermediate-term, high-quality variety; and a money market fund.
- You can, and should, manage your savings with this simple mix in about five minutes a year.

Now, many will argue that these choices will not squeeze every last potential penny out of their respective markets. They will argue that there are mutual funds or other investment products or strategies that have been proven to perform better. They will argue that it's not in your absolute, to-the-nickel best interest (pun intended) to follow this simple advice. They'll produce charts and graphs to prove it. And guess what? Maybe they'll be right. But frankly, I don't care. Because I'm certain that people who use this mix will accomplish their goals, and do it with a lot less effort than those who chase their tails and spend their time, money, and energy reading *Money Magazine*, watching CNBC, and listening to sales pitches from commission-seeking investment advisers.

Bottom line? Charts and graphs exist in a vacuum and you don't. You exist in a world that paints investments as part of a canvas so complex that it can only be understood with an artist standing at your side. Hogwash. I believe that compared to strategies assembled with the assistance of paid experts, the simple mix of investments I've suggested will give you 90 percent of the return with 1 percent of the effort. Need every penny? Go back to school and get a graduate degree in finance. But don't be surprised when your English major cousins do better, since fewer choices mean fewer possible mistakes, not to mention a whole lot less stress.

Now that we know how and why to buy stocks, bonds, and money market funds, we still have to decide how much of each we should own. In other words, we need to know how to allocate our assets. But before we do, let's learn about an entirely different type of investment: options and futures.

6

Stupid Investment Tricks I: Futures and Options

There was a time when a fool and his money were soon parted, but now it happens to everybody.

—Adlai Stevenson

I can't imagine why you would, but if you ever think about how to make a bunch of money as a commission-based financial adviser, you'll come to a quick conclusion: The more often your customer buys and sells, the more often you make money. The act of exchanging one investment for another is called "turnover," a term perhaps derived from the observation that frequent trading results in your money turning over and landing in a salesperson's pocket.

Back when I was a financial adviser, a diligent stockbroker would seek to transform about 2 percent of the assets he controlled into commissions each year. So, for example, if your clients had deposited $10 million with your firm, you were expected to generate about $200,000 worth of commissions each year. Bring in only one hundred grand in commissions while in control of that amount and the implication would be that you were a slacker in danger of losing your job. Bring in five hundred grand and the implication would be that you were trading your accounts excessively (called "churning") and likely to win a trip to Hawaii.

Options and futures are investments that offer a great deal of turnover for a commission-based financial adviser, and a great deal of excitement for investors. Both reasons why sooner or later you're bound to hear about them. Just say no.

Since options and futures are horrible investments, I'm not going to waste your time explaining what they are and how they work. All you need to know is that both represent leveraged bets on the short-term value of some underlying asset. For example, options allow you to bet that within a few weeks or months, the price of a stock is going to be higher or lower than it is today. Futures allow you to make the same kind of bet on something like gold, interest rates, or oil. And since it's virtually impossible to know what's going to happen in the short term, these are stupid bets.

But gambling on an uncertain outcome isn't the only reason to avoid options and futures. Here's a story that will help illuminate another more fundamental flaw.

When I met Gunter Kangyal, he was one of the best poker players in the United States. He had recently won the World Series of Poker—an annual event held in Las Vegas that attracts gamblers from all over the world. Gunter could have made his living at cards, but didn't have to because he was already wealthy from developing real estate.

A client who likes gambling is a wonderful opportunity for any commission-based financial adviser, because short-term, gambling-type investments guarantee turnover. And based on both his vocation and avocation, this guy had gambler written all over him. So prior to my first meeting with Gunter Kangyal, I spent a lot of time preparing. By the time the appointed day rolled around, I was ready to demonstrate my prowess in options, futures, and options on futures: the highest-turnover, highest-risk investments available on Wall Street.

As I pulled up to the Kangyal home, I was practically salivating with anticipation. Not just because this guy alone could double my commission income virtually overnight, but because of the referral opportunities. He undoubtedly had a passel of gunslinger buddies who were just like him. I pictured myself sitting around the poker table with my new client and a bunch of his buddies. "Hey, partner . . . ain't you that broker who's been making Gunter beaucoup bucks in soybeans?" one of them would say as I raked in yet another pot. "I'm going to have my gal shoot you a check for $200,000 tomorrow. See what you can do with it, okay?" "Well," I'd say, "I reckon I can give it a go."

My fantasy began to cave in the instant Gunter answered the door. As we made small talk, I realized that it would be tough to pick him out of a lineup of librarians. Not exactly the gunslinger I'd pictured: more Mister Rogers than Cool Hand Luke. Nonetheless, I knew he was a risk taker, so I started talking trading. But I didn't get far.

"Hey . . . hold on there!" Gunter interrupted. "Maybe you've gotten the wrong idea about me. You must be talking options, futures, and such because you know I'm a cardplayer, right?"

This was so unexpected, I hadn't the time to respond with anything more clever than the truth. "Well . . . yes. I assumed that someone who likes action in cards would like action in the markets, too."

He smiled. "Well, I guess that's a reasonable assumption. But rather than waste your time, let me tell you what I really wanted to talk to you about. I just want to set up a safe, secure account of some kind for my granddaughter. She's two, and I'd like to make sure that when college rolls around, the funds will be there to pay for it. In any case, I wouldn't consider gambling with any of those risky investments you're talking about."

This was odd. An aversion to risk sounded pretty strange coming from one of the best poker players in the world! I wanted to learn just what he meant by his statement. "Mr. Kangyal, before we discuss your granddaughter, mind if I ask why you don't invest in the Wall Street equivalent of poker?"

He responded, "No problem. You see, Stacy, whether you're in Vegas or on Wall Street, there are only three types of games you can possibly play. Positive-sum games, zero-sum games, and negative-sum games. The stock market is the only investment, at least that I'm aware of, that operates within the parameters of positive sum. What I mean by positive sum is that since wealth is actually created in the American economy, nobody has to lose for someone else to win. Think about it . . . when a company is formed, the stockholders put up the money, the factory is built, and the company starts to manufacture and sell its products. If the products are successful, profits are made, the shares of stock become more valuable, and all shareholders benefit in relation to their investment. But the money that's making them wealthy isn't coming at anybody else's expense. In a positive-sum game, nobody has to lose money in order for somebody else to win, because money is actually created from profits. In fact, a positive-sum game, one that potentially creates only winners, isn't really gambling at all. No matter how much the stock market may look scary or fluctuate in value, since it's positive sum it's by definition not gambling, at least when taken as a whole within the context of a growing economy. Clear so far?"

"Crystal," I responded.

"Okay," he said, "now let's consider a zero-sum game. If we were playing poker here at my house, we'd be playing a zero-sum game. It's zero sum because the only money you can win is money somebody else loses. See, in this game, no wealth is actually created . . . just transferred from one side of the table to the other. And that's really what we're referring to when we use the word 'gambling.' A transfer of wealth from one player to another: a winner and a loser. Still with me?"

"Absolutely!" This was getting interesting. "So what's a negative-sum game?"

"Well, to understand a negative-sum game, all we've got to do is take our friendly poker game and move it to a Las Vegas casino. A negative-sum game is just like a zero-sum game, with one exception: The house takes a cut. In other words, in this type of game, if all the players sit at the table transferring money back and forth, sooner or later, if they all play with precisely the same skill, they're all going to lose. Because the casino takes a little bit of money out of each pot. Which means that the amount of money that's available for the players to transfer to one another is gradually shrinking. Negative sum."

"Fascinating," I responded. "But what does that have to do with stock options and commodity futures?"

"Well, you probably know a lot more about options and futures than I do," Gunter said. "But have you stopped to consider what types of games these things represent? Tell me. Are they positive sum, zero sum, or negative sum?"

"They should be positive sum," I confidently concluded. "Because when you're dealing with stock options, you're dealing with stocks, and as you just said that's positive sum. And commodities deal with stuff like crude oil, soybeans, gold, and pork bellies. These are all sources of wealth creation, just like stocks, right?"

Mr. Kangyal looked at me with obvious disappointment. "Wrong. Stock options aren't stocks: They're bets on short-term price fluctuations of stocks. You're betting $500 that a stock's going to go up by enough to make your bet profitable, and the seller of that option is betting it won't. It's just that simple. True, there may be wealth created in the underlying company that issued the stock, and that wealth may ultimately be reflected in the stock price, but that's over the long term. You're not buying the stock, and you don't have years to wait. You're simply betting on what the stock price will be in the short term, and that's no different from betting on a horse race.

"If that's not clear to you, think about it this way. Knowledge is actually created at a university. And since nobody has to get dumber for someone else to get smarter, when you attend a university, you're in a positive-sum game. But if you're just betting on one of that university's football games, you're in a zero-sum game. You don't belong to the university and you're not participating in the knowledge being created there. You're just betting on some short-term event remotely connected to the university. Just because you stamp that bet with the university's name doesn't make it any less a zero-sum game. Furthermore, make that bet through a Las Vegas sports book and you're betting in a negative-sum game. Same thing with stock options purchased through a broker."

"Okay," I said. "You're right. Options and commodities are zero-sum games because the only money you can possibly make is money somebody else loses. Actually, though, they're negative-sum games, right? Because you can't buy options or futures contracts without going through a broker, and brokers are exactly like the house in a Las Vegas casino. Win, lose, or draw, the broker's getting a piece of the action. So these things are all negative sum. You're right. But that doesn't necessarily make them a bad thing, does it? I mean, people do make money with these things. Some of my clients have made money at them!"

Gunter smiled and said, "When I was defining what type of game the options and futures markets represent, I wasn't saying they were bad. Nor was I saying that you couldn't win. But there's one thing you have to concede anytime you're in a zero- or negative-sum game. And that is simply this: If you sit at the table long enough, sooner or later all the money's going to end up in the hands of the smartest player. If we took out a deck of cards right now and starting playing Texas hold 'em, think you could win a hand or two?"

"Sure."

"Of course you could," he agreed. "But poker is a game that I've studied backward and forward for more than thirty years. I've played millions of hands with thousands of people. And I've got a pretty decent bankroll to carry me through the spells when your luck wins out over my superior knowledge and experience. So let me ask you this. How good do you think your odds are of beating me at seven-card stud if we played for, say, three days? Want to put your life savings on that bet?"

"No way," I responded.

"Good answer. Boil it down, son, and it's as simple as this. If you're going to play in a zero- or negative-sum game and expect to win, at least over the long term, you'd better do everything you can to make sure that you're the best player at the table. Because that's the player who's ultimately going home happy. And when you're betting on things like options and futures, who do you think is the smartest player? Me? I'm a real estate developer. You? You're a twenty-seven-year-old securities salesman. And who's on the other side of this table? People who are professionals at these games: full-time traders and institutional investors. This is all they do. They've traded millions of contracts with thousands of people. They've got billion-dollar bankrolls to carry them through the brief periods when our luck wins out over their superior knowledge and experience. They've got every conceivable technological edge to ensure that their information is both accurate and instant. Could we win the occasional bet? Sure: Even the blind squirrel finds the occasional acorn. But you tell me. Would you consider putting up your life savings to bet against people who you know for an absolute certainty are better at these games than you are? And more to the point . . . why would you want to put *my* life savings on bets like that?"

"Well," I stammered, "I just thought that since you obviously have a feel for gambling, maybe you'd like to consider these things. And I certainly wasn't going to suggest putting up your life savings. Just a small portion, like you'd take to Vegas . . . fun money."

"I don't have any 'fun' money," Gunter said. "Because I can't remember having all that much fun making it, and I sure as hell don't have fun losing it. You may think I'm a gambler, and I guess you're right. By definition I am. But let me tell you something about gamblers, at least good ones. They reduce chance to an absolute minimum by increasing their knowledge and experience to an absolute maximum. They don't have fun playing cards. They have fun winning at cards. Granted, I don't know these professional players in New York and Chicago who make their living as traders and institutional investors, but I'd be willing to bet they approach their games the same way. And if there's one thing I don't enjoy, it's being regarded as a rube by allowing myself to get taken to the cleaners by a bunch of genuine professionals. That's a loser's game, and I've never met anyone who thought being a loser was fun. Okay . . . enough about all that. Now can we talk about how to set up an account for my granddaughter?"

While I droned on about the mechanics of 529 college savings plans, uniform gifts to minors accounts, and various other strategies for Mr. Kangyal's granddaughter, I reflected on this simple and powerful lesson. Smart investors should realize that there's no future in futures, and options aren't an option. Because all the chips are ultimately destined to land on the side of the table where the professionals sit. While I hadn't lied when I told Gunter that I had clients who made money in futures and options, what I left out was that the number of my clients who had won consistently and long term was zero. So why was I out trying to sell bad things to good people? That was the last time I did.[19]

Of course, options and futures are only the tip of the iceberg when it comes to investments that are long on sizzle and short on steak. Let's look at some others.

[19] While Gunter Kangyal is a real person (is that a name I could make up?), he's never won the World Series of Poker. This story is fictitious. The fundamental facts, however, are totally true. And my total disdain for options and futures is as real as it gets.

7

Stupid Investment Tricks II: Other Stuff

Money, it turned out, was exactly like sex,
you thought of nothing else if you didn't have it
and thought of other things if you did.

—James Arthur Baldwin

Since the early 1980s, Wall Street investment houses have positioned themselves as financial supermarkets where small investors can find any kind of investment their hearts desire: real estate, money market funds, certificates of deposit, debit or credit cards, life insurance, gold, annuities, unit trusts . . . every conceivable place to drop a dollar.

If you offer only a few products—say, stocks, bonds, and mutual funds—you're not a supermarket, you're a kiosk. So if you're going to bill yourself as a supermarket, better cram your shelves with lots of products and hire a bunch of clerks to show customers around. And when you stock up, don't forget to include lots of stuff that says "New!" "Improved!" and "New and Improved!!"

Let's take a quick walk down the aisles of your local financial supermarket and see what's on the shelves.

Limited Partnerships

Like many things in the investment world, limited partnerships appear to be a perfectly logical approach to making money. The concept is not unlike a mutual fund. Get a bunch of small investors to pool their money, hire an expert, and let the expert invest and manage the dough. Rather than stocks, however, limited partnerships invest in real estate, oil wells, or other specific physical property. Investor money buys the designated property, the property is held for a period of years, income is received and/or the property appreciates, and profits are distributed among the investors, called limited partners. When all the property is gone, the partnership is dissolved. As an incentive for picking the right properties and managing them well, our manager, known as the general partner, receives a share of the profits. Sounds good on the drawing board, doesn't it? The problem comes when we take these investments off the drawing board and put them into real life.

In chapter 4, on mutual funds, we learned that expert selection and management come at a price. We learned that we don't want to part with any of our money up front by paying a sales load, and that we want to keep management fees to a minimum. Well, if you think paying 5 percent up front to a mutual fund company is bad, you haven't seen anything yet. When it comes to limited partnerships you're often going to pay your local salesperson in the neighborhood of 8 percent. Then in many cases you also pay the firm that employs your salesperson and sponsors the partnership. Then comes the "acquisition fee" collected by the general partner for finding and purchasing the real estate or whatever it is he's supposed to be buying. When I was an investment salesman, these upfront charges commonly totaled close to 20 percent, often more. Which means that only 80 cents of every dollar you were investing was ever invested.

The general partner in these deals would also get a management fee every year in exchange for his expertise in the day-to-day oversight of your property. His take there was in the 5 percent range.

When the property was finally sold, the general partner would receive 20 percent of the profits, leaving the investors who put up the money to split the rest among them. This back-end incentive for the general manager was the primary sizzle of these deals. "Hey, Mr. Investor. If you don't make money, they don't make money!" Wink, wink.

Typical limited partnerships offered by the major financial supermarkets were often in the $100 million range, meaning $100 million was raised from the limited partners. In the case of real estate, this money was often magnified by the use of leverage. In other words, mortgages would be taken out so the $100 million might actually end up buying $200 or $300 million worth of property.

In the 1980s when these types of deals were at their zenith, the real estate market and oil markets were appreciating rapidly, and because of the leverage involved in these deals, they could have theoretically worked out despite their high fees. Unhappily, however, real estate stagnated and the bottom fell out of the oil market.

It's unfortunate that these partnerships weren't formed to corner the market in toilets, because that's where lots of limited-partner money ended up. In the case of failed deals, of course, that also meant no back-end profit for the general partner. But the sting was presumably a bit less painful because of the huge fees collected up front and the ongoing management fees. After all, if you're buying $200 million worth of property, a 5 percent acquisition fee would net ten million bucks . . . ditto if you're charging 5 percent annually to manage the investment. So let's add it up. Starting with the people who had no money at risk, we have the salesperson: He got paid. The firm sponsoring the deal: paid. The general partner: paid. Now, as to the people who put up every iota of the money, the limited partners: not paid.

Bottom line? The problems with most limited partnerships are: First and foremost, the fees are simply too high. Second, the asset class they're chasing could very well be on its way downhill. This is because the assets being acquired have probably been enjoying growth healthy enough to garner the attention of small investors for some time before the partnership is formed. ("Hey, Mr. Investor! You've seen how oil prices have been zooming the last couple of years! Why let Exxon have all the fun?") Which means the train may have already left the station by the time a small investor has the opportunity to hop on.

If you want to own real estate, learn about it and buy it. If you want to drill for oil, learn the nuances of that business and drill away. But no matter what you buy, here's some advice: Don't ever trust your savings to an "expert" who has no money of his own in the deal. Think about it: If the deal's really that hot, and he's really such an expert, what the heck does he need you for?

Annuities

Annuities are a classic example of old investments with new wrappers. If you understand a certificate of deposit, you know what a fixed annuity is: a fixed rate of interest paid on a lump-sum investment. If you know what a mutual fund is, you know what a variable annuity is: a collection of stocks, bonds, or both selected and managed by an expert. The only difference between annuities and their CD or mutual fund cousins is that annuities come from insurance companies. And insurance companies offer a tax benefit or two not available from banks or mutual fund companies. Like your retirement plan, interest and profits collected on annuity contracts aren't taxable until they're withdrawn. In other words, your earnings compound tax-deferred. Also like your retirement account, if you take your money out of an annuity contract prior to age fifty-nine and a half, you're penalized. Unlike your retirement accounts, however, there's no limit to the amount of money you can invest in fixed or variable annuities. That's because there's no deduction for the money you're investing.

The problem with annuities is the same as the problem with limited partnerships, albeit not as pronounced. That problem is fees. Most annuities will not have an upfront fee, so its salesperson can and will claim such. What he may forget to mention, however, is that there are often high fees for surrendering the contract for up to a decade. In the case of a variable annuity, high management fees are levied that will negatively impact the returns of the mutual fund it contains. The annual fees on variable annuities for management and administration are typically twice those of a comparable mutual fund. In the case of a fixed annuity, the interest rate you lock in may not last nearly as long as the surrender penalties, leaving you stuck in a low-yielding investment. For example, a typical fixed annuity may offer a first-year rate of 5 percent. But after the first year, the interest rate is reset annually. If you don't like the new rate, and want to exchange your contract for a better deal (possible without incurring tax penalties by transferring your money directly to a new insurance company), you'll have to pay huge surrender penalties to do it. So you'd always want a contract with a fixed interest rate that would match the surrender penalty—period.

Because of the fees involved, approach annuities with caution. If somebody is trying to sell you one, the fees and surrender penalties are probably higher than necessary, since the salesperson's commission has to come from somewhere. Like mutual funds, there are no-load annuities, which should have better returns due to lower fees. Vanguard, Scudder, and other no-load mutual companies also offer no-load annuities.

Let's look at offerings from Vanguard to get a clearer picture of what fixed and variable annuities actually look like.

The Vanguard fixed annuity locks in a rate of 3.5 percent for five years. (It's good that my rate is locked in for five years, because that's how long the surrender penalties last.) Since a fixed annuity is basically like a CD, for comparison purposes I do a search at bankrate.com and see what rates are on five-year certificates of deposit. The best rate available nationwide is 4.08 percent. So 3.5 percent is in the ballpark. Unlike bank CDs, Uncle Sam doesn't insure annuities. So the quality of the insurance company that issues them becomes paramount. Who's issuing this one? Vanguard tells us that its annuity comes from Jefferson Pilot LifeAmerica Insurance Company. It's rated AAA by Standard & Poor's and A++ by A. M. Best: the highest possible ratings. So I can feel pretty comfortable with this company and this rate. What about surrender penalties? The penalty if I decide to surrender before five years is up is 6 percent for the first two years, 5 percent the third year, 4 percent the fourth year, and 3 percent the fifth year. So I know I'm going to want to leave my money there for the full five years to avoid paying the exit fee.

Okay, that's all there is to a fixed annuity. Let's look at a variable. Vanguard's variable annuity offers thirteen different mutual funds to choose from. It has a money market fund, a short-term bond fund, a couple of index funds . . . everything I'd need. As to cost, there's no load to buy and no surrender penalty to sell. The annual fees total 0.62 percent, which is tiny compared to the average variable annuity's nearly 2.5 percent annual fees. However, it's also three times higher than the annual fee in the Vanguard 500 Index Fund (this fund has a fee of just 0.18 percent). All in all, however, this variable annuity looks pretty good, especially when compared to others available.

So this is how we'd approach shopping for fixed and variable annuities if we wanted one: We'd look at rates, fees, and investment options and compare them to other investments. But now comes the question: Do we want one?

Annuities are not necessarily a stupid investment, especially if you keep your costs down by going the no-load route. What we're getting is tax deferral. What we're giving up is the ability to reclaim that money should the need arise, since these investments come with retirement-plan-like penalties for early withdrawal. We're also going to have additional envelopes to open and statements to decipher and store. On the other hand, we're not going to have 1099 tax forms every January from these funds.

What's the final verdict? At this moment, I wouldn't buy a fixed annuity simply because I don't want to lock in 3.5 percent for five years. As to variable annuities, I can see the logic. However, I'd certainly first want to make sure I'm using every possible retirement plan available to me: IRA, 401(k), and so forth. Because these accounts offer the additional benefit of potential income tax deductions, and I can conceivably have these benefits at a lower cost.

Gold and Precious Metals

Gold has historically been used as a hedge against two things: inflation and world chaos. The word "hedge" means an investment that moves in the opposite direction from most other investments. In other words, inflation and its cousin, high interest rates, are normally bad news for stocks and bonds. So is political uncertainty. Therefore, when we encounter periods of global tension or inflation, we'd expect stocks and bonds to do poorly, and we'd expect gold to do well. That's why we'd conceivably use gold to hedge our stock and bond bets. We can buy gold in several forms: coins, bullion, mutual funds, and futures contracts. We already know that futures contracts are a stupid idea. Coins and bullion have very high transaction costs and obviously don't pay interest while they're lying in our safe deposit box (although they are fun to look at and rub all over your body). Mutual funds that own stock in gold mining companies are notoriously volatile. Forty percent annual price swings in these funds aren't at all unusual. So however we choose to invest in gold, we're going to pay the price in lost income, high transaction costs, or extra stress.

Is it worth it? In a word, no. First, while gold may still act as a shelter in the storm, it's not the investment it once was. Because these days people running scared can run to other places. For example, other currencies. If the outlook in America is clouded by a pending war or high inflation, professional money managers can now easily invest in Swiss francs, Japanese yen, or a host of other possibilities. All they have to do is buy bonds denominated in these currencies, which they can do with the click of a mouse, incurring lower transaction costs and picking up higher interest than they'd get from gold. And small investors don't move markets: Professional money managers do. So there's not as much action in gold these days.

Second, storms of the severity that make gold glitter are few and far between. In times of turmoil you'll look like a genius, but your investment will do nothing except stink in every other scenario. For example, in the late 1970s and early 1980s, inflation was rampant and gold was soaring. The average price for an ounce of gold in 1979 was $306.[20] In 1980, it was $612. In 1981, it was $460. But then inflation and interest rates finally settled down, and so did gold prices. In fact, gold hasn't even driven by the $400 neighborhood in twenty years. In December 2001, the average price for gold was around $280 an ounce. Can you really afford the premiums on that kind of insurance policy?

Finally, the whole idea of buying gold runs contrary to simple money management. An effective manager knows better than to try to time markets and develop intricate strategies to offset any potential problem. She knows the economy goes in cycles, she knows there will be bad times along with the good, and she's got better things to do than run around sticking stuff here and there. She ignores the short-term background noise and simply keeps showing up.

If you really think the world is falling apart, guns are a better investment.

Unit Trusts

You know that a mutual fund is an ongoing, dynamic portfolio of stocks, bonds, or both that employs a professional manager to buy and sell the right securities at the right time. What if, instead of hiring him on an ongoing basis, we just hired him for a day? We tell him to pick a perfect portfolio, after which he's sent packing. We then hold on to those stocks and/or bonds for a certain period of time, then sell them. This will eliminate that pesky ongoing management fee.

What we've just invented is a unit trust. The problem? Fees. Unit trusts often come with 4 percent upfront loads. So while we've successfully avoided ongoing management fees, we've still managed to make a Porsche payment for our friendly investment salesperson. Not to mention only investing 96 cents of every dollar we hand over. Unit trusts are the epitome of cramming an old idea

[20] http://www.kitco.com/scripts/hist_charts/yearly_graphs.cgi.

into a new box, labeling it "New and Improved!" and charging more money. A silly idea.

Preferred Stocks, Convertible Bonds, Et Cetera, Et Cetera

There are several types of investments that could be considered hybrids of other investments. For example, a stock that pays interest like a bond (preferred stock), or a bond that has the option of being converted into a certain quantity of stock (convertible bond). If what you're after is a way to complicate your life for no apparent reason, esoteric investments like these are exactly what you're looking for. Collecting investments like these is like collecting GI Joes. You probably won't come out ahead, you'll spend a lot of time learning subtle nuances, and the only one who could possibly understand why you're doing it at all is you.

Zero-Coupon Bonds

As you know, bonds pay interest, and that's why people buy them. But what if you had a bond that didn't pay interest? You'd have a zero-coupon bond. Since they don't pay periodic interest, zero coupons are issued at a discount of their maturity, or face value. A prime example of a zero-coupon bond is the EE savings bond we discussed in chapter 5. They cost $25, but they mature at $50 years later.

The advantage of zero coupons is that the bond interest you're earning is effectively compounding at whatever interest rate you've locked in. In other words, if you invest in a regular garden-variety bond that pays 10 percent interest, you're going to be getting interest checks in the mail every six months. If you're not spending this money, you might not be able to earn the same 10 percent on it when you deposit the check in your savings account. A 10 percent zero coupon is essentially taking the interest and compounding it at this rate.

The primary disadvantage of zeros is that the advantages gained aren't sufficient to justify the time spent finding and keeping track of them. In addition, depending on the type of zero and the type of account it's held in, there can be income tax consequences to owning them. (To be specific, unless the bond is held in a retirement account, you may have to pay taxes on the interest you're not receiving. Not true in the case of U.S. Savings Bonds, but true with some other types of zeros.)

Back in the early 1980s when interest rates were soaring, I had clients who bought twenty-year, AAA-rated zero-coupon municipal bonds with locked-in, totally tax-free interest rates of 13 percent. If this situation presents itself again in my lifetime (doubtful), I may ignore my own advice and hop on board the zero-coupon bandwagon. But absent superhigh interest rates, I think I'd rather just stick with an intermediate bond fund and watch Jerry Springer instead.

Okay, now we've walked down the aisles of our friendly local financial supermarket and found that many of the products here are either irrelevant or silly, designed more to enhance sales than customer satisfaction. So we'll leave them on the shelves for people with an appetite for that sort of thing. In the meantime, we'll stick with what's always worked: a plain vanilla no-load stock index fund, a high-quality, no-load intermediate-term bond fund, and a generic money market fund. Meat and potatoes never hurt anybody.

Now that we've gotten that out of the way, let's talk about dividing our savings among our wholesome and delicious choices. It's a process called asset allocation.

8

Dividing Up the Dough: Asset Allocation

Money can't buy love,
but it improves your bargaining position.
—CHRISTOPHER MARLOWE

Since stocks return about twice as much as bonds and other less risky investments, it may seem that we should have all our savings in stocks. But that would be dumb, because stock prices fluctuate too much, and we'd be nauseous with 100 percent of our savings riding on a stock market roller coaster. We just learned that we can radically reduce the risk we assume in the stock market by investing in a diversified portfolio of giant companies, like the S&P 500 index. This pretty much eliminates the type of risk associated with one company screwing up. But there's no way to eliminate the risk of the entire stock market tanking. And as you probably already know too well, the stock market will tank from time to time, and usually with the precision necessary to disappoint the largest possible number of investors, professional and amateur alike. It's kind of magic that way.

At the same time, because the stock market gyrates, it may seem that we should have none of our savings in stocks. Equally dumb, because the potential returns, especially relative to other investments, are too good too pass up. So the trick is to determine just how much of our money belongs in the stock market. This process is known as asset allocation.

Before we get into asset allocation, however, let's address something that you might be wondering. What about timing the stock market so we're in when it's going up, and out when it's going down? Great concept, except for one problem. You can't do it. Many people will tell you they can time the market, but when it's all said and done nobody has proven that he can consistently do so for any length of time. And there's a good reason for this: Much of the money you'll make in the stock market happens in very short, often unpredictable periods of time. This has been well documented by numerous authors more astute than me. I'll turn to just one: Charles Ellis, whom I've mentioned before, author of *Winning the Loser's Game*. Mr. Ellis examines the period from 1928 to 2000, a period of seventy-two years. During this period of time, $1 fully invested in stocks and left alone would have grown to $1,600. Removing just one year, 1933, from the mix would have resulted in that same $1 growing to just $1,037. Removing two years, 1933 and 1954, would have resulted in a final number of $682. And removing three years out of the seventy-two—1933, 1935, and 1954—would have left you with only $463.[21] Bottom line? If you were on the sidelines for just 36 of the 864 months from 1928 to 2000 (4 percent of the time), you'd have missed about three-quarters of the profits available in stocks during this period. What was happening in these few key years? As you might imagine, huge rallies. And odds are good that every single one of them was totally unexpected.

See why timing the market is so hard? You can't afford to miss the sweet spots, so any attempt to avoid the sour ones by being out of the market is too risky. And remember what I said near the beginning of this chapter. I told you that the market will do whatever it can to disappoint the greatest possible number of investors. I wasn't just trying to be cute. It's true, and for a logical reason. If

[21] *Winning the Loser's Game,* figure 2-2, page 15.

the vast majority of investors are absolutely certain that things can only get worse, they've sold their stocks. Which means the only people left in the game are buyers. And when you've got an auction with only buyers, prices are bound to rise. The converse is also true: When everybody is convinced that trees will grow to the sky, as they were in the late 1990s, they're in with both feet. And when the buyers have no money left to buy with, the sellers are the only players left and the rug is about to be pulled out. Make sense? That's the way Wall Street works, and that's why timing the market is not only difficult, it's dumb.

Okay . . . so we know we're going to have to stay pretty much invested with the part of our savings that we've allocated to stocks. But how do we decide how much this is?

Virtually everyone remotely involved in offering investment advice has devised some sophisticated formula for determining what part of your savings should be in stocks as well as where to put the rest. The giant Wall Street firms offer computer programs. Personal finance magazines offer calculators on their respective Web sites. It's all magical and mysterious, with the implication that it's a task best left to the experts. But most of these asset allocation formulas are nothing more than smoke and mirrors designed to conceal common sense behind a curtain so you'll think those responsible are wizards. Let's look at a couple of asset allocation models, see what they suggest, then compare a simpler and infinitely less time-consuming method to allocate your assets.

Before we begin, let's assume you're thirty-five years old, you've got a good job, and you have an extra twenty grand lying around that you're wondering what to do with. You have vague opinions on the economy (seems like it should be getting better soon . . . doesn't it?), but when you're in leisure mode you'd rather watch *Bewitched* reruns on Nickelodeon than CNBC. In other words, although you know money is important, you'd rather spend your time elsewhere. Sound familiar?

Let's begin!

First we'll have a look at *Money Magazine*'s asset allocation calculator.[22] I've paraphrased the wording, but essentially the calculator asks us the following multiple-choice questions:

1. How long can you wait for your dough?
   a. 3–5 years.
   b. 5–10 years.
   c. 10+ years.

(We don't need the money, or at least not for a while. Of the three alternatives offered, we'll select the longest period, which is 10+ years.)

2. What's your tolerance level for risk?
   a. Not much at all.
   b. A reasonable amount.
   c. As much as possible.

(While I know you'd prefer balancing on a tightrope while juggling chain saws, let's opt for the middle of the road answer, which is a reasonable amount.)

3. How much wiggle room can you afford?
   a. If I miss my goal by a year or two, I'll still be okay.
   b. I can't afford to miss my target.

(A trick question: You thought it related to the size of your living room, but they're really inquiring about risk. Let's be flexible and assume that a year or two past the goal is going to be okay.)

4. The last time the market tanked, did you do nothing, sell your stocks on the theory that worse is in store, or buy more stocks because you saw an investment opportunity?
   a. See an opportunity to buy more stocks.

[22] http://cgi.money.cnn.com/tools/assetallocwizard/assetallocwizard.html, performed November 4, 2002.

b. Sell stocks, thinking things would only get worse.
c. Do nothing.

(Hmmm . . . what if we've never even thought of owning stocks? Whatever. Anyway, doing nothing is obviously our choice here; if we knew what to do, we probably wouldn't be doing this!)

Now all we have to do is click on the "get allocation" button and within seconds we have our suggested asset allocation. It suggests we need to have 20 percent of our savings in bonds, and the remaining 80 percent in stocks. The total stock portion is supposed to be 40 percent large-cap stocks, 20 percent small-cap stocks, and 20 percent foreign stocks. (Remember from our discussion of mutual funds, "cap" refers not to hats, but capitalization. So "large-cap stocks" is the fancy way of saying stocks of big companies. "Small-cap" refers to the stocks of small companies, and of course "foreign stocks" refers to non-U.S. companies.) In addition to a colorful pie chart and allocation percentages, *Money* also gives us a list of suggested mutual funds in each category, so we'll be ready to act immediately on its recommended allocation. It gives us thirty-seven large-cap funds, fifteen small-cap funds, seventeen foreign stock funds, and eight bond funds.

So let's summarize. *Money Magazine* asked us four questions, each ambiguous in its own way. The result we got did include a specific allocation percentage for our money, but I wonder how easily we would have been able to make a choice among the total of seventy-seven recommended mutual funds? In addition, we have no idea why the magazine recommended the funds it did. Were they the best in their class? Did they have the lowest expense ratios? *Money* doesn't say, so we don't know.

Now here's a little pop quiz from me.

1. How comfortable would you feel investing your life savings via the results of this calculator?
   a. Very comfortable. What a great calculator! I've never felt so self-actualized. Can I watch *Monday Night Football* now?
   b. Better than nothing. And hey, it's only money, right?

c. Not comfortable at all. In fact, I'm exactly where I started: at square one. Can I watch *Monday Night Football* now?

Now let's try another cutting-edge calculator, this time from *Smart Money* magazine.[23] This calculator is a lot different from *Money*'s version. This one wants to know how much money we have now in each type of investment and what our tax bracket is. We'll say we're in the 27.5 percent tax bracket (which means if we're filing a joint return, our taxable income is around fifty grand a year) although we actually don't have the foggiest notion. Next, we get to use clever little adjustable arrows to indicate the following additional information:

- How much of our twenty grand we intend to spend within two years. (Let's say zero.)
- How much we intend to spend within ten years. (Again, we'll say zero.)
- How much we intend to leave to our heirs. (Let's say 0 percent . . . we'll have whatever's left buried with us.)
- Years to retirement. (Let's say twenty-five.)
- How much we have in tax-deferred accounts. (This refers to retirement accounts, like a 401(k) plan. Let's say half.)
- How much equity we have in our home. (We'll say 30 percent.)
- How many dependents we have. (Let's say two.)
- Volatility tolerance. (What's volatility? We don't know, so we'll say right in between low and high.)
- Economic outlook. (Search me . . . we'll indicate between weak and strong.)
- Inflation forecast. (What are we, economists? Okay, 3 percent is the middle of this scale, so let's use that number.)

That's it . . . ready to hit the compute button? Drumroll, please . . . *Smart Money* recommends that we put 64 percent of our cash into

[23] http://www.smartmoney.com/oneasset/, performed November 5, 2002.

stocks, 18 percent into bonds, and leave the other 18 percent where it is. And like *Money Magazine*'s online calculator, this one also suggests splitting our stock investment into three categories: large cap, small cap, and international. Again, the result is beautifully displayed in a multicolored pie chart. Here's how the suggested mix shakes out:

Cash $3,600 (18%)
Bonds $3,600 (18%)
Large caps $5,600 (28%)
Small caps $3,400 (17%)
International $3,800 (19%)

So let's see . . . *Money*'s calculator had us put 80 percent of our savings in stocks; *Smart Money*'s says 64 percent. This difference is primarily because *Smart Money* urges us to leave 18 percent of our money in cash, while *Money* apparently doesn't care for cash. The percentages they had us put into foreign stocks was similar (*Money* says 20 percent; *Smart Money*, 18 percent). Likewise for small-cap stocks and bonds.

What's remarkable when considering the similarity of the conclusions is the lack of similarity of the questions leading to them. *Money* didn't care how much we intend to leave to our heirs, how many years we have till retirement, how much we have in tax-deferred accounts, how much equity we have in our home, or how many dependents we have. And yet we got almost the same results. Looks like smoke and mirrors to me.

The Money Made Simple Method of Asset Allocation

Now that we've explored what the wizards say we should do with our money, let's pull back the curtain and check out my method. Before we begin, however, you'll need to gather some information. Here's what you'll need to know: your age. Got it? (Hint: Check your driver's license.) Now, subtract your age from 100. The result is the percentage that you should have in stocks or other ownership-type investments. What's left you should divide equally between bonds and cash (money market). Since this method of asset allocation is so complicated, let's use an example.

Your age 35
Your age from 100 65
Percent of your savings that you should have in ownership assets 65%

The remaining amount of your assets, 35 percent, you will equally divide between cash (meaning money market funds) and bonds (meaning a high-quality intermediate-term bond mutual fund). So 17.5 percent in cash, 17.5 percent in bonds.

Let's now compare the results of the Money Made Simple Asset Allocation Formula with the ones we got from our Wall Street Wizards.

Asset Class	***Money Mag***	***Smart Money Mag***	**Money Made Simple**
Cash	0	18%	17.5%
Bonds	20%	18%	17.5%
Stocks	80%	64%	65%
Colorful pie chart	Yes	Yes	No

Let's also scope out another scenario so we can address more mature readers. This time we'll assume we're seventy years old instead of thirty-five, and therefore a lot more cautious. Here are the results:

Asset Class	***Money Mag****	***Smart Money Mag*****	**Money Made Simple**
Cash	0	28%	35%
Bonds	70%	20%	35%
Stocks	30%	52%	30%

* Answers to *Money Magazine* Calculator: First question: need money in 3–5 years. Second question: Not much risk at all. Third question: Can't afford to miss target. Fourth question: Sell stocks in market decline.

** Answers to *Smart Money* questions: 2-year spending: 0. 10-year spending: half. Leaving to heirs: all. Years to retirement: 0. In tax-deferred accounts: 0. Equity in home: 100%. Dependents: 0. Volatility tolerance: low. Economic outlook: medium. Inflation forecast: 3%.

Okay . . . now imagine that you're seventy years old. If you're nowhere near that old, imagine your parents, grandparents—whatever. Which asset allocation would appeal most to a seventy-year-old? Let me tell you one thing for sure: It's not the one that has half the money in the stock market. And while I'm being emphatic, I'll add that it's also not the one that leaves zero in cash. Having worked as a stockbroker for more than a decade, primarily with seniors, let me assure you that your average senior will pick the Money Made Simple allocation every single time. And if he doesn't, he should. Because the large amount in money market will give him ready cash if an emergency arises (always a concern as we age) while offering the ability to take advantage of interest rate hikes. The large amount in bonds gives him relative safety and a monthly check. And the remainder in stocks will give him a much-needed hedge against inflation.

There . . . the curtain is drawn and the wizards are exposed. At least, these particular wizards. Subtracting your age from 100, then dividing the rest between intermediate bonds and money market funds, is perfectly fine when it comes to allocating your assets. You don't need *Money Magazine*, *Smart Money* magazine, or a securities salesperson in the guise of investment adviser.

Are there asset allocation models that will more accurately reflect your personal, specific risk tolerance, desires, and needs? I certainly wouldn't doubt it. When I was discussing stocks, I promised that if you chose a different path, I wouldn't chop off your foot with a dull ax. Now I'll tell you that if you feel like modifying the Money Made Simple Asset Allocation Formula to suit your own needs, fine. Use this method as a starting point and modify away. In that vein, here are some other things to consider while allocating.

- Exclude money that you might need for a car or some other imminent purpose before you start allocating your savings. This is for long-term investing only.
- Instead of using stocks, you could use another ownership asset, like real estate.

- If the recommended stock allocation is too high for your comfort level, lower it. In fact, here's a good rule of thumb: You should never expose more to the stock market than you can stand to see temporarily fall by 50 percent. In other words, if you have fifty grand in stocks, you could open a statement one day that says that your account has dropped to twenty-five grand. You're in the world's biggest companies, so you know the loss is temporary, and you know it's just a paper loss. Still, can you handle it? If the answer is no, don't put fifty grand in stocks, no matter what any calculator says. There is no amount of money worth trading for a good night's sleep.
- Maybe you're convinced that interest rates have nowhere to go but up. (As I write this, in fact, that seems like a good bet.[24]) Since even intermediate-term bonds can, and will, decline in value as interest rates rise, maybe you should opt for a short-term bond fund instead. Go ahead. See if I care!

Bottom line? The Money Made Simple Asset Allocation Formula isn't supposed to be everybody's everything. It's supposed to be what it is: a way for you to allocate your assets according to some measure of common sense in a few minutes a year. And it will do that quite nicely, thank you.

Like I said when we were talking about stock mutual funds, the goal here is to get 90 percent of the result with 1 percent of the effort. This will do it for you.

Now let's move on to the only investment system you'll ever need.

[24] It's November 6, 2002, and the Fed just lowered the discount rate to 1.25 percent. Interest rates can't go lower than zero, a figure they are now approaching.

The Only Investment System You'll Ever Need

Money talks . . .
but all mine ever says is good-bye.
—ANONYMOUS

Do a Web search for the term "investment system" and you'll get more than three million Web pages that feature these words. There are an awful lot of people out there who claim they've devised a way to make money by using some unique method of investing in stocks, bonds, commodities, or some other financial market. Some rely on fundamental analysis (the study of a company's financial results and projections), some rely on technical analysis (the study of a security's trading history), and there are even some that rely on astrology. But while all systems differ in approach, they have three things in common. Their authors all swear they work, they all cost you money to find out, and they all feature a lot of exclamation points!!!

Want to be a successful purveyor of an investment system? Don't worry about knowledge or experience. I'll hook you up with everything you need to know right now.[25]

[25] A sad commentary on our society. At this point I have to make the following statement: This example is made as an illustration only, and in no way, shape, or form am I encouraging or inducing you to engage in a con scheme. In other words, DO NOT TRY THIS AT HOME.

First, buy a mailing list of people who are suitable candidates for your new system. It's not hard to find a list of people who have bought investments, or even people who have thrown money at other people's investment systems.

Next, randomly select four stocks. Just get the listing of stocks from the local paper, close your eyes, and take four stabs.

Now write a letter proclaiming the benefits of the *Turbo-Charged Super-Stock Selection System.* Make up a bunch of hoo-ha about how the system has worked for thousands of investors who were willing to gamble a mere $500 in exchange for learning the secrets of turbo-charged investing. Put in some charts and graphs showing how $5 invested using this system ten years ago would now be worth $5 million. Don't forget to use lots of exclamation points! Close your letter with a few sentences something like this: But wait, friend! I DON'T WANT YOU TO SEND MONEY TODAY! I know you have no reason to believe me! Instead, just watch one stock, the one mentioned at the bottom of this page, for the next few weeks. The Turbo-Charged Super-Stock Selection Model SAYS IT'S GOING HIGHER!!! SEE THE RESULTS FOR YOURSELF!!! Who else would offer you FREE TIPS THAT PROVE THEIR SYSTEM WORKS? NOBODY, THAT'S WHO!!!

Now divide your list into four groups, and suggest one of the four stocks you selected to each group. Wait a month. Odds are that at least one of the four stocks you blindly selected will have gone higher. If the market is generally rising (a safe bet, since on an annual basis the stock market goes up about 75 percent of the time), they may all go up.

Throw out the group to whom you mailed bad suggestions. Write a second letter to the groups that got profitable suggestions. Basically just restate the benefits of the *Turbo-Charged Super-Stock Selection System* and sprinkle in a few more outlandish claims. This time, include some testimonials from "real" people who have used the system. At the end, include something like this: I STILL DON'T WANT YOUR $500! NOT UNTIL I'VE PROVEN WITHOUT A DOUBT THAT THE SYSTEM

WORKS!!! AT THE BOTTOM OF THIS PAGE IS YET ANOTHER STOCK THAT THE TURBO-CHARGED SUPERSTOCK SELECTION SYSTEM SAYS IS GOING HIGHER!!! WATCH IT FOR ONE MONTH FOR MORE PROOF THAT THE SYSTEM WORKS!!!

Use the blindfold-and-point system to select four more stocks. Divide your list of remaining prospects into four groups, giving each group one of your new suggestions.

Repeat this process two more times, until you've arrived at a list of prospects to whom you've mailed four consecutive winning stocks. Each time, you'll be including more hyperbole and exclamation points. Ask for $500 from each of these people. Many will bite. Congratulations! You're in the investment system business! Continue to take in checks and send out randomly chosen stock selections until you screw up. Don't worry about people hating you when this inevitably happens, because this ultimately happens to honestly developed investment systems, too.

If you happen to accidentally continue to pick winners for any length of time, hire a publicist, write a book, and hit the talk-show circuit. When the money starts petering out, simply expose yourself for the fraud you are and write another book. Call it *There's One Born Every Day: The Story of* ____________ [your name here].

There. You're rich and famous. And now that you've got some money to invest, maybe you'd like to know about an investment system that really does work. And this system is simple, free, involves no smoke and mirrors, and can be proven in less than a minute. Not only that, you're probably already using it. It's called dollar cost averaging, or systematic investing.

Both dollar cost averaging and systematic investing are $10 words for a 50-cent concept: investing fixed amounts of money at regular intervals over periods of time. In other words, doing what you may already be doing in your 401(k) or other savings account: putting $50, $300 or whatever you can every month into a fluctuating investment. The concept is simple. When you put a fixed amount of money into a fluctuating investment, you're automatically buying fewer units when prices are high and more units when prices are low. Do this over time and you'll find that you create wealth even if the investment ultimately doesn't go up in value! Impossible? Check this out:

Date	Investment	Price	Shares
January	$100	$10	10
February	$100	$8	12.5
March	$100	$15	6.7
April	$100	$7	14.3
May	$100	$8	12.5
June	$100	$10	10
Totals	**$600**		**66**
Result	**$600**		**$660**

This chart shows what happens if you invest a fixed amount ($100) in a hypothetical stock (or mutual fund, or gold coin, or tulip bulb . . . anything that fluctuates in value) every month for six months. When you start, the price is $10, so your C-note buys ten shares. The next month the price drops to $8, so that same one hundred bucks buys 12.5 shares. In the third month, the price zooms to $15, so your money only buys 6.7 shares. Yada, yada, yada . . . six months go by. At the end, the stock is back where it started: ten bucks. But you've accumulated sixty-six shares, now worth $660. You've made 10 percent on your money, even though the stock is exactly where it started. How did this happen? Because your investment was fixed, you automatically bought more shares when prices were low and fewer when prices were high. And you didn't need to write a check to some phony wizard or obtain an MBA to do it. All you had to do was keep showing up.

You'll recall that earlier I told you that since 1929, the stock market has averaged about 10 percent a year. But even if you've never gone near a stock, you know that the market doesn't grow steadily by 10 percent year in and year out. The stock market's going to go down 10 percent one year, up 20 percent another year, be flat another year, and basically do whatever is necessary to make complete idiots out of as many people as possible. While it may seem unsettling, this volatility isn't a bad thing; it's a great thing. It's exactly why systematic investing works. Because when prices are low you're going to buy more shares, and when prices rebound these shares are going to make you much wealthier than you'd have been with a steady 10 percent.

Let's use an example from real life to see how using systematic investing in a fluctuating stock market compares to earning a steady, consistent rate of return. Say we travel back in time to January 1, 1980. (While we're here, let's pick up a few shares of Microsoft and Wal-Mart, okay?) We're both going to start putting $500 each and every month into separate investment accounts. You're going to put your money in the bank and earn a steady 10 percent, year in and year out, on some type of loaner investment. And I'm going to invest in the Vanguard 500 Index Fund. Now fast-forward twenty years to December 31, 1999. How much have we accumulated? We've both invested $120,000 ($500 per month = $6,000 per year x 20 years). At a steady 10 percent, you'd have about $363,000. But I'd have ended up with about $987,000! Why did I beat you? Primarily because the S&P 500 did a lot better than its historical average of 10 percent per year: During this particular time period, it actually averaged more than 17 percent per year. But some of the difference comes from investing fixed amounts of money over fixed periods of time—in other words, from buying more shares of the fund when they were cheap and fewer when they weren't.[26]

It's also important to note that there's no way you'd have been earning anything like 10 percent in a high-quality loaner-type investment. You'd have probably averaged something more like 5 per-

[26] How much of the difference comes from return and how much from the dollar cost averaging effect? To find out, we assume a $500-per-month investment into a savings account earning a steady 17.56 percent, so we can compare apples to apples. The result is about $918,000. As noted, investing in an S&P index fund would have returned $987,000. So the amount added by market volatility, by buying more shares low and fewer when prices were high, is about $69,000.

cent, which would have brought your final balance down to about $204,000.

I could leave this example alone, since it presents dollar cost averaging as a great system in the most dramatic way. But I think to do so would be misleading. In doing the research to investigate this example, I also obtained data for other twenty-year periods in addition to the one I just used, and they're illuminating enough to briefly sidetrack us. Let's have a look.[27]

Growth of $500/Month Invested for 20 Years in S&P 500 Index Fund

Period Starting	Period Ending	Ending Value	Average Annual Return
Jan. 1, 1980	Dec. 31, 1999	$986,734	17.56%
Jan. 1, 1981	Dec. 31, 2000	$777,052	15.39%
Jan. 1, 1982	Dec. 31, 2001	$593,923	14.96%
Jan. 1, 1983	Dec. 31, 2002	$390,976	12.46%

Adjusting our starting and ending points by just a few years changes the outcome dramatically. If we stop our experiment in 1999, we end up with more than twice the money we'd have by ending in December 2002. You probably already know why: The stock market lost oodles in the first two years of the new millennium. From January 1, 2000, to December 31, 2002, the S&P 500 index lost 40 percent of its value, one of the biggest setbacks since the Great Depression. In addition, a large rally began in August 1982, so by starting our program after this point we miss some of that gain as well.

The purpose of looking at these additional scenarios is to drive home a point: The stock market is unpredictable. That's why it pays more than other investments, that's why we don't put all our eggs in this basket, that's why we don't try to time this type of investing,

[27] All this information regarding various returns on $500 per month invested for twenty years in the Vanguard 500 Index Fund came from conversations with Rebecca Cohen of Vanguard mutual funds.

that's why we commit to it only with long-term money, and that's why we reduce our exposure to stocks as we get older.

Still, when you use dollar cost averaging, you *want* the market to go down, at least occasionally and especially in the early going. Because that's where you get your advantage. As long as the market ultimately goes higher, you're making money. People who have been consistent with such a program during the monster downturn of the last few years will ultimately be rewarded. The stock market is nothing more or less than a proxy of the American economy. And if you don't have enough faith in the American economy to believe that it will ultimately grow, then you shouldn't be investing in stocks. For that matter, the only investments that really make sense in a permanently contracting economy are canned food or a ticket to somewhere else.

This is a simple system, and it probably makes perfect sense to you. So the question arises, "Why do I feel upset when my 401(k) statements reflect a quarterly or annual loss?" The reason is because you're focused on the short term. In fact, it's short-term focus that makes investing seem so complicated in the first place. Because over the short term, things often change in scary ways. And with infinite variables to try to take into account, who can assess the possible impact of each one and create scenarios to account for them all? Nobody. That's why Wall Street professionals don't outperform unmanaged indexes, why complex investment systems don't work, and why today's investment guru is tomorrow's loser.[28] It's also why you should ignore all these sources, forget short-term events, focus on the long term, use systematic investing, and sit around and watch Jerry Springer instead.

Imagine if your happiness were measured every day on a scale of 1 to 10. Every morning you awoke to a printout of the previous day's events and their effect on your sense of well-being. What

[28] Remember Joe Granville? Marlon Brando had nothing on him in the late 1970s. How about Elaine Garzarelli or Robert Prechter? Huge stars in the 1980s. Just a few of many examples of widely popular market mavens who once captivated Wall Street with eerily accurate predictions. Until they were wrong, that is.

would happen? You'd lose sight of the big picture and start micro-managing everything in anticipation of tomorrow morning's report. But ultimately this wouldn't be in your best interest. Because the universe dictates that it's often necessary to endure short-term pain in order to capture long-term gain. Grope around trying to readjust your life for momentary pleasure and you're almost certain to miss long-term fulfillment.

The rules are the same where your investment life is concerned. You don't need to grope around trying to adjust your savings for short-term pain avoidance. What you need to do is find a simple, eminently manageable way to invest your money, focus on the long term, then let everyone else wail and gnash their teeth at every little bump in the road. In the meantime, you'll be relaxed because you know exactly what you're doing and why you're doing it. You're using investments that make sense within a system that makes sense over the only period of time that makes sense, the long term.

There. Now you can ignore the ridiculous noise pertaining to your financial life that you're being bombarded with every day. What do I mean by "noise"? I mean things like Web sites, magazines, newspapers, and TV shows whose purported purpose is to provide you with valuable investment advice, but whose genuine mission is to receive checks in the mail from advertisers in exchange for your attention. And, as anyone in the news business can tell you, the most effective way to retain the attention of an audience, short of sex and violence, is fear.

To illustrate how providers of investment information attempt to capture your attention by making you afraid, I was prepared to present an unabridged article from one of the more popular financial Web sites, CNN/*Money Magazine* (http://money.cnn.com). I can't do that however, because, ironically enough, they were frightened to let me.[29] For that reason, I'm afraid I'll have to paraphrase.

[29] Several weeks after requesting reprint permission from CNN/Money, I got an e-mail back from their permissions people that said, in part, "(Your) request has been declined because of the negative association [presumably meaning suggestion] that these types of articles [presumably meaning the type of article I was seeking permission to reprint] are of little benefit to average investors."

The article with which I was going to fill this space was published on August 6, 2003, and was titled "Hold Onto Your Hat."[30] The headline and first paragraph suggest that the stock market is in deep doo-doo: ". . . the talk on Wall Street is that stocks may be in for a very tough time." But as we continue reading, we find that what the article really says about the short-term direction of the stock market is . . . nothing at all. It quotes some professionals who say that since the S&P 500 has fallen below a key level, it's undoubtedly heading lower. But then it goes on to quote other professionals who say the pessimists may be wrong. "So, is the market about to treat us to one of its dramatic interpretations of the lemming? Not necessarily." It ends by telling us that "up or down, investors should put their helmets on."

This story is typical of the dozens we're exposed to daily, which capture our attention by scaring us, but in the final analysis do little more than waste our time. That being said, there are several valuable lessons we can indeed take from this article and others like it.

First, even if you're in the habit of mixing metaphors ("Hold Onto Your Hat" and "put [your] helmet on") you may still find a career in journalism.

Second, the "expert" advice we receive in these stories is often wrong. When this article was published on August 6, the S&P 500 was at 965. As I write this (November 21, 2003), the S&P 500 is at 1036. So had we been scared out of our stocks by reading these "experts," we'd have left a 7 percent gain on the table. Mind you, I'm not suggesting the typical expert quoted in financial stories is stupid. I'm suggesting the stories are stupid, because they're implying they're about to predict the unpredictable. It's not the expert's fault that this promise can't be fulfilled. And you can't blame 'em for trying. They want their fifteen minutes of fame, and they're not going to end up first in the CNN interview Rolodex by throwing around quotes like, "Where's the stock market going? In the short term? Hmmm . . . great question!"

[30] Here's the link to the article, which, thus far at least, they can't stop me from providing: http://money.cnn.com/2003/08/06/commentary/bidask/bidask/index.htm.

Third, keep in mind that many experts showing up in print, online, on radio, or on TV have their own personal ax to grind, which is related to your personal ax only coincidentally. In many cases, these folks have serious money bet on the opinion you're hearing, and the only reason they're talking to the media at all is to try to positively influence the outcome of that bet. Which makes their advice non-objective, and therefore useless to you.

Finally, fear may be a fun emotion, but only when it involves horror movies or roller coasters. If financial news is interesting to you, cool. But one of the primary reasons many people pour over boring financial stories is because they're afraid of losing the money they've invested in this, that, or the other. They're not seeking to satisfy their curiosity; they're seeking an "expert" who they hope will validate decisions they've already made concerning money that's already at risk. But you won't allay your fears this way, because the experts will disagree, they'll be wrong, and when they are, they won't share your losses. If you're legitimately afraid of losing the money you've got in any investment, it simply means you have too much money there. Forget trying to find some talking head to validate your decision. Simply remove enough money from the investment in question until the amount that's left isn't enough to scare you, but is enough to keep you interested.

You may recall that in the beginning of this book, I said that paying too much attention to things like investing is often detrimental to your financial health. This is precisely what I was talking about. This is one area of your life where less can be more. Less time spent, fewer terms learned, less anxiety to deal with . . . more money in the long run. What could be better?

Now let's talk about investing for retirement.

10

Investing for Retirement

Life is a game.
Money is how we keep score.
—TED TURNER

There have been many books written on retirement investing, and there will be many more. But I really don't understand why a distinction is so often made regarding investing for your golden years, because basically all the investing you're ever doing is for retirement. In other words, the whole point of investing is to make money, and the whole point of making money is so you can stretch out on the sand at the earliest possible moment. So in terms of strategy, there's really no need to distinguish between investing for retirement and any other kind.

That being said, there are a few characteristics specific to retirement investing that do merit mention. For example, the types of accounts you use. Notice I'm saying "accounts," not "investments." The investments are the same either way. But there are types of accounts that are unique to retirement investing, and you do need to know about the ones that might be available to you.

Just to make sure that we're on the same page when I'm talking about accounts versus investments, let's use an example. Picture a Mason jar filled with beets. The Mason jar is like an account: a place to hold something . . . in this case beets. The beets are like stocks and bonds: something that needs to be put somewhere.

The point is that an IRA isn't an investment, and neither is a 401(k) or its nonprofit cousin, the 403(b).[31] Like a joint account, a trust account, a uniform gift to minors account, or any other type of account, they do have certain unique characteristics. But when you shift to retirement investing, you're not reinventing the wheel. The accounts you're dealing with may be a little different from your garden-variety nonretirement accounts, but the investments won't be. Beets are beets whether they're in a Mason jar or Tupperware. So when you're investing for retirement, keep your life simple by sticking with the investments you just learned about: a stock index mutual fund for the owner portion of your savings, and an intermediate-term, high-quality bond fund, coupled with a money market fund, for the loaner part. If you're in an employer-sponsored plan that doesn't offer these specific options, you'll just select the options that most closely resemble them.

If all this talk about investments versus accounts seems too confusing, just remember this: You can put a stock certificate in a Mason jar, but you can't deposit beets into your IRA.

Now that we've cleared that up, let's look at what makes retirement accounts different. There are five main things, many of which you may already know.

- Sometimes you get free money when you put money in a retirement account.
- If you take money out of your retirement account before retirement age, you'll probably pay a penalty to do it.
- You don't pay income taxes on the money you invest in most retirement accounts. (Or, if you're investing money that's already been taxed, you could get a write-off on your income taxes.)
- You don't have to pay income taxes on the profits you make in retirement accounts, at least until you take the money out of the account. The other side of this coin, however, is

[31] These things get their idiotic names from the tax codes that enabled them.

that you also don't get to deduct any losses you suffer in these accounts.
- Because retirement accounts have these tax advantages, you're limited as to how much money you can put in them in any given year, and how long you can ultimately leave it there.

Okay, let's go over these distinctions one by one, starting with my personal favorite, free money.

Let's say you work at a company with a 401(k) retirement plan. If so, it's likely that your company is handing out money for nothing. For some reason, however, it doesn't call it that. It calls this a company match, because for every dollar you put into your 401(k) account, it'll match your dollar with some money of its own. For example, you put in a buck of your money, it puts in 50 cents of its cash. Some companies match dollar for dollar, some match 50 cents to the dollar, and a few, like mine, offer no match at all. If they do match, they'll put a limit on the total you're eligible to get in matching money in any one year—typically 6 percent of your salary. But however you slice it or dice it, a company match is free money. And since free money is the easiest you'll ever make, my advice is, whenever it's offered, take it. If you have to contribute 6 percent of your salary to pick up every cent your employer is putting down, do it. Because getting 50 cents for every $1 you invest is like earning a guaranteed 50 percent on the first day. Think you can do better than that in some other form of investment? Think again. The only scenario in which you wouldn't contribute enough to get the entire company match is if you can't possibly survive parting with that much of your salary. Even then, I'd rather see you collecting aluminum cans on the side of the road to make ends meet than to leave free money on the table.

The second unique characteristic of most retirement accounts is that if you take your money out before you reach retirement age, you'll have to pay a penalty. When the government says "retirement age," it doesn't mean the age at which you choose to retire. When it comes to retirement accounts, this means age fifty-nine and a half. This may strike you as confusing, since when it comes to Social Security, the government apparently thinks that retirement age is either sixty-two or sixty-five. Then why is retirement age fifty-nine and a half for retirement accounts? The only explanation I can offer is that perhaps when you're in Congress, and therefore don't actually work for a living, the term "retirement age" is a bit more slippery to wrap your mind around.

In any case, the penalty for withdrawing money from a voluntary retirement account is typically 10 percent of the amount you withdraw, and this penalty isn't deductible. In addition, since you most likely haven't paid taxes on that money yet (we'll get to this in a second), you'll also have to pay taxes on money you prematurely remove. Bottom line? You're better off collecting aluminum cans on the side of the road than taking money out of your retirement plan early.

Depending on the type of retirement plan you're in, there could be a few situations in which Uncle Sam would waive the early-withdrawal penalty, but if your contributions weren't taxed going in (like in a 401(k) or tax-deductible IRA) they'll always be taxed coming out. For example, you can take out up to ten grand from an IRA—but not a 401(k)—without penalty to buy your first house. Meet the requirements and you won't have to pay a $1,000 penalty. But you'll still have to add $10,000 to your income when you file your taxes that year. Which conceivably means increasing your tax bill by thousands of dollars.

Suffice to say your retirement account should be considered in the same vein as a roach motel: Your money checks in, but it doesn't check out. Until you're at least fifty-nine and a half, that is.

The third thing that makes retirement accounts unique is that you don't pay income taxes on the money you put into them. Take Sanford Weill. If he earns $30,000,000 this year, and contributes $13,000 of it to the Citicorp 401(k) plan (that's the maximum contribution allowed for 2004), the W-2 that he gets at the end of the year will show earnings of only $29,987,000. Not paying taxes on that $13,000 will save him more than $5,000 in federal taxes alone.[32] Smart move, Sandy! Now you can buy that boss skateboard you've been dreaming about.

What if you're self-employed, and therefore don't have access to an employer-sponsored retirement account like a 401(k) or 403(b) plan? You can still get a tax break. If you contribute $3,000 to an IRA (the maximum for 2004, unless you're over age fifty, in which case the maximum is $3,500), you get to deduct your investment, which is the same thing as not paying taxes on that much income. In fact, even if you have a 401(k) plan with your employer, you can still put money into an IRA and deduct it, providing your income isn't too high.[33]

In addition to being able to exclude retirement account contributions from our income, we also don't have to pay taxes on any earnings that we make in these accounts until we see that money again. This is a very cool benefit when we're kicking butt in the stock market, because we could be making money but getting no 1099 tax form at the end of the year—and therefore paying no taxes. But there's no free lunch, either. Because when we ultimately take that money out, it's going to be taxed as ordinary income. If it were outside our retirement account, we might be eligible for capital gains tax rates, which means we'd pay less tax. In addition, while gains aren't taxable in our retirement accounts, losses that we incur in these accounts won't give us any write-offs, either. And losses outside these accounts *would* give us write-offs. We'll talk more about these topics in chapter 15, on income taxes, but keep in mind that a retirement account is no place to lose money. But then again, there is no good place to lose money.

Now we arrive at the final thing that makes retirement accounts

[32] The top federal tax bracket is 38.6 percent; $13,000 x 38.6% = $5,018. His savings will actually be a lot more, because he'll also avoid New York State taxes and New York City taxes.

[33] For joint filers in 2002, your adjusted gross income has to be no more than $54,000 to get the full deduction. After $54,000, the deduction starts phasing out and is gone entirely if your income exceeds $64,000. This amount will be indexed to inflation in years after 2002. http://www.taxplanet.com/newtaxlaws/newlaws2002/iraded2002.html.

a little different. Because of all these tax advantages, Uncle Sam will let you put aside only so much every year. This amount changes, but for 2004 the maximum you can sock away in a 401(k) or 403(b) or 457 is $13,000[34] and the maximum amount for a traditional IRA is $3,000.[35] Keeping in mind that this is roach-motel money, we'd like to put as much money as possible in these accounts because of the tax advantages. Think of the example with Sandy Weill that I used a little while ago. Socking $13,000 into a 401(k) saves him five grand in taxes. That's a lot! And even though he'll eventually be paying taxes on the money when he reclaims it, he's compounding it in the meantime. In other words, deferring taxes is like getting an interest-free loan from Uncle Sam: You're "borrowing" the money you'd otherwise be sending to Washington, and using it to make more money.

Before we conclude this chapter, let's go over a few more salient points. First, you've probably heard of Roth IRAs. What are they? Simple. Hold a traditional, deductible IRA up to a mirror and you've got a Roth IRA. A Roth doesn't let you deduct the money you're putting in. Instead, it lets you not pay taxes on the money you're taking out. There's also such a thing as a Roth 401(k), but they won't be available until 2006. But the concept will be the same. After-tax money in, tax-free money out.

So do you want a Roth IRA? Is it better than a regular IRA? The definitive answer is that there's no definitive answer. This is because to determine the correct answer, you'd have to know things that you can't know. For example, most financial planners will assume that you'll be in a lower tax bracket when you retire than you are now. If this is indeed the case, then you'd be better off taking tax deductions now with a regular IRA, then paying taxes on the gains in your lower tax bracket when you retire. But you can't know what tax brackets will be when you retire, much less which one you'll find yourself in. For all we know, the United States will have a socialist government when you retire and you'll

[34] Unless you turn fifty before December 31. Then "catch-up" provisions allow you an extra $3,000.

[35] Again, "catch-up" provisions allow workers over fifty to put in an extra $500.

be in a 90 percent tax bracket. Or you'll die when you're fifty-nine and a quarter and taxes will be of no concern to you.

I've read a lot of articles on this Roth-versus-regular-IRA thing and I've come to the conclusion that if there is a difference, either it's based on assumptions that are none too reliable or it's not enough of a difference to worry about. The one thing that we can say about a Roth IRA, however, is that it's more flexible than a regular IRA. Because the money that's going in has already been taxed, Uncle Sam doesn't get as hinky penalty-wise if you have to start withdrawing it early.

One additional note about 401(k)s: If you happen to work for a publicly traded company and your employer offers its own stock as an investment option within your 401(k) plan, treat this stock like you would any other individual stock. Just say no. The fact that the stock being offered is your own company's doesn't make it any safer than any other individual stock. And the fact that you're already staking your paycheck on the bottom line of your company means that putting your retirement eggs into this same basket doesn't make you the brightest bulb in the box. The only exceptions? When your employer gives you its stock free, since we love free stuff. Or when you have legitimate inside information and are willing to illegally profit from it. In the latter case, remember: Sharing is caring. Please let me know. (Just kidding. See the footnote on page 89.)

One more retirement issue, then we'll call it a chapter. This issue is other sources of retirement income that we normally don't think about.

When I was a commission-based investment adviser—that is, a salesman—I was thoroughly trained in the use of fear as a motivator. And what's more fear inspiring than the thought of spending your retirement years living in a cardboard box and pushing a shopping cart around? Consider the following sample conversation . . .

ME: So, Ms. Prospect, how old are you?

YOU: I'm thirty-five.

ME: And how much have you put away for retirement so far?

YOU: Well, let's see . . . total? About $1,500. But I'm adding $100 a month to that.

ME: Congratulations! That's great! If you retire at sixty-five, that means you've still got thirty years to go. Let's see how much you'll save. [At this point, I pull out my calculator and start tapping away.] Hmmm . . . $1,500 . . . $100 a month . . . we'll assume a 10 percent annual return . . . alrighty then! Keep it up and by the time you retire, you'll have a whopping $255,805! Of course, thirty years from now that amount of money will probably only buy a candy bar. But let's look at a best-case scenario and assume that there won't be any inflation at all. And we'll assume that when you turn sixty-five, you'll start using the interest on your savings to generate retirement income. This means you'll be getting $25,580 a year . . . 10 percent of your $255,000. You won't have any problem living on a couple grand a month will you?

YOU: Live on $2,000 a month? Of course I can't live on $2,000 a month! What are you, nuts?

ME: Then I guess we'd better start saving a bit more, wouldn't you say?

YOU: Well, I guess so. I'll just cut back on a few expenses. Electricity and water are really just foolish luxuries anyway, right? And, now that I think about it, who needs a phone?

ME: Now you're talking! Let me just get your signature on a few papers here . . .

What's wrong with this picture? Plenty. First, I conveniently forgot to mention one major retirement plan you're already contributing to. Namely, Social Security. If you go to www.ssa.gov/planners, you'll find a lot of very useful information, including calculators that will help you estimate what you'll be getting when retirement rolls around. For example, simply input the age of thirty-five and the annual income of $50,000, choose to see your estimated benefit in future (inflated) dollars, and in the blink of an eye you'll see that at age sixty-seven, you could be receiving $5,000 a month in Social Security benefits. If you choose "today's dollars" instead of "future dollars" (future dollars reflect the probable result of inflation), you could be getting an extra $1,500 a month. Granted, $1,500 a month isn't radical wealth, but it's certainly not something to ignore when you're planning your retirement. And if estimated amounts aren't good enough, the Social Security Web site also allows you to request your own Social Security benefits statement, which will reveal more precisely how much you're personally likely to receive.

Another thing that I forgot to ask my prospect is what she might stand to inherit. Even if you come from modest means, it's certainly possible that at some point prior to reaching retirement age you'll get a cash injection by inheriting some money. How many financial advisers ask this question and add the answer into the mix? It's important . . . so when you're doing your own retirement planning, don't forget it.

In conclusion, the point of this chapter is to illustrate that investing for retirement is no different from any other kind of investing, and therefore should require little additional time and little additional knowledge. As you may have noticed as I went over various retirement accounts, these plans have tons of niggling rules attached, and these rules are always changing. Therefore nobody knows them, at least not for long. While I could have swelled the pages of this book by delving into each variation and specific rule applying to each account, I didn't see the point. Because at the end of the day, the only plan that matters is yours, and the only time that the niggling rules affecting your account matter is when you need to know them. And odds are, that's not now. If you work at a company with a 401(k) plan, there's a person there who will tell you more than you'll ever want to know about the rules affecting your specific account. If you're self-employed and need to know what options you have, ask an accountant, go to a Web site like irs.gov, or do a search for "tax advice" or "retirement plan advice." But once your retirement plan is in place, providing you follow the same simple asset allocation rules that we've already discussed, you don't have to think about it for more than a few minutes a year.

The bottom line is that whether your assets are taxable or tax-deferred, they're still your assets and therefore subject to the same common logic of asset allocation that we've already discussed. Subtract your age from 100. This percentage belongs in ownership stuff. Whether the stuff is a Roth IRA, a 401(k), or a joint account with your aunt Agnes doesn't matter. When you boil it down, the only differences between retirement accounts and any other is tax breaks when you put money in and tough breaks if you need it before retirement.

Use your retirement accounts to get as many tax breaks as you can, and avoid tough breaks by only investing money in these accounts that you probably won't need to withdraw prior to retirement. How much time did that take?

11

Investing for College

No one would remember the Good Samaritan
if he'd only had good intentions.
He had money as well.
—MARGARET THATCHER

There was a time not so long ago that I could have skipped this chapter, saying something like, "Investing for college is like any other long-term investment goal. You simply invest in stocks, bonds, and/or money market funds as you would for retirement or anything else."

These days, however, there are sufficient tax-advantaged scenarios and financing alternatives to necessitate a full class on the subject. This is sad for me, since I now have to write an additional chapter. But it's good for you, because if you've got kids heading off to college next month or seventeen years from now, you're going to be able to save some serious money.

The first piece of advice I have regarding finding the dough for college is this: Don't ever pay anyone to help you find the money. You don't need to pay for financial advice, and you don't need to pay for help in finding scholarships or other sources of aid. There's more free information on the Web than you can shake a mouse at, not to mention plenty of face-to-face advice at your favorite high school or college. Besides, paying for help in this area is like paying for help with your taxes: The hardest part is filling out the forms, and nobody's going to help you with that anyway.

As you can imagine or perhaps recall, partying nonstop for four years is an expensive proposition, especially if you spend your off hours in classrooms. And it's getting more expensive all the time. From 1979 to 2001, tuition costs increased an average of 8 percent per year,[36] which equates to the price doubling every nine years. If the trend continues, kids born this year will require close to four times today's prices to attend their four-year party. The good news is that in recent years, the level of tuition inflation has fallen, perhaps because colleges are pricing people out of the market and are doing what they can to control costs.

Thinking the army doesn't sound so bad after all? Well, take heart. It's because college costs have mushroomed that federal and state bureaucrats have rallied around and tried to make it easier for us by coming up with things like low-interest loans and special savings programs.

Before we get too far into saving for college, let's get something out of the way. The biggest mistake we can make when it comes to saving for a college education is to be too conservative. While it's certainly correct that this isn't a place for rolling the dice, it's incorrect to assume that this means we should stick with ultraconservative investments. So let's take a quick pop quiz:

1. Providing we have time on our side, the investment that earns the most money over time, and is therefore appropriate for college savings, is:
   a. Stocks.
   b. Bonds.
   c. Money markets.

If you answered "a," you get a gold star. Plus, your kids have a better chance of not having to get a scholarship, beg for loans, deal drugs, dance in topless bars, or otherwise attempt to help finance their college years.

[36] http://www.finaid.org/savings/. The site credits the Bureau of Labor Statistics.

If stocks are the investment of choice for a long-term goal like retirement, it would follow that they would also be good for a long-term goal like college. But remember, since stocks fluctuate in value, they're only appropriate when you've got lots of time: at least five years. So ideally, the time to start investing is the morning after conception. Also keep in mind that as your kids reach their mid- to late teens, you may not like them all that much anymore, which is another reason to start when they're cute and cuddly.

Ten years ago, that's kind of all there was to say about saving for college. But since then a bunch of different savings plans have popped up that are intriguing for three reasons. First, some of these things can help you save money for your kids' education. Second, many will help you save money on your income taxes. Third, trying to understand these relatively new investment options will serve as a reminder that even though you graduated from college, you're not nearly as smart as you think you are.

Let's start with 529 savings plans, then have a brief look at some other possibilities.

529 Savings Plans

Anytime you see any type of plan or account that begins with a string of meaningless numbers—say, 401(k)—it's a safe bet you're about to be confronted with something related to our income tax code. Which means the investment plan in question must have something to do with saving money on income taxes. Otherwise nobody would be stupid enough to saddle some poor investment account with such a boring name. Such is the case with 529 savings plans, also known as qualified tuition programs. This doesn't mean you have to qualify; it means the IRS has approved of the plan—the same deal as with IRAs, 401(k)s, and so on, which are called qualified retirement plans.

Since qualified tuition programs are distant cousins of qualified retirement plans, let's do a quick refresher on what makes retirement plans cool, then see how tuition plans compare. With retirement plans:

- Sometimes you get free money when you put money in a retirement account, because your employer matches your contribution.
- If you take money out of your retirement account before retirement age, you'll probably pay a penalty to do it.
- You don't pay income taxes on the money you invest in most retirement accounts. (Or, if you're investing money that's already been taxed, you could get a deduction on your income taxes.)
- You don't have to pay income taxes on the profits you make in retirement accounts, at least until you take the money out of the account. The other side of this coin, however, is that you also don't get to deduct any losses you suffer in these accounts.
- Because retirement accounts have these tax advantages, you're limited as to how much money you can put in them in any given year, and how long you can ultimately leave it there.

Remember all that? I didn't . . . I had to go back to the chapter on retirement and cut and paste. But now we're ready to see how qualified tuition accounts compare with retirement accounts.

With qualified tuition programs:

- Sometimes you get free money when you put money in a tuition program because your state matches part of your contribution. Matching dollars in these accounts, however, are normally reserved for lower-income families, are much harder to find, and aren't as generous. Nevertheless, anytime there's even a whiff of free money in the air, you should check (in this case with the state you live in) and see if you can snatch it up.
- If you take money out of a 529 plan that isn't being spent for college costs, you'll probably pay a penalty to do it.
- You will pay federal income taxes on the money you invest in 529 plans. No federal tax deduction.
- Depending on where you live, however, you may get a full or partial state income tax deduction on your contributions.
- You don't have to pay state or federal income taxes on the

profits you make in 529 plans. Not when it's growing, and not when you take it out, either, providing you're using your withdrawals to pay college bills.[37] As with retirement accounts, you don't get to deduct your losses.

- Because 529 accounts have these tax advantages, you're limited as to how much money you can put in them per year and in total, as well as how long you can leave it there. These limits, however, are much more generous than with retirement accounts. For example, you can normally contribute hundreds of thousands of dollars. Reasonable, since that's how much some colleges cost.

Now you see how seemingly unrelated things like retirement investing and college investing can be related after all. Both are the result of tweaking a six thousand–page tax code to motivate citizens.

There is a major difference between 529 plans and 401(k) plans, however, that makes them harder to describe in general terms. While federal law authorizes both, 529 plans are offered through individual states. When you're talking retirement plans, the same stuff is going to apply in Maine and in California. But when you're talking tuition plans, those offered by Maine may be subtly different from those offered by California. This is why I'm going to have to use annoying words like "generally" and "usually" when I talk about tuition plans, and you're going to have to scout for details when you actually go on the hunt.

There are two basic types of qualified tuition, or 529 plans: the prepaid tuition program and the college savings plan. Boil it down and the real difference between them is how the rate of return is computed. Let's start with the prepaid tuition program.

PREPAID TUITION PROGRAMS

As the name implies, prepaid tuition allows you to lock in tomorrow's tuition at today's rates. That's the basic idea. Even if your kid

[37] Unless Congress acts to maintain this benefit, however, the federal tax exemption of withdrawals from 529 plans will expire in 2010. Presumably they'd still be state-tax-free.

was born five minutes ago, you can pay the cover charge now and she's guaranteed admittance to her personal four-year party when the time comes. So here's one solution if you're lying awake at night worried about inflation. Getting a life would be another possibility.

While the idea of locking in tomorrow's tuition at today's rates sounds good, keep in mind that what you're really doing with a prepaid tuition program is earning a guaranteed rate of interest; you just don't know what it is yet. The interest you'll earn is simply the inflation rate of tuition at colleges in your state. Sound good? It's no big deal. But before we get into that, let's delve a little deeper into these programs so you'll know exactly how they work.

While the idea of locking in today's rates is a simple concept to grasp, upon further reflection it's likely to raise questions, such as, "What if my kid doesn't go to college?" "What if she gets a scholarship?" "What if he dies?" "What if she wants to go to an out-of-state school?"

Here are common terms for prepaid tuition programs.

While you're investing in only one plan with one state, the money you set aside can often be used at any qualified institution of higher education, public or private, anywhere in the country. So if you put money in your state's plan, intending for your offspring to party at the local state university—only to have her later decide to party elsewhere—no sweat.

You can often change plans (say, to another state's prepaid tuition program or college savings program) anytime until your student begins to take money out. You can normally get a refund with no penalty if your partier receives a scholarship, dies, or becomes disabled and cannot attend school.

Parents, grandparents, or other sympathetic sources can also contribute, either by paying tuition in one lump sum or making monthly payments until the party starts.

Once an account is paid in full, the state prepaid tuition program guarantees payment of full tuition at any public college or university in that state, or will give you that amount of money to use elsewhere. Plus, benefits can usually be transferred among siblings, cousins, and other eligible family members with no penalties.

As noted above, withdrawals for tuition are state- and federal-tax-free, and so are the earnings in the account. If there's extra money left over after tuition is paid for, it can be used to pay other qualified bills like room, board; and books.

That should answer some of your questions. Let's try an example and see if that will pick up the rest.[38]

Robert and Cheryl Coggins live in Kentucky and are therefore eligible for Kentucky's prepaid tuition program. It is their intention to use the plan to pay for the education of their son Austin, who is now seven years old. There are three prepaid plans available in Kentucky: the value plan, the standard plan, and the premium plan. The value plan is designed to pay tuition for Kentucky's technical and community (two-year) colleges. The standard plan is for public four-year universities, and the premium plan is designed for Kentucky's private universities. Robert, who has made a perfectly good living in diesel repair, likes the idea of technical school and the value plan. Cheryl, however, likes the idea of a Vanderbilt man in the family, and thus favors the premium plan. In the end, they compromise on the standard plan.

The target tuition for the standard plan is the average expected tuition for Kentucky's most expensive public university, which that year happens to be the University of Louisville. According to the pencil pushers, the four-year tuition for the University of Louisville, if paid today, would be $15,000. The Cogginses go for it. They sign up today, locking in the fifteen-grand tuition. They pay it off by making monthly payments for the next five years. (Because they choose to make payments rather than paying in a lump sum, they also have to pay what amounts to a finance charge, although it's called an "annual investment premium.")

When they started the plan, Austin was seven. Fast-forward ten years: Austin is now seventeen and ready to party like a rock star at

[38] I changed the wording, but a lot of this example came from Kentucky's prepaid tuition Web site, which you can find at http://www.getkapt.com/.

his parents' expense. Now it's time to see just how much money he's going to have. The most expensive tuition at a public university in Kentucky is no longer at the University of Louisville. Now the priciest campus is the University of Kentucky, where the four-year tuition is $34,000. Bingo. That's the amount Austin now has at his disposal: the most expensive public school tuition in the state. (By the way, if you grow $15,000 to $34,000 in ten years, you've earned about 8.5 percent.) If he decides on a two-year technical school that costs only $9,000, he's got money left over that he can either pass down to sister Anna or use for books or other qualified expenses. And if he decides to be a Vanderbilt man after all, he's got $34,000 to apply toward the estimated $290,000 tuition bill. In this case, of course, Robert can forget about ever retiring, but that's not Austin's problem.

Getting a clearer picture now? What happens with a prepaid tuition program is that you're going to buck up now, then earn whatever the inflation rate is for tuition in your state until college starts. If inflation is a million percent, you come out smelling like a rose. If it's 2 percent, you could have done a lot better. But at least you got some tax breaks, and you know that should your kid desire to attend a four-year party close to home, she'll be able to.

As I write this, there are nineteen states offering prepaid tuition programs, but no matter when you're reading it that number will undoubtedly have grown. So rather than just give you the current states, I'll give you a place to find an updated list instead: www.collegesavings.org. (This is one of many sites that devote lots of cyber-ink to what appears to be objective information about every aspect of financing a college education. Another one is www.finaid.org. I'll sprinkle in more as we plod along.) And as I mentioned, there are differences among plans, so be sure to study the one offered by the state where you live, which is most likely the only one you'll be eligible for and therefore the only one you'll care about. And don't forget to see if there are matching funds available. But don't hold your breath.

COLLEGE SAVINGS PROGRAMS

When I was eighteen, my parents said they'd pay for college, but only if I agreed to go at least one thousand miles away and stay there until after I graduated, joined the army, or turned forty, whichever came first. Since keeping a kid that far away for that long is an expensive proposition (trust me; no way I was joining the army), they needed maximum bang for their buck. Too bad they didn't have college savings plans back then.

A prepaid tuition program is like a certificate of deposit: Your return is guaranteed, and you earn whatever the inflation rate is. A college savings program is more like a 401(k) plan: You put in what you put in, decide which options to choose, and it earns what it earns. So unlike a prepaid tuition program, you're not locking in today's tuition. No guarantees; you're just setting aside money that will hopefully grow enough to pay the future tab. Also like 401(k) plans, you'll be asked to choose among investment options including various stock, bond, and/or money market funds. Unlike your 401(k) plan, however, most plans suggest a predetermined mix of stock and bond funds based on your kid's age to save you the trouble of dealing with it. (Hopefully this sounds like a familiar strategy by now.) As with any configuration of mutual funds, there are fees attached. And as we learned when we discussed mutual funds, management fees erode fund performance. So it's important to look at fees and performance in whatever plans you're considering, and remember: No two are exactly alike.

So that we can better understand college savings programs, and so that I can squeeze more of my friends' names into this book, let's use another example.

Olaf and Frauke Haas are natives of Germany now living in Florida. In the families where they grew up college was mandatory, and that's a tradition they plan to continue with their four-year-old son Charles. The only unknowns as far as they're concerned are where he'll end up attending and how they'll pay for it. They like the idea of college savings programs, and find no shortage of information on the subject. In fact, they find Web sites that offer textbooks full of information: explanations of the various plans; rankings according to investment performance, fees, and lots of other criteria; links to each state's plan; pluses and minuses of using these plans; tax advantages; and so on, and so on, and so on. Some sites they visited: www.morningstar.com, www.kiplinger.com, www.finaid.org, www.savingforcollege.com, and www.collegejournal.com. They also found some useful information at *Money Magazine*'s Web site (http://money.cnn.com/) and by looking up archived articles in the online edition of their local paper and *USA Today* (www.usatoday.com).

As with prepaid tuition programs, the first place to look for a college savings plan is the state where you live. So that's where Frauke and Olaf started. If they lived in a state with high state taxes, they'd be sorely tempted to use that state's plan because it may have offered them state tax deductions for money they invest. (As I write this, twenty-five states offer at least some benefit. Five offer a full deduction; twenty offer a partial deduction.) Happily, however, they live in Florida where there are no state income taxes. There's another reason to check out their state plan, however. As I mentioned earlier, some states also offer matching money, especially for families whose incomes fall below a certain threshold. Unhappily, this opportunity doesn't exist in Florida's plan.

So after checking Florida's college savings program, Olaf and Frauke learned that there was no reason to stick close to home for Charlie's savings plan. Which left them with a lot of flexibility, since most states welcome out-of-state investors in their college savings programs.

At finaid.org, they found a ranking of plans specifically for out-of-state investors that considered a slew of factors like account performance, fees, and minimum contribution requirements. In just a few seconds, they learned that California, Connecticut, Georgia, Hawaii, Idaho, Illinois, Iowa, Michigan, Minnesota, Mississippi, Missouri, Nebraska, New York, Oklahoma, Tennessee, Utah, and Vermont all had good grades. That's still a lot of choices, so they looked for ways to narrow it down. They turned to savingforcollege.com for another ranking of plans based on similar factors. They compared the two lists and found that the following plans appeared on both: California, Connecticut, Georgia, Hawaii, Illinois, Michigan, Minnesota, Missouri, Nebraska, New York, Oklahoma, Utah, and Vermont. Still a lot to consider. Now they headed to Kiplinger.com to see what was recommended there. The only plans that appeared on all three sites were the ones from Michigan, Minnesota, and Utah. Now they had a manageable number to look at and compare individually.

Of the three plans remaining on their list, the Michigan and Minnesota plans were almost identical, which comes as no surprise because they're both managed by TIAA-CREF, the monster investment company originally set up to invest retirement money for teachers. TIAA-CREF is a great investment manager for two reasons: It's good performance-wise, and it's cheap fee-wise. For example, these plans had expenses of only 0.65 percent per year. Pretty good considering many plans have expenses as high as 2 percent. And who wants his return reduced by 2 percent when it could be shaved by a fraction of that amount? Another plus for the Michigan and Minnesota plans was a minimum contribution of just $25. Can't get much lower than that. Okay, now it was time to see what Utah had to offer. The asset manager was a name they recognized: Vanguard. And as with Vanguard mutual funds, the expenses here were scraping the bottom of the barrel: just 0.35 percent. In addition, the Utah/Vanguard plan was also the simplest, since it offered only three basic investment options: a stock fund, a bond fund and a money market fund (which also should ring a bell). The minimum contribution was higher than the other finalists: $300. But this wasn't a deal breaker: They could invest in that increment. They decided to take a closer look.

A link on the Kiplinger.com Web site took them directly to the Utah Educational Savings Plan Trust Web site (www.uesp.org), where they learned exactly what the plan looked like. Let's look over their shoulder and check it out.

The Utah plan, as with most other college savings plans, invests in a mix of stocks and bonds depending on the age of the future student. In addition, the mix can be further refined based on the risk tolerance of the investor, leaving you with four separate possibilities.

Here's a table laying them out, condensed from the plan's online brochure:

Age	Option 1	Option 2			Option 3		Option 4
	Money Market	Stocks	Bonds	Money Market	Stocks	Bonds	Stocks
0–3	100%	95%	5%		100%		100%
4–6	100%	85%	15%		100%		100%
7–9	100%	75%	25%		100%		100%
10–12	100%	65%	35%		95%	5%	100%
13–15	100%	50%	40%	10%	85%	15%	100%
16+	100%	25%	50%	25%	75%	25%	100%
Enrolled	100%			100%	65%	35%	100%

When you first look at this chart, it's confusing, but stare for a second or two and it comes into focus. On the left, we have the age of our future student (known in plan lingo as the beneficiary). As with the ultrasimple formula that we used to divide up our personal savings in the chapter on asset allocation, we see that college savings plans use the same criterion—age—to divide up our kid's savings.

The options get more risky (and therefore more potentially rewarding) as you read from left to right. Option 1 is for the superconservative: No matter what the kid's age, the money's staying in money market funds[39] from birth through graduation. Option 2 starts off heavy in stocks, then reduces the amount as college age rolls around, ending up entirely in money market funds during college. Option 3 gets a little dicier: heavy in stocks pretty much the whole time. Even while the student is enrolled, 35 percent of the savings are still in stocks. And Option 4 is strictly for those who eat razor blades for breakfast: all stocks all the time.

Olaf and Frauke felt that the most prudent course for them was

[39] The Utah plan actually calls this option the Public Treasurer's Investment Fund, or PTIF. But a footnote in the brochure assures us that this money is indeed invested in short-term money market funds.

Option 2, because it felt a lot like their own investment planning: more stocks when time is on their side and less as the target date approaches. Perfectly logical. And it's even simpler than their retirement investing because Utah's investment managers reallocate the funds automatically as Charlie ages. All they had to do was sign up (they can download the application online) and start investing (can be done with automatic withdrawals so they don't have to remember to write a check). What could be simpler? They created a miniature version of their own investment mix that was just as simple and just as low cost. They spent not much time, got what's very likely to be the biggest bang for their buck, and ended up with a plan that's exceedingly simple.

As we prepare to leave our discussion on prepaid tuition and college savings plans, let's stop and reflect for a moment on why Olaf and Frauke might have opted for a college savings plan instead of the prepaid tuition version. First, Frauke considered that while the average inflation rate for tuition over the last twenty years was 8 percent, the stock market averaged more than 10 percent during this same period. Furthermore, Olaf noted that the inflation rate for college costs had declined in recent years: Numbers he found at the finaid.org Web site indicated that the rate from 1996 through 2001 had averaged only about 6 percent. Finally, the asset allocation model that they discovered in college savings programs closely resembled their 401(k) and other long-term investment plans. If it's good enough for them, shouldn't it be good enough for Charles?

When you opt for a college savings program over a prepaid tuition plan, what you're doing is opting for an uncertain return (more risk) in exchange for additional potential profit (more reward). A prepaid tuition program is doing nothing more than locking in a rate of return that's equal to the inflation rate of that state's tuition. If stocks and/or bonds outperform this rate (likely, at least over time), you'll be leaving money on the table and would have been better off in a college savings program. If stocks and/or bonds underperform the state's tuition inflation rate, you'd have been better off in a prepaid tuition program. Since stocks historically have outperformed inflation (including the higher rate of inflation relating to tuition), a college savings program should be the logical option, especially if you start early. Deposit $300 a month for thirteen years and earn 6 percent, and you'll end up with $71,000. But earn 9 percent and your four-year-old will start partying with $87,000.

I hasten to add, however, what I've said before when it comes to the stock market: The goal isn't just maximum return. Because just as important is comfort. If you're more comfortable knowing that you've got your costs covered, then prepaid tuition is for you. If you like the idea of more risk for more reward, then you should consider a college savings program. Neither is a stupid choice, and both offer good tax breaks. Just make sure that your kid goes to college, or someone in your family does, because the penalty for non-college-related withdrawals is 10 percent, just like early withdrawals from qualified retirement plans. And since flawless money management means never paying penalties, you know what you'll have to do if none of your kids uses the money? That's right . . . you'll have to go back to school yourself to make sure that money gets used. And now that you're older, four years is a long time to party.

I think I've droned on long enough regarding 529 plans. I've told you where to find plenty of information to study, and if one of these plans sounds interesting, study you should. Just remember the key benefits of both plans:

- Your money grows tax-deferred (like an IRA, 401(k), or other retirement plan).
- Depending on the state you live in, you may get a state tax deduction for money you invest. You won't, however, get a federal tax deduction.
- When the money comes out to pay for tuition or other qualified college costs, it will do so free of both state and federal income taxes. (But remember that the federal tax benefit will expire in 2010 unless Congress does something to make it last.)

You may think class is now dismissed, but it's not, so stop fidgeting and looking at the clock. There are still a few other tax-saving, college-related investments to study. But we'll hit them quickly, along with sources for finding the details when you're good and ready to look at them.

U.S. Savings Bonds

You already learned about savings bonds back in chapter 5, "Bonds," but since that was more than fifty pages ago, here's the down and dirty: They're safe, they pay decent interest, you don't have to pay federal taxes on the interest until you cash them in, and you never have to pay state taxes at all. What could be better?

Here's what could be better: a program that makes the interest from U.S. Savings Bonds federally tax-free when you cash them in. And what do you know . . . there is such a program! It's called the education bond program. Use the interest you earn on Series I or EE savings bonds for expenses related to higher education, and you get to bypass federal income taxes on the interest. One caveat, however: If you make too much money, you don't get to skip the federal taxman after all. In this case, Uncle Sam considers you rich if you're single and have a modified adjusted gross income of more than $58,500, or if you're filing jointly and have a modified adjusted gross income of $87,700.[40] This is just when the federal tax exemption starts fading, however. It doesn't disappear entirely until you reach $73,500 single and $117,750 joint. In case you're wondering what the heck "modified adjusted gross" income is, wonder no more: It's basically just adjusted gross income plus the interest you're earning on these otherwise tax-free savings bonds. And in case you're wondering what "adjusted gross income" is, don't sweat it; that's coming up soon in the chapter on income taxes. But if you can't wait, you can just look at the first page of any 1040 tax form and you'll immediately see how gross income becomes adjusted gross income.

[40] These are the income limits for 2003, but they rise by the inflation rate. So unless you're reading this way after I wrote it, they're probably still in the ballpark.

Dying to learn more about the education bond program? God help you. But if that's your itch, here's where to scratch: Download IRS form 970 at irs.gov, go to savingsbonds.gov, or visit finaid.org.

Education IRAs

These are actually not called education IRAs anymore. When the government realized it had named something simply and in a cleverly descriptive fashion, it rushed to change the name to something more obtuse. So now they're called Coverdell Education Savings Accounts.[41] If you're up to speed on the basics of IRAs and the other education-related investments we've already discussed, you'll easily master the rules concerning Coverdells. Max amount any beneficiary (translation: student) can have invested on her behalf in any given year is $2,000. Money going in isn't deductible; money earned isn't taxed while it accumulates; money coming out is tax-free providing it's used for education-related expenses. And guess what happens if you take money out that isn't used for educational expenses? If you answered, "10 percent penalty, and you have to pay taxes on the earnings," you've made me very proud indeed.

One thing that makes Coverdells a little different from savings bonds or other education savings vehicles is that these accounts don't have to be used for higher education. They can be used for any kind of education, including elementary and high school.

As with our education bond program and some other types of IRAs, Uncle Sam takes back his promise of tax-free withdrawals from Coverdell accounts if you make too much money. How does Uncle Sam define "rich" this time? Tax-free withdrawals start phasing out for single filers with modified adjusted gross income of $95,000 and joint filers who hit modified adjusted gross of $190,000. And they disappear entirely when that rich single filer hits $110,000 and the joint filers arrive at $220,000. The definition of rich changes more often than a chameleon in a plaid factory, doesn't it?

[41] I'm sure the name was actually changed to honor some person who fiddled around with education IRAs, but to be honest, I really just don't care enough to find out.

For those who are planning to actually use one of these accounts or are really hurting for reading material, download IRS Publication 970 at irs.gov. You can also get the details at college-related Web sites like finaid.org.

Traditional and Roth IRAs

If you're under fifty-nine and a half, you can still take money out of traditional and Roth IRAs without triggering the 10 percent penalty if the money is going to be used for qualified education expenses. Fine, but you still have to pay taxes on the withdrawal: taxes on the whole amount if it's a traditional IRA, and taxes on the earnings if it's a Roth. So this is obviously not your best choice, and should probably be reserved for those whose children are unwilling or unable to forage for aluminum cans on the side of the highway.

Other Stuff

I could ramble on practically forever when it comes to financing a college education, because while we've talked about the basics of different investments, we haven't even touched on financial aid in the form of scholarships, loans, and grants. Nor have we talked about the tax breaks you get by being able to deduct interest on student loans, or collect credits like the hope credit and the lifetime learning credit. The problem is that if I cover everything, we'd be looking at a book here rather than a chapter, so I'm going to have to stop soon. But before I do, a few more notes.

When you start your college planning, become acquainted with the possible ownership of college-related savings accounts, as well as the advantages and disadvantages of each. This is important because sometimes who owns investments will radically affect your future partier's ability to get aid. We're often tempted to put savings accounts and such in our kids' names because they're in lower tax brackets than we are. But this can be a bad strategy, because students are normally required to contribute a much greater portion of their savings (typically 35 percent) before qualifying for aid, while their parents are required to contribute a much lower percentage (not more than 6 percent). So you're probably better off keeping college savings in your name rather than mini Einstein's, at least if there's a ghost of a chance that she'll someday qualify for aid. In any case, read about it at any of the college Web sites I've mentioned before you forge ahead.

One of the first things I said in this chapter was that you never, ever pay for help in finding scholarship or grant money, because there's nothing you can pay for that you can't get free. For example, you can do a free scholarship search at sites like www.fastweb.com, www.scholarship.com, www.collegeboard.com, and a ton of others. (I just did a search for "college scholarship search" and got more than a million hits.) You can go to the public library and check out any of dozens of books on the subject. You can contact any high school counseling or college financial aid office for ideas. Trust me: There are far more free sources for college scholarship assistance than there are hours left to use them, no matter how old your kid is. All this information used to require a degree to assimilate. Now it just takes a few clicks of a mouse.

As to the tax deductions and credits available for those readers already laboring under the tuition burden, I really don't have to explain much. Because your $20 tax preparation software program never sleeps, and it wouldn't think of letting anything claimable slip by.

In conclusion, while saving for college seems to be an onerous task, it's really no big deal. Yes, the ramp-up process does require a bit of extra effort. But as you've seen, most of the options are basic, are logical, and resemble other things we've already encountered. And once you've made your selections, they're pretty low maintenance. A small price to pay for a four-year party!

12

Deflating Inflation

Certainly there are things in life that money can't buy,
but it's very funny—Did you ever try
buying them without money?
—Ogden Nash

If you've ever been through any type of financial planning, you've probably heard all about, and been duly frightened by, inflation. The word "inflation" refers to the gradual erosion of the purchasing power of money due to rising prices over time. In other words, your money is worth less because stuff costs more. While it may seem that rising prices are bad, actually the folks who guide our economy like a little inflation. That's because the opposite of inflation, deflation, is the stuff that nightmares are made of. Deflation, or falling prices, nearly always accompanies a severe economic downturn, like our Great Depression of the 1930s or the great Japanese depression that's still ongoing. Since soup lines aren't considered the result of sound fiscal policy, inflation, as long as it stays in the 1 to 3 percent range, is fine by most economists.

The problem with inflation, even if it's just a couple of percent a year, is that over long periods of time it can hurt your ability to maintain your standard of living. We've all heard stories of (or maybe even personally remember) loaves of bread that cost a nickel, cars that cost $2,000, houses that cost $5,000, and executive salaries of $3,000 a year. And it's not hard to imagine that living on $3,000 a year these days would be quite a trick. So inflation quickly becomes public enemy number one when retirement investing is the topic of conversation, and that's why it's always mentioned in books like this.

While inflation is certainly a real and potentially serious barrier to your financial security, I'm going to tell you something that you'll probably never read anywhere else. It may not be as big a deal as you think. Inflation is not cast in stone, nor is it automatic, despite what many financial planners would lead you to believe. And it's quite possible that it's not nearly as big a threat as you might expect. Why? Because *your* rate of inflation, which is the only one that really matters, largely depends on you personally. It depends on whether you're choosing to spend your money on things that are increasing rapidly in cost and if so, what you're willing to do about it.

Consider the consumer price index, or CPI, by far the most popular gauge of inflation at the consumer level. Every month, the CPI is computed by the Department of Labor and announced on the national news with varying degrees of fanfare. But when Tom Brokaw tells you that your cost of living went up by an annual rate of 3 percent last month, is he being accurate?

As I explained earlier, the Dow Jones Industrial Average is not the stock market. It's only thirty stocks out of about six thousand that trade on any given day. But because it's a decent proxy for the overall market (meaning that it often does represent the same percentage move that the overall market made that day), it's used to help us understand at a glance what happened in a particular trading session. The consumer price index is the same kind of thing, at least theoretically. Here's how the Department of Labor describes the CPI: "changes in the prices paid by urban consumers for a representative basket of goods and services."

But even if you're an urban consumer, the question remains . . . is it representative of you?

If your family buys all the representative goods and services that the Labor Department tracks every month, the CPI does indeed accurately depict your personal inflation rate. But if you don't, it doesn't. So wouldn't it make sense to see what goods and services the Department of Labor is tracking before we go around scaring ourselves to death with these numbers? When you go to the department's CPI Web site (http://www.bls.gov/cpi/), one of the things you'll find is a calculator that will tell you how much money you need today to buy the same stuff you could buy in 1980. For example, plug in $10,000 and the calculator will instantly tell you that if that's how much you had in 1980, you'll need $22,000 to buy the same stuff today. This kind of information certainly helps sell investments because it convinces people that not doing something immediate and commission-generating in order to increase their net worth will ultimately result in their eating out of Dumpsters.

Inflation is most often used to scare people who are either retired or on the verge of retirement. Why? Because they're the ones who will no longer have the ability to increase their income or their savings and thereby offset it. They're no longer getting a salary that will keep pace with the spiraling cost of living. (They do, however, often receive Social Security, which in fact does have cost-of-living increases.) They've been gathering acorns all their lives, and now they've reached the time when they're going to have to start eating them. So their greatest fear is that they'll run out of acorns before they run out of time, especially since their acorn-gathering days are behind them. And this is a legitimate fear, since according to IRS life-expectancy tables, the average sixty-five-year-old will live for another twenty-one years.[42] So if you're an investment salesperson, demonstrating how the purchasing power of the dollar is reduced by half every twenty years is a great way to get stubborn seniors off their duffs and into stocks, which have proven to be long-term inflation beaters.

But before we start freaking out about inflation, let's see what's being measured.

[42] http://www.irs.gov/pub/irs-pdf/p590supp.pdf.

Prices for the goods and services used to calculate the CPI are collected in eighty-seven urban areas throughout the country from about twenty-three thousand retail and service establishments. There are more than two hundred products and services sampled, but they can be broken down into the following eight categories. Here they are, along with the weighting that each category receives in determining the final overall inflation number.[43]

- ***Food and Beverages.*** **Percentage of CPI: 16 percent.** All manner of food and drink, including full-service meals, snacks, and alcoholic beverages. A little more than half of this total comes from food and beverages at home; a little less than half comes from price changes in restaurant meals. In terms of overall percentages, alcohol and meat are about equally weighted.
- ***Housing.*** **Percentage of CPI: 40 percent.** About three-quarters of this number comes from rent and owner's equivalent rent. The rest is roughly divided equally between utilities and furnishings.
- ***Apparel.*** **Percentage of CPI: 4 percent.** Men's shirts and sweaters, women's dresses, shoes, jewelry. Women's stuff is a bigger chunk than men's. (Astounding!)
- ***Transportation.*** **Percentage of CPI: 17 percent.** Little bit gas, little bit maintenance, little bit car insurance, little bit airfares, but mostly new and used car prices.
- ***Medical Care.*** **Percentage of CPI: 6 percent.** Prescription drugs and medical supplies, physicians' services, eyeglasses and eye care, hospital services.
- ***Recreation.*** **Percentage of CPI: 6 percent.** Television sets, cable television, pets and pet products, sports equipment, movie and theater admissions.
- ***Education and Communication.*** **Percentage of CPI: 6 percent.** About half is college related, and the other half is postage, telephone services, and computer stuff.

[43] http://www.bls.gov/cpi/cpiri_2001.pdf, pages 6–10. These are for the year ending 2001. Percentages don't quite equal 100 due to rounding errors.

- *Other Goods and Services.* Percentage of CPI: 4 percent. Tobacco and smoking products, haircuts and other personal services, funeral expenses.

So how will our average retired person be affected by changes in the consumer price index? The fact is that there's no such thing as an average retired person, but let's have a look and see if we can draw some general conclusions. Nearly half of the food component of the CPI involves eating out, so if I were concerned about keeping that inflation cost down, I might eat a meal at home, then go out for dessert. When it comes to housing, people who own their own homes (whether they're retired or not) aren't affected by this at all, unless maybe they've got an adjustable mortgage. And this is by far the biggest single category of CPI. In fact, homeowners should really want this part of the index to skyrocket, since that would reflect higher home values. Ditto if our average retiree happens to be a landlord. Fact is, real estate, whether rental or owner occupied, is the single biggest savings account most of us will ever have. So inflation in this category, as long as we already own some real estate, is more good than bad.

Clothing isn't a very big component of CPI, but you could easily keep your costs down by buying on sale, buying used, or using my method and simply not buying at all. (Virtually everything I wear I've received as Christmas presents, mostly from my sister-in-law Marcie. And I wear it until it completely dissolves.)

Next to housing, transportation is the largest component of what we regard as inflation, and most of that is made up of how new cars escalate in price. Since buying a new car is pretty much a waste of money anyway, this part of the CPI could be addressed by buying used. Airline tickets certainly aren't taking wing, are they? Gas prices have clearly gone up over the years, but the availability of more economical cars has also increased. Insurance goes ever higher, but as you'll see in chapter 16, on insurance, there are many ways to lower this cost.

Medical expenses are huge for seniors, but then again they also have access to Medicare, which covers a large part of medical expenses. Drugs aren't covered by Medicare, but then drugs are also less than 1 percent of the CPI. If I wanted to cut my costs on prescription drugs, I'd either try to get generics or visit Mexico and/or Canada every now and then, where prices are about half what they are in the United States.

Recreation costs are about as heavily weighted in CPI as medical costs. (I'm not sure which category recreational drugs fall into.) One of the largest components of recreation is television sets, which are certainly getting cheaper all the time. Cable is going up in price, but it's hardly a necessity. I'd rather read a good book myself, and they're still free at the library. Another big component of recreation is club membership, and I certainly wouldn't consider joining any club that would consider having me as a member.

Education is probably not a major issue for seniors. (I know it isn't for my parents, because, judging by the advice they're always handing out, they already know everything. Just kidding, Mom.) Obviously rising education costs are a huge concern for people with young children, but as you learned in chapter 11 on saving for college, there are ways to deal with them that didn't exist a few years ago. As for communication, long distance is a small fraction of what it used to cost, and there's no such thing as postage in cyberspace. Computers are getting cheaper all the time, especially if you're willing to settle for second generation. So in this overall category, with the exception of tuition, there's more deflation happening than inflation.

Most of the "other" category concerns itself with toiletries (can you say "Sam's Club"?), tobacco (roll yer own!), and services like funerals (note that cremations, which cost a fraction of burials, are growing in popularity) and legal (software is certainly cheaper than a lawyer).

So where am I going with all this? I'm not suggesting that inflation shouldn't be a factor in your financial planning. It most definitely should be. But inflation depends largely on the type of discretionary spending you do—therefore you have a great deal of influence on how much influence it has on you. There are certainly components that are pretty much out of your control (property taxes come to mind), but the next time Tom Brokaw tells you what the CPI did last month, don't automatically assume that that's what it did to you or your savings. And as you'll see when you read through other parts of this book, and/or check out other sources for saving money, there are ways to compromise many price increases that come along.

13

Setting Goals

It would be nice if the poor were to get even half of the money that is spent studying them.

—Bill Vaughan

Hey, let's go for a ride! Where do you want to go? Nowhere? Okay, we'll just drive around aimlessly and hope we accidentally end up somewhere interesting. Hop in!

That's the way most people plan their financial life. They may have a vague idea of where they want to go, but they're not really sure in which direction to point or how long the trip will take. Then they spend the rest of their lives zigging, zagging, asking directions, and wondering, "Are we there yet?"

If you feel like you're not getting what you want, or feel confused about money, this could be one reason why. Because if you don't know what your specific goals are, they obviously can't be achieved.

If you want something from life, no matter what it is, the fastest way to get it is to describe what it is you want as specifically as possible, visualize it, understand why it's important, define the tasks required to achieve it, divide those tasks into manageable steps, and follow through. If you don't do each and every one of these steps, you'll either never get what you want, or you'll take longer than necessary to do it. These steps are the road map that represents the shortest path from where you are now to where you want to go. And a map is the only thing that keeps you from driving around in circles.

Okay . . . so where do you want to go? Do you want to be self-employed? Do you want to retire at age fifty? Do you want to send your kids to Yale? Do you want to pay off your house? Write a book? Be an actor? What you want from life is a unique and very personal reflection of who you are. Most people never even think about what they really want, much less do anything to make it happen. Oh, sure, when pressed most of us will spit out some canned answer to the question of what we want. "I want to be rich!" "I want to go fishing every day!" "I want to be a Stanford professor!" "I wanna be a rock star!" But that's about as far as it goes. One major reason is probably because a dream that's not acted on can remain a dream. In other words, if you never attempt to make your dreams into reality, you can't fail. Of course, you can't succeed, either, but for most people avoiding failure is more important than not getting what they want. Pain avoidance is human nature, which is a shame since the pain of repeated failure is incredibly insignificant when measured against the pleasure of ultimate victory.

But let's assume that we're sufficiently self-actualized to risk failure and we're ready to attempt to turn a vague image, which is another name for a dream, into something we actually intend to achieve, which is another name for a goal. Let's pick something, follow the steps, and see what happens.

Let's become rock stars. Time to describe, visualize, understand, define tasks, create a list of specific steps, and follow through.

First, we describe what it means to be a rock star. "Rock" obviously implies what kind of music we play, but what's a "star"? Our thesaurus tells us that synonyms for "star" include dominant, main, major, outstanding, predominant, preeminent, and principal. And from our dictionary we find several fitting definitions: a highly publicized theatrical or motion-picture performer: an outstandingly talented performer <a track *star*> : a person who is preeminent in a particular field.[44]

Cool. That's what *Webster's* says, but let's see exactly what *we* mean when we use the words "rock star" by visualizing what a rock star looks like in our mind's eye. There we are on stage, in tight leather pants, belting out the blues. Now we're sitting on a bar stool in our private studio, guitar in hand, putting the finishing touches on our latest creation. And there we are getting out of our limousine and being mobbed by adoring fans.

Now we've got a clear picture of what we mean by rock star. Let's use this to see if we can understand why this whole thing is so important. In other words, what are we *really* after? Rock stars are rich. Is it the security that comes with money that we're after? Well, security is certainly appealing, of course, but when we honestly assess it, that's the icing, not the cake. Rock stars create original works of art. Is it artistic expression that we yearn for? Hmm . . . that rings true. Yes, definitely part of what makes being a rock star so appealing. Of course, we could be creative without being a star, so there must be something else. What about fame? Eureka! This is definitely the core of our desire; the crux of the biscuit.[45] When we visualize being a rock star, the clearest and most appealing image we have is the throngs of people pressing their eager faces against the windows of our limo, desperate to catch a glimpse of us. So what we really want is the immediate recognition and respect that comes with fame. We want to be the center of attention for a change. Yep, that's it. Anything else? Well, since this is our personal, private visualization, let's come completely clean: a few dozen groupies never hurt.

Fine. Now we know exactly what we want and what it looks like—and more important, we know exactly *why* we want it. We know what spiritual need is being met by accomplishing our goal: the need for recognition. Now that we know this, we might want to

[44] Merriam-Webster online dictionary.

[45] In case you're not familiar with the term "crux of the biscuit," it comes from the lyrics to a song by one of my personal heroes, Frank Zappa. Hey, if you're going to be a rock star, you should know stuff like this!

figure out why this spiritual need is so important for us, or we might not. Either way, we're ready to take the next step.

We've described what we want, we've visualized it, and we understand why this goal is so important. It's time to define the steps to make it happen. Step 1: Best we learn to play a guitar and sing. Step 2: We need to figure out how one goes about cutting an album and do it. Step 3: We need to figure out how we're going to get noticed so that we can get our big break.

These are the broad strokes. Now we've got to make an itemized list of specific tasks to accomplish these steps. Since this isn't my goal, I'm not sure what these steps might be, but maybe they would include things like signing up for guitar and singing lessons, reading a book or two about how other people have done it, finding other musicians to hang out and jam with, forming a band, looking up theatrical agents, playing in the right nightclubs, contacting a recording studio, entering a battle of the bands, getting our demo into the hands of a major record label . . . et cetera, et cetera.

As we list each specific task, we record exactly by what date we'll have it done. As we proceed, we periodically review our progress, add steps if necessary, and adjust our deadlines to conform to an ever-changing reality.

Now all that's left is to follow through. Easy to say, tough to do. In fact, simply showing up, persevering, is without a doubt the least understood component of success.

I've been successful at two careers in my life: stockbrokerage and TV news. While these careers have almost nothing in common, interestingly enough both took around five years of failure, of daily rejection, before anything appeared that even slightly resembled success. In both careers, during these five-year periods I watched the vast majority of my peers quit and go elsewhere. I'm not suggesting that success always takes five years, nor am I saying that if something isn't working out you should stick to it regardless. I'm simply saying that nothing worth having is easy to obtain, and complete commitment is the only way to obtain it, at least in my experience. I'll bet you won't find a rock star who argues this point.

On the off chance that being a rock star isn't your primary goal, maybe we should include a quick example of something that may relate more closely to the subject at hand. Say, retiring early.

First, we've got to describe exactly what "retiring" means, and then what "early" means. I've often mentioned to my wife that I'd like to retire sometime soon, and she just laughs. She laughs because when I use the word "retire" she visualizes someone sitting on the front porch in a rocking chair. And she knows that I'm definitely off my rocker. I'm more like a shark: If I'm not moving, it can only be because I'm dead. Therefore she knows there's no way I'm retiring, at least not anytime soon. But that's not the vision of retiring that I had in mind. I'm talking about having the *ability* to do things other than face deadlines. If I want to work, which I undoubtedly will, fine. But I want to have enough so that regular, intense work is optional. So my vision of retirement is actually having the financial security that affords us the freedom to do what we want, when we want. And if what we want to do is nothing, we can. As to understanding why I want to accomplish this, the spiritual goal I'm striving for is security: to know that if push comes to shove, I'm going to be okay. And just as important, I need to know that if something should happen to me, Gina will be okay. Finally, to be brutally honest, I kind of like the ego gratification that I'd get when someone asks me what I do and I respond, "Whatever I like." It's that recognition-and-respect thing.

Now I understand why my goal is important to me. I've described and visualized, but I'm not done yet. Because I still haven't defined how much money I'll need to meet my definition of retiring. To do this, I'll have to know the approximate amount of money I'll be spending when I'm retired. Once I know this, I can extrapolate how much principal will be required to throw off that much income. I can subtract what I already have from what I need, see what the shortfall is, and then figure out how to fill the gap with monthly contributions to savings. When I've done all this, I'll know exactly how much time it's going to take. Only then can I know whether my goal of retiring early is possible and, if so, what "early" will look like.

Before we can plug in some numbers, we first have to get specific about what our retired life will look like. Gina and I talk it over and think out loud about what we'd do if we had more free time. We both love traveling, so we'll definitely be doing some of that. We also like boating, motorcycle riding, and dancing in our favorite honky-tonks. As we think it through together, we come to grips with the kind of people we are. We realize that we don't require expensive toys; nor do we need to do our traveling in a limo or private jet. But we're not hitchhikers or panhandlers, either, and the occasional big splurge is something we both enjoy. We think this kind of stuff through thoroughly, estimate what we'd like to spend having fun every month, and combine that with more mundane expenses, like keeping the lights on and eating. We arrive at a monthly income requirement of $6,000, which we think will do the job once our mortgage is paid off. We also factor in that we could be earning additional money by things like the occasional public speaking engagement or royalty check. But since these things are uncertain, they're icing, not cake.

So now we've described what we want, visualized what it's going to look like, and understand why we want to accomplish this goal. Time to build a road map by defining the steps to get there.

The steps to saving for an early retirement are pretty basic. Actually, there's only one: We need to know how much principal we'll need to generate an income of $6,000 a month.

In days gone by, this would have been the start of a daunting task. On the surface, it's no biggie: If I need $6,000 a month, that's $72,000 a year. And if I assume that I can earn 7 percent on my money, all I have to do is divide 72,000 by 7 percent and I arrive at $1,028,571. So, all things being equal, I need about a million bucks to spend $72,000 every year without putting a dent in the principal. But all things aren't equal. Because we also have to factor in things like Social Security, which we won't be getting until our midsixties. We have money in retirement plans that we can't touch without penalty until we turn fifty-nine and a half. There's inflation to consider. Income taxes. We don't know how long we're going to live. And we don't necessarily need to die with a million dollars in the bank, which means that we could ultimately choose at some point to spend our principal. Add up all the variables and you have trouble adding up all the variables. In the days before technology, the resulting confusion might have sent us to a securities salesperson disguised as a financial planner.

These days, however, we can quickly find free and accurate help to do all this number crunching for us. There are plenty of calculators online; let's use the one I found at the CNN/*Money Magazine* Web site (http://cgi.money.cnn.com).

In the first section, the calculator asks me to input the following information: both of our current ages (I'm forty-seven, but I'm way too smart to tell you how old Gina is), our desired retirement ages (I said fifty-five for me, which is eight years from now), our life expectancies (I said eighty-five), our current income (none of your beeswax), what kind of annual raises we expect (I said 3 percent), and our desired income at retirement ($72,000).

The next section of the calculator starts by telling me what we can expect from Social Security, but allows me to make adjustments if I think it's wrong. (Remember, I can go to ssa.gov for projections, or even request a personal benefits statement if I choose.) Then it asks if I've got other sources for retirement income, like maybe a pension plan. (No such luck.) On to the next section, which concerns itself with what I already have in savings.

In this section of the calculator, I input the current balances in my 401(k), how much I'm contributing as a percentage of my annual pay, and any company match I'm getting. It also asks about any IRAs, SEPs, or other retirement accounts. Then it asks about our nonretirement savings accounts: what we have now and how much we're adding to them every year. Finally, it wants to know what tax bracket we're in on both the federal and state level.

The next question our calculator asks is what type of investing we're doing: very conservative, conservative, passive, balanced, active, aggressive, or very aggressive. It describes what it means for each category by offering an investment mix. We don't really fit exactly into any of the seven possible categories, but I choose "active."

All the information required was readily available, and filling in the blanks took only a few minutes—easily accomplished during one commercial break. Now all that's left is the results. A click of a mouse and there it is: I'll need to have a total of $1,236,003 to retire in eight years, and given what I've told the calculator about what I already have in savings, what I'm adding every year, and how much the whole enchilada is earning, I have a 71 percent chance of making it.

The calculator also provides me with a detailed breakdown of the income I'll be getting, including Social Security, and tells me how much we'll have left over when we die. It allows me to make adjustments. For example, I can tell it to increase my annual savings contributions so that my probability of success goes from 71 percent to 90 percent. (This would require my saving an additional two grand a month.) It factors in inflation. So we've arrived at a decent, but not perfect, conclusion.

Why isn't the conclusion perfect? Because there's no calculator that can know me personally or ask every possible question that could potentially influence the outcome. For example, this model assumes I'll only be earning about 3 percent on my savings—realistic, perhaps, but I think that by using rental real estate or other slightly less conservative investments I can do better. The calculator also doesn't know that I might be earning some additional income during my retirement years, nor does it consider that I'm willing to make lifestyle adjustments to counteract part of the inflation it's assuming. It didn't ask if I'd be inheriting. It can't know how long I'll actually live, nor did it allow me to make adjustments to the amount we want to have left over when we die. (Since we don't have any kids, I don't have a compelling desire to die with half a million bucks, which is how much it said we'd have.) It didn't ask whether I'd be willing to sell my home at some point and move to something smaller, thus adding to savings. There's no way for any calculator, or its human counterpart, to factor in every variable, account for every possibility, or know my personal capabilities. So they can only be used as a starting point, albeit a solid one.

Bottom line? This calculator was a huge help in defining the steps (in other words, telling us how much we'll have to save) to achieve our goal of retirement when I turn fifty-five. If I want to get more detailed—and I probably would if this were a true goal for me—I could do additional things like try other calculators or fiddle around with these results to make them more accurately reflect our personal situation.

The result of this exercise, however, is that we now have a much clearer picture of what our goal is, why we have it, and what we'll need to do to accomplish it. So our odds of achieving this goal just went up radically. As for the next step in the process, dividing the steps into manageable tasks, that's simple enough. Once I've fine-tuned what we need, we'll make sure we put aside the amount required every month to succeed. And we'll follow through, which will mean putting aside this amount and forgoing spending money, if we can help it, on anything that might keep us from doing this. And unless our goal changes, we'll do it consistently for the next eight years. We'll periodically review our progress, say every four months. We'll make adjustments if necessary and do whatever it takes to keep on keeping on. And when we're tempted to do something that might screw up the odds of reaching our goal, we'll stay on track by calling to mind our well-defined, crystal-clear vision of what we think is most important.

I hope these examples demonstrate the importance of goal setting as well as the process of doing it. The point is that if you want to accomplish something, take it out of your dreams and make it a goal by planning it out in detail and writing it down. Because dreams only come true by accident; goals are achieved by design. Accept the fact that failure is always a possibility and goals are dynamic; they often change. Also accept the fact that, as in the preceding example, most of the time you can't factor in every conceivable variable. You can radically reduce your odds of failing by first discovering what it is you're actually attempting to achieve. For example, when we defined and visualized being a rock star, we discovered what we really wanted was recognition, not a limousine. Well, there are other ways of gaining recognition than being a rock star. Like writing a book, for example, or starring in a community play. Granted, this isn't the same level of recognition, but maybe when we weigh the probability of success and the time and effort required, it's a spiritual compromise we can live with. How we'll survive without groupies, however, I haven't the foggiest.

But as you go through the organizational process of becoming a flawless money manager, remember that what you're doing is enhancing your ability to get where you want to go. Goals are destinations. And without destinations, there's nothing for a money manager to manage. So go places; set some goals.

14

Getting Organized

The person who doesn't know where his next dollar
is coming from usually doesn't know
where his last dollar went.

—ANONYMOUS

As the twenty-first century dawned, the world was aglow over the Internet. The Internet was going to make the invention of things like TV, radio, and personal computers pale in comparison. This technology, like the Industrial Revolution, marked a quantum leap in human productivity. It would forever connect businesses with suppliers and us with everyone else on the planet. We would throw away our TVs and telephones, because the Internet was going to supply us with video and allow us to communicate globally at little or no cost. We wouldn't need libraries, since the Internet would offer free access to all information known to humankind. We weren't going to need books, because we could read anything by anybody anytime in any room of the house. We weren't going to need stores, because we could order everything from groceries to jet planes and have it delivered right to our door (or hangar, as the case may be).

The Internet was going to allow us to shrink the planet to the size of a golf ball and make us all wealthier, healthier, happier, more productive, and better informed. Forget sliced bread; this was the best thing since oxygen.

What happened? As with many things in life, the promise outstripped the reality. Because of the hype, companies with little more than a stupid idea were able to raise billions of dollars, which certainly changed their world, but not anyone else's. In many cases, these companies went out of business, leaving small investors holding the bag. (See chapter 1, "A Tale of Two Pities.") Result? What felt just a few years ago like a revolution in evolution now feels more like a pyramid scheme.

Hype aside, the truth is that the Internet *is* a revolution and *does* represent a quantum leap in productivity. Because in many ways, the Internet has lived up to the promise, especially as it applies to your becoming a flawless financial manager. So if you don't have a computer, get one. And if you're not hooked up to the Internet, get that way. Don't have the money? Then become acquainted with your local library. Computers there are hooked up to the Internet, and the reason they're there is because you and your neighbors paid for them.[46]

Managing your money quickly and effectively means keeping your fingers on the pulse of your financial world. In other words, knowing where your money is, making sure you're getting what you're paying for, being able to quickly and accurately comparison-shop, and avoiding paying for services you don't need. With a computer and the Internet, you'll always know where your money is and where it's going. You'll be able to do your income taxes in a few minutes every year, and comparison-shop for everything from a picture frame to life insurance in less than a minute. Thanks to technology, you'll be fast, accurate, knowledgeable, and in control in a way that was completely impossible just a few short years ago.

Can you do all this without a computer and/or the World Wide Web? Some things you can . . . for example, you can certainly keep

[46] A portion of your local phone bill goes to pay for computers and Internet access for public libraries. So if you have a phone, you're paying for public Internet access.

track of where your money is coming from and where it's going, because all you need for that is a piece of paper and a pencil. But will you be able to shop ten long-distance service providers in ten seconds? Nope. Will you be able to do your taxes in ten minutes? Fahgiddaboutit.

Two hundred years ago, it took weeks to travel from New York to San Francisco, because the only way of getting there was on either a horse or a ship. Then trains came along, which made the trip much faster. Then planes, which ultimately condensed the trip to its current five or six hours. But while I'm describing these changes as if they happened in the blink of an eye, the truth is much different. People didn't stop using horses the instant the first train rolled down the tracks. It took time for the new technology to gain a foothold. It took time for trains to become economically feasible, reliable, and safe, and more time for people to become comfortable with them. Only then could less efficient technologies begin fading away. Same thing with air travel. And this is exactly where we are right now with computers and the Internet. Computerized financial management has now proved its worth and is officially accepted as a mode of getting you from A to B financially. Pencil and paper are wagon trains. So is ignorance, because the Internet is chock-full of information. So is overpaying, because the Internet is such a great source of comparison-shopping. It's only been within the last ten years that the trip from Chaos to Control shrank from weeks to minutes.

All aboard! Here are the steps to prepare for your journey.

- ***Step 1:*** Either get a computer or get access to one. If you decide to buy a computer, it doesn't have to be the latest, fastest, whiz-bang model with a P-9 chip, two gigs of RAM, and a twenty-one-inch flat-screen monitor. It just has to be able to run a couple of simple programs. One of the great things about rapidly evolving technology like computers, especially in consumer economies like ours, is that the value of yesterday's technology is practically zero. So if money is tight, go for yesterday's technology and you'll probably get paid to haul it away. In other words, don't be afraid to buy used or slightly out of date. And if only free is cheap enough, go to the local library.

- *Step 2:* Get some personal finance software. Because you'll want your software to be supported for a long time and have the ability to communicate with other programs (like tax preparation software), I'd advise sticking to one of the biggies in the software business: Intuit's Quicken and Microsoft's Money. As with a computer, you don't need the deluxe version; nor do you need the most current version.[47] Shop around and you should be able to get by with twenty bucks or less. Of course, you could further reduce this price all the way to zero by borrowing the program from a friend or downloading it from a peer-to-peer Web site like KaZaA.com, but I won't suggest you do that because to do so would be to encourage theft. Besides, Microsoft only made $3 billion last quarter,[48] and Intuit (maker of Quicken) made just $70 million all of last year.[49] They obviously need the money more than you.
- *Step 3:* Get an Internet connection up and running. If you want to swell the coffers at AOL Time Warner, pay $23 every month to subscribe to America Online for dial-up service. If you want to swell your own coffers, however, pay less. At cnet.com, you can do a search by area code that will list all the Internet service providers (ISPs) in your area. In my area code, for example, I found dial-up services for as little as $8 a month. If you want to surf the Web really fast, and are willing to pony up hundreds of extra dollars every year to do it, get DSL or cable service. But for our purposes, you can use a cheap dial-up and be fine.
- *Step 4:* Boot up your computer, install your software, fire up the Internet, and start inputting your financial life. This is a time-consuming process, and while you're doing it, you

[47] I've noticed that both Quicken and Microsoft have started putting the year after their respective programs—say, Quicken 2004. This, I assume, is designed specifically to make you feel that if you're using Quicken 2003, you're using something old that needs to be replaced. However, the only thing that probably needs updating is Quicken's bottom line. My advice? If it ain't broke, don't upgrade it.

[48] Microsoft net income for quarter ending September 30, 2002: $2.73 billion.

[49] Intuit net income for fiscal year ending July 31, 2002: $69.8 million.

may feel like a nitpicking, anal-retentive, arm-gartered, Coke-bottle-glasses-wearing, boring geek. I'm sorry. When I figure out a way to track your financial activity with power tools, I'll let you know. For now, however, you'll have to use a keyboard.

That's it. You're ready to roll! As you begin to assemble the paperwork that represents where your money is coming from and where it's going, you'll soon appreciate why the mere act of looking at things will help you feel more in control. You'll also start seeing how you've made your life so complicated and how to make it less so. First, you'll input all your checking, savings, and investment accounts. In other words, what you own. Then you'll put in all your credit card and loan accounts: what you owe. Then you'll tell your program (and yourself) where your money comes from and where it goes. And then you'll be in the same position as any successful business: able to set goals, fine-tune, and review what's happening to maximize your odds of reaching them. We're going to go over each of these things in detail. But before we start inputting all your financial information, let's go off on a brief tangent to discuss general organization.

Using Spreadsheets

If your car won't start, who do you call? What if you've got a leaky pipe? You want to find someone to help you build some shelves? Where do you go when it's time to shop for insurance? A mortgage? How much are your property taxes? Where do you keep all the serial numbers of your electronic equipment? What does your spouse do if you should die unexpectedly?

If you were asking me these or many other questions regarding my household and financial life, I could answer any of them virtually instantly. Because these are some examples of information that I keep forever at my fingertips in spreadsheets. If the word "spreadsheet" sounds a little hoity-toity, use "list." It doesn't matter. I'm just suggesting that if you keep the answers to questions like these in your computer, you'll spend a lot more time riding your Harley and a lot less rifling drawers and looking for stuff.

Let me give you examples of spreadsheets that I refer to often. (I build my spreadsheets on Microsoft Excel, but what you use doesn't matter a whit.) The title of one of my spreadsheets is "Household." Within this spreadsheet are separate pages for mortgage (you'll see this sheet when we get to the real estate section), insurance (you're going to see that as well), property taxes, inventory, vehicle info, vehicle repair, and utilities. Whenever I begin some chore regarding my house or transportation, this is where I go. Another spreadsheet is called "Production Equipment and Supplies." This is where I keep information regarding equipment I use to produce my TV news stories. Here's an example of how they save me time.

Earlier this week, I decided it was time to do three chores. First, one of our cars was running like crap, so I needed to take it to a mechanic. Second, I noticed that the registration for our other car was missing. (How did that happen? Must have been Gina.) Third, I needed to order additional batteries for our production video camera.

First, a mechanic: I went to the car section of my household spreadsheet and there found the names and phone numbers of the two mechanics I've used. I also had brief notes regarding what they'd done, what they'd charged, and how I felt about them. I decided that Mario at A-1 Service was the right guy for this job because my latest note indicated that he does good work at reasonable prices. I called him up and arranged to bring my car in. That took less than a minute.

As for my missing registration, I had a Web site address built into my vehicle info spreadsheet that took me directly to the Department of Motor Vehicles Web site. There I downloaded the form for lost registration and printed it. I sent it in, along with a check for $16. This took about five minutes, much of which was spent on the DMV Web site trying to figure out which form I needed.

Now time for camera batteries. These things are expensive, but I already knew where I could get the best price. How? Months before, I'd used a Web shopping bot to comb the Internet in search of the best deals. Now all I had to do was open the "battery" section of my production equipment spreadsheet. There I found a link to batteries4everything.com. I clicked on it, copied the description of the batteries I needed from my spreadsheet, pasted it into the Web site's search engine, found the batteries, made sure the price was the same as last time, and ordered four. The entire process took about two minutes. I could have done a new Internet search to see if I could find them cheaper still, but I didn't feel like it at that moment. I already knew that the price I was paying was about half of what I'd have paid locally, and that was good enough. While I'm not above scrounging for pennies, I was too busy at that moment to bother.

Now compare what I've just described to what probably would have happened in the days before I was organized and the Internet wasn't standing by to help me. When it came to repairing my car, I'd have gone into the glove compartment, the phone book, or a file folder, desperately seeking Mario. I might have been lucky enough to ultimately find or remember the name of his shop, but I certainly wouldn't have remembered his name, and I certainly would have increased my blood pressure trying because I like to maintain the personal touch when it comes to services like this.

In the days prior to the Internet, there would have been only one way to deal with a lost registration: Call or visit the DMV. I won't waste words reminding you what that's like.

When it comes to camera batteries, I'd have been faced with driving either my sick car or the one with the lost registration to a local store so that I could wait in line to pay twice the price. If they'd had them, that is.

Having information like this at your fingertips will keep repairs, maintenance, and all manner of errands from becoming more stressful, expensive, and time-consuming than they already are. When I'm writing down the names of people and stores I deal with, I don't record all of them—just the ones that do good work or provide good products at reasonable prices, which automatically eliminates most. But over the months, my list of good people and products has gotten longer in each category, which has saved me huge time and aggravation by having to start from scratch every time I need something. And because I strive to keep my relationships friendly by injecting just a pinch of personal touch—easy with a few notes on my spreadsheets—I probably also end up with better service and lower prices to boot.

When it's time to shop for a mortgage or insurance, I'm ready because I've written down where I got the best quotes last time, and I've already got notes and explanations of all the components of every policy I have. Same with mortgage shopping. Because these types of services are shopped so infrequently, not having this stuff written down would mean relearning it every time and starting the whole process from square one. Having it all written down and instantly accessible means less time shopping and more time watching Jerry Springer. And just as important, it also allows my wife to step into my shoes anytime. Me: "Hey baby, I'm going for a motorcycle ride. Would you mind getting a new mortgage while I'm out? You know where the info is." Gina: "Sure, honey. By the way, where do we keep our list of lawyers?"

As I said, you'll soon see some examples of spreadsheets I use, so don't worry about the details right now. But if this concept makes sense, do what I did. As you're going through your life and getting it together, start a spreadsheet collection of your own. Will it take more time in the short run? Most definitely. But the next time a friend asks you for a mechanic, your spouse wants new shelves, or you want a new mortgage, you'll save a ton of time and look like the organized genius that you are.

Now we've completed our little side trip. Let's get back to organizing your financial life by inputting everything about you into personal finance software.

Where's Your Money Hiding Out? What You Own

This part of the process begins by telling your money management software where all your money is right now. You're going to find it scattered among one or more checking accounts, one or more savings accounts, one or more investment accounts, in your pocket, and under your sofa cushions. While you're inputting all this minutiae, be thinking about how to get rid of some accounts. Do you have several checking accounts? Savings accounts? Investment accounts? Perhaps you only need one of each. Because when it comes to being a flawless money manager, less is definitely more. In fact, no matter how long you'd care to pore over your financial life, recognize early on that there's an inverse relationship between your effectiveness as a manager and the number of accounts you're expected to oversee. So do a better job by eliminating as many accounts as you can. This will not only improve your efficiency, but also radically enhance your speed.

When I reached this step in my personal process, I found that between my wife, myself, and our business, we had three savings accounts, four checking accounts, and twelve investment accounts! And don't think this has anything to do with being rich. I wish. Most of these accounts had very little money in them. Our accounts had made like bunnies primarily due to nothing more than mental meandering—in other words, opening an account here and an account there in search of some short-term bell or whistle, the details of which had long since faded, leaving nothing in their tracks but lots of little balances stretched over a plethora of places.

Since I already work about fifty hours a week, I didn't really need the added hobby of trying to keep up with twenty-two accounts. So I started hacking away. How? First, by thinking hard about what I really needed, then eliminating things I didn't.

The first thing I tackled was the four checking accounts. We had one local commercial checking account for our business, another local checking account for personal stuff, a third checking account with a credit union where we used to live, and a final checking account with a cyberbank. There's no question that the cyberbank (we use E*Trade Bank) offered the best deal: no monthly fees, unlimited checking, free online bill paying,[50] debit card, free local ATM machines, and interest that rivals a money market fund. So the ideal scenario would have been to just keep that account and get rid of everything else. Except I couldn't do this, because I had to have a separate checking account for our business. In addition, I wanted to be able to make business deposits locally. In other words, I didn't want to have to use the mail to send my deposits to a distant cyberbank, and most of the businesses we get checks from won't deposit electronically for us. So the local business checking stayed. But we decided to get rid of our local personal checking account and the credit union checking account. Two accounts down, twenty to go.

Trimming our savings accounts was relatively easy. Two of them were money market accounts for the business, which I combined into one. The third was with the credit union, which we combined with our cyber checking account. Like I said, the cyber checking account pays as much as most money market funds anyway. Two more accounts down.

Now to the most onerous task in the simplification process: trying to consolidate some of the dozen investment accounts we had. This was kind of frustrating, because many of our investment accounts had to remain separate. For example, we couldn't mingle business investments with personal investments. Both the wife and I had 401(k) rollover IRA accounts from our days when we were employees, and we both had regular IRA accounts as well. Plus, I had a SEP IRA account that also had to remain separate. So I couldn't do a lot of combining. But I combined what I could, eliminating four accounts. Then I moved what was left into one spot. Vanguard provided a place where I could buy and sell stocks, mutual funds, and money markets for all our accounts. In addition, while I couldn't actually combine many of our accounts, I could combine them for review purposes. In other words, I can now log

[50] Since I first wrote this chapter, E*Trade started charging $6.95 for electronic bill paying. As soon as the book is done, I'm shopping.

onto Vanguard's Web site and with the click of a mouse see all our investment and savings accounts on one page: Gina's retirement investments, my retirement investments, our joint nonretirement investments, and our business's investments. (Again, this isn't a commercial for Vanguard. While I don't know this for a fact, I assume that many other no-load fund families offer the same services.) This is a tremendous time saver when review time rolls around.

While I was whittling our accounts down to a manageable number, I also put another time saver into place. I signed paperwork so that I could move money electronically from one account to another. In other words, whenever our business checking account balance grows too large, I can electronically move money from my local bank to the Vanguard money market. Whenever we need money in our E*Trade checking account, we can move it from either the local bank or the Vanguard money market. And we can make these transfers free 24/7 by simply logging onto the Internet. In addition to being able to manually transfer money, I now have the ability to automatically transfer money as well, both from our local checking account to Vanguard's money market, and from Vanguard's money market to its 500 Index Fund. In other words, my money moves all by itself while I'm watching TV.

Making all these changes took a lot of time, effort, and focus. I had to invest hours learning what I wanted and where it was available. I had to invest effort requesting, obtaining, signing, and returning forms. And I had to focus to figure out what I was trying to accomplish and the best method for achieving it. But after all the changes were made, my life got a whole lot simpler. I became a much better manager, and the time required to keep track of everything shrank dramatically.

The process of inputting all of your checking, savings, and investment accounts will probably be easier for you than it was for me, since you're probably not suffering from the same degree of attention deficit disorder as I was. In addition, if you're not self-employed, that will also reduce the number of accounts you have to deal with. But if you're deciding where to put your money, keep a few things in mind:

- In terms of fees, large national banks will generally charge the highest fees and have more of them. As a rule of thumb, you'll find lower fees at local banks, lower still at credit unions, and lowest with online-only banks. But each of these outlets offers different services, so you can't go by price alone. For example, if you travel a lot and need a nationwide network of ATMs, you might have to consider a national bank to avoid foreign ATM fees. If you go with an online-only bank, you may have to maintain a minimum balance to get the services you want without cost. If your employer offers direct deposit, you may be able to have your paychecks electronically deposited to your online bank; otherwise you'll have to mail them . . . a process that can leave you a bit nervous, especially if you're living from paycheck to paycheck.
- If you're borrowing money with credit cards or have other types of loans, you'll usually pay the least interest at credit unions. This is because, unlike banks, they're nonprofit. Credit unions (along with cyberbanks) also generally offer the highest savings rates. The downside of credit unions is that they may not be conveniently located for you, and you have to be a member to use one. Still, if you're not a member of a credit union, you probably should be. Find out if you're eligible to join one by asking people at work and/or people at church. No luck? Surf to the Credit Union National Association's Web site at www.cuna.org. Go to "consumer information" and click on "credit union locator." In many cases, you can tell by the name whether you'll be eligible to join. (Example: When I did a search, I got "American Airlines Federal Credit Union." Although I occasionally fly American, I doubt that's good enough.) Still no luck? Open the yellow pages. If you live in a metropolitan area of any size, you're almost certain to find one that will be happy to have you as a member.
- Finding the best deals on checking is easy, and so is finding

the highest rates on savings accounts and bank money market funds. Simply go to www.bankrate.com.[51] Bankrate offers free, objective information on who's charging what and who's paying what. And it gets its information by doing independent polling of thousands of savings institutions. Most other Web sites display only information from institutions that pay to be represented, which makes their information nonobjective and therefore useless.

- To find the highest interest rates on mutual fund money markets (Bankrate covers only money markets offered by banks), check out Imoney's report. Go to www.ibcdata.com and click on "top money funds."
- Since money market mutual funds are not federally insured, you might want to take a quick look at how safe your current or prospective fund is. Go to standardandpoors.com, click on "funds," then "money market funds." (You'll find that the vast majority are AA and AAA rated.)

Okay . . . now that we've uncovered and rearranged where our money's hiding, let's continue by seeing where our money is going.

Where's Your Money Going? What You Owe

The next thing you'll be required to do to become organized is to tell your personal finance software where your money is going—a process that begins with taking stock of what you owe.

This part of the plan was probably a lot easier for me than it will be for most people, because we don't owe a lot of money. We have a mortgage, which was easily recorded by looking at our most recent statement. But we don't have a car loan. (We have two cars, the newest of which is a 1982 Mercedes. The older one is a 1968 Mercedes. We do have a 1999 Harley, but we paid cash for that.) And compared to most people, we didn't have a lot of credit cards.

[51] Disclosure time: My TV news series, *Money Talks,* is sponsored in seven cities by bankrate.com, or it was as I wrote this. However, the sponsorship arose as a result of my approaching them, not the other way around, and in no way did that sponsorship influence their mention here. If you know of another objective source of similar information, let me know (my e-mail address is in this book's conclusion), and I'll include it next time.

But we still had three, and that was one too many. Gina kept one, I kept one (the one that gives frequent flier miles), and the last one got sliced and diced. We probably could have gotten rid of another one, especially since we also have our trusty debit card. But Gina likes to have a credit card of her own "just in case." (Which means just in case I do something to make her mad, she can retaliate by going to the mall and buying a new outfit. Since half of the money she's spending is hers, I've never really understood why shopping constitutes a fitting reprisal. But I'm a money expert, not a wife expert.)

While we're on the subject of debt, this is a good time to tell you something very important that will reduce your stress, increase your bank balance, and make you a better money manager. Here it is: By and large, it doesn't make sense to invest money when you owe money. If you've got money in savings and a balance on your Visa, instead of shopping for the best savings rates or considering which mutual fund to buy, consider paying off your Visa instead. Think about it. If you're paying 15 percent interest on credit cards, paying them off is like earning 15 percent—after taxes and risk-free. And in case you haven't noticed, that's pretty hard to do. If you've got money in a money market fund, you're lucky (as I write this anyway) to be earning 2 percent on it. And if you've got to pay 30 percent taxes on the interest you're earning, you're actually only bringing home 1.4 percent. The 15 percent interest you're paying on your credit card, on the other hand, isn't deductible. You're out the full 15 percent.

So paying off your debts is almost always a much better use of money than investing it. Are there exceptions? Sure, but not many. If you're paying 6 percent on your mortgage, and have enough deductions to itemize, your after-tax cost of borrowing this money is only 4.2 percent. (If you're in a 30 percent tax bracket, 30 percent of what you're paying you'll get back as a reduction of the tax you owe, meaning you're only out of pocket by 70 percent of the 6 percent you're paying: 70 percent x 6 percent = 4.2 percent.) And it's a pretty safe bet that over the long term, money you're putting in the stock market will return better than 4.2 percent after taxes. In addition, your house is hopefully going up in value every year, and if you're lucky by more than 4.2 percent. So at least in this scenario, there's a logical argument for borrowing. But this argument is hard to make with almost any other debt you have. Credit cards? No way. Car loan? Not likely.

Since it's pretty obvious that paying 15 percent while earning 2 percent is walking backward, we're left to wonder why so many of us keep money in a savings account while owing money on a Visa. I believe there are two reasons for this. The first is that human beings as a group are pretty sharp at remembering what we own, but we're a little hazy when it comes to remembering what we owe. In other words, it feels good to have money in the bank, and it's easy to forget we owe money on the car we use to get there. We're optimists by nature, so we tend to look at our savings glass as half full even as we owe a glass and a half to various lenders. The second reason we save while owing is that this is the advice we nearly always get from securities salespeople disguised as investment advisers. In other words, we've always been advised to keep some money set aside for "emergencies." While there's nothing wrong with having an emergency fund, when you're paying interest on debt, the argument gets weak. I have a $19,000 credit line on my Visa. If I have an emergency, I'll pay 15 percent in order to access that cash. But why the heck would I walk backward to the tune of 13 percent (paying 15 percent, earning 2 percent) when there's no emergency? Keep doing that and I'll kindle an emergency long before I extinguish one.

About the only exception to this rule is if your prospects for continued employment are bleak. If you're about to be laid off, then it makes sense to stockpile cash while you can. This is because you only have to repay a portion of what you've borrowed every month, and if you have zero cash with which to make payments, you're sunk. But if you've just celebrated your fifteenth anniversary with the Department of Motor Vehicles, you're probably better off paying off your debt than building your savings.

Paying off debt instead of adding to savings makes even more sense when you consider flawless control in minutes a year. Because it will also result in a lot less time spent figuring things out. Things like where to put your savings. Reporting what you earn on your income taxes. Deciding whether you should refinance your debt. Figuring out how to make the interest on your debt tax-deductible. Making payments on the debt. Worrying about what will happen if you should be unable to make the payments. All this is nonsense. If you owe $5,000 on your Visa and you have $5,000 in the bank, kill two statements with one stone by paying off the debt. Now you can watch *Oprah* instead of opening envelopes, writing checks, and worrying about earning more interest and/or paying less interest. You've still got an emergency source of cash, and the math handily proves that you've made the right choice. Even if you don't have enough sitting in savings to completely pay off a debt, it makes sense to divert any extra cash you accumulate on a monthly basis to paying off debt rather than investing. The worst thing you can ever do debt-wise is to make minimum payments. Despite what lenders may imply, minimum payments are in no way related to convenience for you. They are all about profits for them. The longer you pay, the more they make, and that's all there is to it. So forget what your lender tells you. There's only one minimum payment on a debt, and that's the maximum that you can possibly afford to pay.

As you're recording all your debts and thinking about how to reduce them, here are some things to keep in mind.

- As with your savings accounts, credit unions are one of the best places to have your loan accounts. Nonprofit often means lower rates. In addition, credit unions are normally easier to borrow from paperwork-wise. Since they tend to be smaller, community-based organizations, they often have fewer hoops for you to jump through. This applies to every type of loan: credit card, auto, signature, and sometimes even mortgages.
- Consolidating your various loans with a home equity loan makes sense for at least three reasons: These loans are often tax-deductible, they normally have lower interest rates than other types of loans, and consolidating means fewer state-

ments for you to open, examine, file, and lose every month. However, you should also keep in mind a pet expression of mine: "Buy a blouse, lose a house." In other words, when you borrow against your home's equity, what you're doing is putting your shelter up as collateral. If you're borrowing to support a lifestyle that you can't afford, don't be an even bigger dope by putting your home at risk. Get your act together spending-wise before you start consolidating. I'll have more on this topic in chapter 19, "Bringing It All Together."

- If you close credit accounts, you're not done when you've paid off the debt and/or cut up the credit card. You still have to inform the lender in writing that you want the account closed. Otherwise, your credit report will show that you have open accounts when you thought they were gone. This is bad because it will appear from your credit report that you already have too much available credit, which lowers your credit score and makes borrowing more difficult and more expensive.
- Speaking of credit reports, when was the last time you looked at yours? The number of mistakes in credit reports is a national disgrace. Depending on whom you choose to believe, estimates suggest that up to 70 percent of credit files contain errors. Why does this matter? One reason is obvious: Black marks on your credit history make it harder to borrow. But your insurance company could also use your credit report to set your car, life, and/or homeowner's insurance rates. (They've found that people who irresponsibly use credit could be irresponsible in other areas . . . go figure.) Even your current or prospective employer could access your credit report as it decides whether to hire or promote you. If something bad has happened to you as a result of your credit report (say, you're turned down for a loan, a job, or an insurance policy), you can request a free copy of the report that caused the problem, providing you do it within sixty days of the rejection. You can also get one free credit report per year if you're (1) unemployed and plan to look for work within sixty days; (2) on welfare; or, (3)

your report is inaccurate because of fraud. Otherwise, a credit reporting agency is allowed to charge you up to $9 for a copy of your report. That's the federal law. But there are also certain states that have passed laws that allow you to get a free copy of your credit report once every year just for the asking. They are Colorado, Georgia, Maryland, Massachusetts, New Jersey, and Vermont. Here's how to contact the big three credit reporting agencies:

EQUIFAX
P.O. Box 740241
Atlanta, GA 30374-0241
800-685-1111
www.equifax.com

EXPERIAN
P.O. Box 949
Allen, TX 75013-0949
888-397-3742
www.experian.com

TRANS UNION
P.O. Box 1000
Chester, PA 19022
800-916-8800
www.tuc.com

And while you're on the Web, learn more about your credit report and how to fix errors by going to www.ftc.gov.

- When you're looking for the best loan rates for cars and homes, bankrate.com can help. As I said before, this Web site will hook you up with both national and local lenders so you can see at a glance who's got the best rates. But don't stop there. Check with your current lender. Let the folks there know that you're considering refinancing and see if they'll match or beat offers from the competition. And ask if they'll do it with fewer fees and less paperwork. After all, they already know you. Finally, open the phone book, call a few other lenders, and make sure you're getting the best possible deal—and don't forget credit unions.

- When you borrow money, especially on a home, you'll be faced with a frenzy of fees. Just say no, or at least make the lender earn the fees by having it explain each and every one in enough detail so you'll understand what you're paying for and it'll regret answering the phone. Once you understand the fees, attempt to eliminate, or at least reduce, each and every one. The easiest way to do this is to tell your prospective lender that its competitor isn't charging that fee, or isn't charging as much. (Hopefully this will be true, because it's quite possible they'll check.) More on this in chapter 17, "Real Estate."
- If loans come with fees, try to avoid putting them on the back end of the loan by including them in the amount financed. Like minimum payments, this ploy appears to be a convenience for you, but it's really simply a method of increasing your lender's bottom line. You probably already know that if you borrow $100,000 to buy a house, by the time you make minimum payments for thirty years, you'll have paid close to $250,000: $100,000 in principal and $150,000 in interest. Well, if you finance $3,000 of closing costs, you'll end up paying $7,000 by stretching them out over that same payback period. If you can't afford the closing costs, then you have no choice. And if rates are really low, fine . . . maybe you can earn more after taxes by investing this money than you're paying after taxes by borrowing it. But go into the transaction with your eyes open.
- How do you know when refinancing is in your best interest? Simple. Take the cost to refinance and divide it by the money you'll save every month. The result is the number of months it will take to recover the cost of the refinancing. If you're planning on staying in your home for longer than this number of months, you'll come out ahead.

Where's Your Money Coming From and Where's It Going? Your Revenue and Expenses

After you've understood, recorded, rearranged, and consolidated your debts, it's time to see where else your money is arriving from and where it's heading.

Recording your income is pretty straightforward. You'll simply plug the numbers into the software in appropriate revenue accounts conveniently provided. If you're an employee who receives a regular income, you can tell your software how much that is and it will input it for you automatically from that day forward, along with any regular deductions for savings, 401(k), taxes, health insurance, and so on. If your income and other paycheck items are less certain due to commission sales or self-employment, no biggie; just tell your software whenever you get a check. In either case, whenever money arrives in your life, you'll tell your program and it will keep tabs.

Now comes the main event: where your money is going. This will include recurring, unavoidable expenses like utilities, insurance, and taxes, as well as sporadic, theoretically avoidable ones such as trips to the mall and single-malt scotch. Personal finance programs come complete with expense accounts that will help you categorize your expenses. And if a category that is uniquely you isn't included, you can easily add it. Tracking where your money is going is the single most important thing you can do to control your financial life. And doing it with a personal finance computer program is especially helpful, because in an instant you can see what amount and what percent of your money is going for what expenditure, making the creation of a spending plan much easier to do. For example, if you find that 8 percent of all the money you make is going to pay for your various insurance policies, you can choose to focus on reducing your cost for insurance. If you're spending $2,500 a month on entertainment, maybe you'll start thinking of ways to entertain yourself without spending so much. The point is that seeing where your money is going in black and white will instantly get you thinking about whether you're getting what you're paying for. If you are, fine. If you're not, change it. If saving for your kid's education has a higher priority than renting movies from Blockbuster, this is where you'll find out. Most of us are never allowed to make decisions like this because we're not confronting ourselves with exactly what we're spending at Blockbuster; nor do we spend a lot of time thinking about how much reward we're actually getting from what we're buying. Again, while this may seem like a method to generate guilt, it isn't. If you'd rather let your kids pay for their own tuition by collecting aluminum cans along the highway so that you can watch the latest DVD, who's to say that's wrong? Recycling is good for the environment and walking along the highway is good exercise, not to mention a great way to develop fast reflexes. So don't sweat it: The only wrong decision when it comes to your money is not making any decisions. And the only way to make informed decisions is to be informed.

So from this day forward, you'll be recording all your expenses in your personal finance software. Every dime, every day. Will it take time? Yes. But less than you think, and besides, this is really important. Keeping track of where your money is going has nothing to do with managing your money quickly. It has to do with going through life with your eyes open, which you should be doing no matter how long you choose to focus on your finances.

A tip or two on expense tracking and making it easier:

- In order to keep track of your cash expenses, you'll need to be able to write them down as you incur them. This can be done with something as simple as a 29-cent pocket-sized notebook or as complex as a $500 Palm Pilot. But record them you must, and you must transfer these cash outlays to the appropriate category of your personal finance software every day. You'll also find that the simple act of recording expenses will cause you to think about them, which in turn may reduce your spending with no effort on your part.
- There's a hidden blessing that comes along with recording your expenses in your personal finance software. Namely, when you record an expense, you'll indicate whether it's tax-deductible. Then, when year end rolls around, you can electronically export this information directly to your tax preparation software (like TurboTax or H&R Block TaxCut) and prepare your tax return in minutes instead of hours. The ability to do this one thing will practically pay for a computer, not to mention the software, in terms of saving time. More on this in the next chapter, on income taxes.

- If for some reason you should decide that you don't want your kids wandering the highway in search of aluminum cans to pay for college, you may find that you want to spend less in some categories in order to save more in others. The trick to doing this is not to deprive yourself, since deprivation takes you down a path that's difficult to follow. So when it comes to saving money, first focus on things that won't leave you feeling deprived. For example, if you pay 4 cents a minute for long distance instead of 10, you won't have any less fun; there will be no noticeable impact on your life. If you bring your lunch from home instead of eating out every day, there may be a minimal impact, but barely noticeable. If you raise the deductible on your insurance policies, you probably won't feel like a second-class citizen. It's little things like this that make saving more money painless. And painless saving is the only kind that works over long periods of time, unless you really choose to focus on changing your belief system about money.
- Speaking of changing your belief system, use a few simple mental techniques that help you spend less money. For example, stop thinking in terms of dollars and start thinking in terms of hours. Start by considering how much money you make for every hour you work. Now subtract 30 percent of that to account for all the taxes you pay. For instance, if you make $40,000 a year, you make about $20 an hour. Subtract 30 percent of that and you're left with $14 an hour. The next time you're at the mall and are tempted to spend $100, stop and think. The store wants you to consider that $100 as $3 per month, the amount that your purchase will cost in terms of minimum payment on your Visa. But what are you really giving up? If you pay cash, you're giving up seven hours of your life working (7 hours x $14 per hour = $98). If you pay with your credit card and make minimum payments, you're giving up fourteen hours of your life. (That's because you'll end up paying two or more times what you spend by the time you pay the interest.) So spending this money means you're retiring one to two days later than you could have. You're surrendering one to two days of doing someone else's bidding. When measured against this yard-

stick, many purchases don't make sense, and you're much more likely to leave your wallet in your pocket or purse. And if you choose to spend the money anyway, odds are good that you're buying something you really want rather than something you impulsively think you want.

- Another mental realization that will positively influence your saving skills is to recognize this simple truth: *Physical possessions cannot meet spiritual needs.* Sound obvious? Let me assure you that it's not obvious to your subconscious, because if it were most advertising wouldn't work. The next time you're watching TV, pay attention and you'll see exactly what I'm talking about. Car ads that promise you'll appear younger if you drive a certain car. Toothpaste that virtually promises you a sexual encounter. A diamond cartel explaining that the only true evidence of love is a gemstone. Once you understand that Madison Avenue is attempting to convince you that your spiritual needs can be met with physical possessions, you'll see this parlor trick for what it is and be better equipped to ignore it.
- Want some simple, specific ways to save money? You won't have any difficulty whatsoever finding them. If books are your preference, you'll find dozens on the subject, including mine: *Life or Debt*. If Web sites are your thing, you will again have no trouble finding more than you can ever review. Rather than listing dozens of frugal-living Web sites, I'll just list a few of my personal favorites. One of the best sites for just about any topic you can think of, including saving money, is www.about.com. For frugal living, go to http://frugalliving.about.com. Along the left-hand side of the page, you'll find a few dozen categories, listed alphabetically, that will zip you to practically every money-saving idea in every topic from appliances to utilities. Another great site for those who want to stretch their dollars: The Dollar Stretcher (www.stretcher.com). Some of the suggestions will seem a bit extreme. ("Learn what cows have known for years . . . eating grass is good for you!") But you're free to ignore these. You're still guaranteed to find some simple ideas that will save you serious bucks.

Creating a Spending Plan

Whether you're talking about a shoeshine stand or General Motors, pretty much every business has a plan of where its money is coming from and where it's going. This involves estimating how much money the business is planning to take in (revenue projections) and how much money it's going to spend (expense projections). The difference between what a company takes in and pays out is its profit. The amount of this profit is a company-wide goal. In other words, a well-defined target, set out in black and white for all to see. Because for most businesses, profits aren't the main thing, they're the only thing. So in every successful business, at least once every year someone sets the profit goal, and someone estimates every potential source of revenue and expenses. And after the year is over, someone sees how close projections came to reality. If the profit goal wasn't met because less revenue came in than expected, someone's going to be explaining why. If the profit goal wasn't met because more money went out than estimated, someone's going to be explaining that. After all the explanations are in, decisions can be made about what to do next.

You may think that nonprofit organizations by their very definition don't fit this mold, but you're wrong. While it's true that profits may not be their stated goal, rest assured, they want to make sure their income is more than their expenses. Otherwise, sooner or later they'll be forced to shut their doors and their nonprofit purpose will no longer be served. To prepare for lean times, nonprofits need . . . profits! They may not call them that, but they certainly want to build a cushion to help them through tough times, and taking in more than they're paying out is the only way to create one. If you doubt that nonprofits are serious about creating a cash cushion, listen to National Public Radio or watch your local PBS station sometime during a fund-raiser. I dare you.

The only type of organization that might accurately say that it has no interest in profits is a governmental organization. Rather than profits, these organizations exist to spend as much money as possible, get as little value for the money they spend as possible, and, in the process, piss off as many people as possible. But even in governmental organizations, you'll find that there are people whose job it is to formulate goals relating to revenue and expenses. It may not be a big deal if their expenses are higher than their revenue, since they're in the unique position of being able to force additional revenue out of their customers. But it's important for them to at least pretend to be accountable.

So if goal setting, estimating revenue and expenses, and comparing estimates to reality is so important where you work, why isn't it where you live? It is. While it's true that your family wasn't formed to make a profit, if its expenses exceed its income it will soon be bankrupt, and at least part of its purpose—food and shelter—will no longer be served. Like any other organization, it needs a cushion to see it through tough times. So business-wise your family is really a nonprofit organization, which probably comes as no surprise. The chief distinction between your family and more traditional nonprofits is that all your employees are tenured so they can't be fired.

The point of all this is that keeping track of what you make, what you spend, and your savings goals is everything when it comes to family finances. Savings are ultimately what's going to allow you to retire. Savings determine how you meet emergencies. Where, when, or whether your kids go to college. In short, savings are the intersection where what you want from life crosses what you get from life. It's just that simple. And let me assure you: ANY increase in your savings that occurs without keeping track of what you make and what you spend is purely coincidental.

If that's not enough to convince you, maybe this will. Not being organized and keeping track is directly related to any anxiety you feel when it comes to finances. Check out the following definition of "anxiety." And as you read it, see if you can relate to how you feel when you think about money:[52]

[52] Merriam-Webster online dictionary.

ANXIETY: painful or apprehensive uneasiness of mind usually over an impending event or anticipated ill.

Does this not fit the vast majority of people when it comes to money? We feel anxiety because sooner or later something expensive is going to happen and we're afraid we might not have sufficient funds, or we won't be organized enough to know what to do. We're going to get sick. Our kids are going to college. Our car's going to break down. We're going to retire. We're going to die. Whatever . . . we know that *something* is going to happen that's going to cost us. But we don't know how much it will be or how we're going to deal with it. And there you have it: anxiety.

Of course, setting goals, staying on top of revenue and expenses, and being organized won't result in an automatic increase of your savings balance. But these things do immediately increase your control and reduce your anxiety, because doing this stuff requires you to review where you've been and think about where you're going. Which means that before you know it, you're aware of exactly what's covered in case of a health care crisis, exactly what you'll be expected to pay, exactly where that money is going to come from, and exactly where to find the pertinent clauses in your insurance policy. You'll have an idea of when you plan to retire, what that retirement will look like, how much you'll have in savings, and the factors that will influence that savings balance. See how this works? Organization and flawless money management are like tattoos and bikers: You won't see one without the other.

Once you've input and organized what you own, what you owe, and where your money is going, you'll probably want to fiddle with your expenses a bit so you can attempt to set savings goals. This entails creating a spending plan.

The key thing to remember when you're talking about planning your spending is that it's a plan. It's not a "budget," which implies deprivation much like "diet" implies going hungry. We talked about allocating your savings in an earlier chapter. Did that sound like deprivation to you? Well, same principle here. Your spending plan is merely a reflection of how you're allocating the money that doesn't find its way to a savings account. If you want to allocate 7 percent of your income to your GI Joe collection, nobody's going to beat you up or call you names. You just need to recognize that you're spending 7 percent of the money you make on GI Joes. That's not screwing up . . . that's learning something. If you get that much pleasure from GI Joes, maybe you should increase the percentage. But if retiring a bit earlier, or owning your own business, or helping your kids with college seems important, too, you're now in a position to review your priorities and make sure your assets are allocated properly to achieve your desired outcome.

In other words, having a spending plan allows us to see where our money is going now, make sure that the current allocation is satisfying our goals, and—if it isn't—try to rearrange things so it is.

And by the way, I was just being polite before: IF you're spending 7 percent of your income on GI Joes, you're screwing up big time.

Okay, now you're almost there! You're a new, organized you. You have the fewest possible number of places to keep your money, and you have the highest interest rates on them. You have the fewest possible debts, and you have the lowest interest rates on those. You know where every penny of your money is going, you have resources to find additional ways to trim your expenses, and you are ready to do your taxes at the push of a button. Isn't life grand? But before we stop talking organization, let's do something else that will make you annoyingly efficient. Let's trash some of the stuff you've been keeping.

Record Keeping

It's necessary to keep some paperwork handy, but the vast majority of us keep a lot more than we should. This causes us to spend time filing when we could be watching TV or fantasizing about the new neighbor across the street.

What do you need to keep? How long do you need to keep it? Well, the first thing to remember is that if something doesn't relate to either taxes or a warranty, there's probably no point in keeping it at all. For example, utility bills. Admit it . . . you send in the check to your power company every month, and then file the portion of the bill that says, "Keep for your records." Good thing the bill didn't say, "Jump off a cliff." Your electric bill isn't tax-deductible (unless perhaps you're working from home), so the IRS doesn't care whether you've paid it or not. If your check doesn't find its way to the electric company, the part of the bill that you've kept for your records isn't proof of anything. So exactly whom are you keeping it for? If you want to see if and when you've paid a bill, look in your check register. If you want to see if anyone cashed the check, look at your bank statement or the canceled check. If you want to see how much electricity you've been using, call the electric company and ask. There are people there who are paid to keep track. You're not.

What about your bank statements? Once you've reconciled your statement and made sure that your balance agrees with the bank's, you really don't need the statement anymore. But that doesn't keep most of us from keeping them all anyway. By the way, your personal finance software will help you reconcile your checking account in a few minutes a month, and thereafter can go online and tell you instantly which checks have cleared and which are outstanding as of that moment. You know as much as the bank does.

As to canceled checks: If you need them, the bank has copies. It's justifiable to keep canceled checks for a month or two in case someone, like the electric company, says that you didn't pay your bill. It's also perhaps understandable to keep those that relate to income taxes, or prove you paid for something that carries a warranty, although store receipts are better for this purpose. But what about everything else? Can you imagine the circumstances that would require you to keep a canceled check for the groceries you bought last year? If you want to know how much you're spending on groceries, get a report from your personal finance software or add up the amounts in your check register.

This is also true of your credit card statements. You only need your monthly statement for as long as it takes to reconcile the receipts for purchases you made that month (you've kept 'em, right?) with the charges reflected on your statement. Again, your personal finance software will keep track of what you bought and put your purchases in the proper categories. It will also show that the credit card bill was paid and the check was cashed. Like canceled checks, if you want to be conservative, keep statements for a month or two in case some payment dispute arises. But how many times have you needed last year's credit card statements?

You may not have noticed this, but many of your investment statements are cumulative, especially in the case of mutual funds. In other words, your December statement shows all the activity in your account from the previous eleven months in addition to what happened in December. The other eleven statements have now outlived their usefulness. And if you've been faithfully updating your personal finance software, you've already got a secondary source for this information anyway, albeit not one suitable for tax purposes. Your 401(k) statements are normally quarterly, but you also get an annual statement. Once you've made sure that the annual accurately reflects the quarterlies, the quarterlies are kindling. In other words, keep statements that summarize your annual activity, but toss substatements after making sure everything's kosher. Statements that show how much you paid for a security, however—including reinvested dividends in the case of mutual funds—should be kept until three years after the security is sold, thereby becoming part of a tax return.

What about receipts? If there's a warranty involved, staple the receipt to the warranty or instruction book so you don't lose it. Receipts are also documentation for your tax records, so you should keep these with the applicable tax return, meaning they'll be around for three years after the return is filed. Receipts or other proof of improvements to your home should be kept until three years after your house is sold, because these expenses could affect the sale price you report, if you have to report one.

Some people like the idea of keeping receipts for big-ticket items indefinitely so they'll have proof for the insurance company if they lose their possessions in a fire or the like. Nothing wrong with that, but I prefer to videotape my possessions while dictating the price I paid and the date I bought them. This is normally adequate for the insurance company. In any case, if you keep receipts for insurance purposes, don't keep them in your house, since if they burn up, they won't do you much good. Unless you've videotaped the receipts, and the tape is someplace safe. But since you can't shoot video of the video camera, you'll need to keep the receipt for that. Isn't this confusing?

Your pay stubs are like your mutual fund statements: cumulative. Make sure your year-to-date numbers add up, then toss prior stubs. Same drill when you get your annual W-2 statement from your employer. Agree with the last December stub you had? The December stub is now toast.

I'm not going to go over every conceivable piece of paper you're storing right now, but see what you're keeping and think about why you're keeping it. If you haven't touched a particular folder in a year or more, odds are that you don't need it. Unless, that is, it relates to taxes.

So how long do you keep your tax returns and the canceled checks, receipts, and other fragments of dead tree that support them? For answers to this burning question, we turn to IRS Publication 552, "Recordkeeping for Individuals." This staple of bathroom reading declares that you should keep your tax stuff (that is, the return and everything that supports it) for three years after the date the return was due. (In other words, if your return is due on April 15, 2004, the clock starts ticking on April 15, 2004, even if you file the return early. If you file it late, the clock starts the day you actually file.) Notable exception? If you cheat on your taxes. If you don't file a return, or file fraudulent returns, the IRS could conceivably audit you for every year since you were born, and maybe even while you were still in the womb. If you under-report your income by 25 percent or more, it can go back six years after the return was filed. But if you're not an outlaw, you only need to keep your tax returns for the three years after you file. That being said, some people counter that since the IRS could conceivably audit you for any year in which you don't file a return, it makes sense to keep a copy of your return forever. Otherwise, Uncle Sam could say you didn't file a return and you won't be able to prove you did. So if you're a pack rat, there's your excuse to keep packing.

There are additional rules for people who own businesses. For example, you should keep all records related to your employees for at least four years. But I'm not going to include everything having to do with those of us who are self-employed. Instead, I'll just tell you where you can go to download it. You want IRS Publication 583, "Starting a Business and Keeping Records," and you can find it at irs.gov. It's free, and perfect to add to your bathroom library, or to keep by the bed if you suffer from insomnia.

Okay, that's that. Now you're organized! As I mentioned at the beginning of this chapter, as you go through the process of keeping track of everything and staying organized, you might be afraid that you'll gradually evolve into a nitpicking, anal-retentive, arm-gartered, Coke-bottle-glasses-wearing, boring geek. This is a perfectly normal concern, but don't worry. Look at me. I'm organized, I track my expenses, and I can provide you with a long list of people who will vouch that I'm none of the above. Well, at least they'll confirm I don't wear glasses.

Now let's move on to how to keep your tax burden as low as possible and make that whole process less confusing.

15

Making Your Life Less Taxing: Income Taxes

A billion here, a couple of billion there,
first thing you know it adds up to be real money.
—EVERETT MCKINLEY DIRKSEN

Let's begin our discussion of income taxes with synonyms for the word "complex," courtesy of *Webster's Collegiate Thesaurus*.

> **COMPLEX:** Byzantine, daedal, elaborate, U.S. income tax laws, Gordian, intricate, involved, knotty, labyrinthine, sophisticated.

Okay, so I took a little literary license by adding "U.S. income tax laws" to the synonyms for "complex." But whether *Webster's* cops to it or not, the U.S. tax code *is* practically a synonym for complex. The complete Internal Revenue Code contains more than 2.8 million words. Printed sixty lines to the page, it would fill almost six thousand letter-sized pages.[53] This is a ridiculously complicated way to express a brutally simple concept, namely that Uncle Sam wants to share in the spoils of your success.

Over the years, a few brave souls have actually tried to tackle

[53] http://www.fourmilab.ch/uscode/26usc/.

our tax laws for the express purpose of making them simpler and therefore fairer. For example, back in 1998 I did TV news stories about a couple of proposals then on the drawing board. The first was a proposal for a flat tax, proposed by Congressmen Dick Armey and Richard Shelby. Under this proposal, our entire tax code would have been shredded and replaced with a simple tax of 17 percent of income. No deductions, no credits, no exceptions. You'd get a big personal exemption, but every dime you made after that would be taxed. For a family of four, for example, the exemption would have meant that only income above $33,800 would have been taxed, but everything beyond that exemption would have been taxed at 17 percent. The major selling point of this proposal was that everyone in America would have been able to file their taxes on one side of a postcard. Proponents of the flat tax claimed that it would result in savings of $100 billion a year in IRS expenses alone. Those opposed said that a 17 percent rate wouldn't be enough, claiming that it would take a rate of more like 22 percent to keep the red, white, and blue in the black.

Also in 1998, Congressmen Billy Tauzin and Dan Schafer proposed an even simpler plan. They wanted to do away with income taxes altogether and replace them with a national sales tax. This plan had some real pizzazz since it repealed all personal taxes, corporate taxes, inheritance taxes, and gift taxes. Better yet, it suggested completely dissolving the IRS by the year 2001. And it was very simple: Income tax was to be replaced with a 15 percent sales tax on all retail purchases of goods and services. Sounded good, at least until you looked under the hood. Because while a national sales tax replaced all income taxes, it didn't do away with Social Security, other employment taxes, or state or local income taxes. And when they said the tax applied to all goods and services, the key word was "all." Houses, cars . . . everything. The final straw was that even with that onerous additional burden, some experts said that 15 percent wouldn't be enough. It would take more like a tax of between 17 and 37 percent to make the system work. Try adding that on top of a new house.

While neither of these ideas ever made it to second base, at least the thought was good. The tax code doesn't need to be complicated to accomplish its mission. If you can put a man on the moon, you should be able to separate a citizen from his money with less than 2.8 million words. So why are taxes so complicated? Let's turn again to *Webster's*:

> **PORK:** government money, jobs, or favors used by politicians as patronage.

Many of the wrinkles in the tax laws are there because some special interest benefits from them. I also believe that another reason our taxes are kept so complicated is the same as why investing is made to appear complicated. Namely, because lots of people make lots of money with the current system. As with investing, there are thriving industries built around interpreting tax laws and offering paid guidance to the less informed multitude. But as with investing, we can pull aside the curtain, blow away the smoke, and break the mirrors. Because the truth is that very few of those 2.8 million words apply to your situation, and you don't need expert help, especially now that personal computers are on the scene.

Most financial planning books drone on with intricate details compiled by close examination of the tax code. While that's a good way to fill up a book, it's kind of self-defeating from an educational perspective. In the first place, there are so many variables in individual situations that no single book can address them all. Plus, the minutiae being described are often so numbingly boring that nobody's going to remember the solutions for more than a few minutes anyway. Which is fine, since a few minutes is about how long tax laws seem to last. The ink wasn't dry on *Taxes for Dummies* before someone in Congress started making the information obsolete. Bottom line? There's no reason for this book or any other to go into intricate detail when it comes to tax law. You're much better served spending the money you'd blow on a book on a computer program instead, because this program will learn your personal situation intimately within half an hour of meeting you. It will know every current law and update itself automatically from the Internet the instant changes are hatched. So forget about investing time, effort, and money buying and reading books like *Income Taxes for Dummies*. Only accountants and insomniacs read books about income taxes. You've got better things to do.

That being said, you do need to understand the broad strokes when it comes to income taxes or, more specifically, reducing your income taxes. When it comes to taxes, a flawless financial planner invests a few minutes a year on strategy, then hits the sofa, leaving the details for his computer.

Even if you know next to nothing about income taxes, you probably do know that the taxes you pay in April are a result of money made and spent the preceding calendar year. This is Factor 1 in determining how much income tax you'll pay. You probably also know that the more income you report, the more taxes you pay. This is Factor 2. Finally, you're most likely aware that you're allowed to reduce your taxable income by subtracting certain allowable expenses, called deductions. This is Factor 3 in determining your personal tax burden. So if you understand these three factors, you're already 90 percent of the way to becoming an effective tax planner. Because the term "tax planning" is really nothing more than a fancy phrase describing the process of reporting as little taxable income as possible and reporting as many tax deductions as possible. No big deal.

Income

The first broad stroke you'll want to master is exactly what the heck tax brackets are all about.

While you may think that tax brackets are hardware used to hold up tax shelves, guess again. Tax brackets describe the percentage of the money we make that Uncle Sam expects to receive. Our tax brackets are called progressive or incremental. That's because the more you make, the higher your rate. Note that I'm not saying "The more you make, the more you pay," although this is also true. I'm saying that as you make more money, the incremental money you make is taxed at a higher rate. This concept becomes clear when you look at projected tax tables for 2003.[54]

Married Filing Jointly

2003 Taxable Income	Tax Rate
$0–12,000	10%
$12,000–47,450	15%
$47,450–114,650	27%
$114,650–174,700	30%
$174,700–311,950	35%
$311,950	38.6%

Single Taxpayers

2003 Taxable Income	Tax Rate
$0–6,000	10%
$6,000–28,400	15%
$28,400–68,800	27%
$68,800–143,500	30%
$143,500–311,950	35%
$311,950	38.6%

There are additional tax tables reflecting other categories of tax filers, like married people filing separate returns and heads of household (translation: unmarried with children). But since we're only trying to grasp a concept or two, let's stick with the two most common: joint filers and single filers. A glimpse at the tables reveals what a progressive tax structure is all about. Looking at the table for single taxpayers, we see that in 2003, if you made $6,000 or less, you were in the 10 percent tax bracket. If you made more than $6,000 but less than $28,401, you were in the 15 percent tax

[54] These are projected tables, but this was the most up-to-date info available when I was writing this. It came from the Commerce Clearing House Web site at http://www.toolkit.cch.com/columns/taxes/02-085brackets.asp. Tax rates going forward will be adjusted for inflation, so will be slightly different. But this is close enough for our purposes.

bracket. And if you made more than $311,950, I hope you paid full retail for this book.

Before we go on, let's make sure we understand what we're looking at. The term "taxable income" in the tables doesn't refer to every dime you made. That would be your "total income," your "gross income," or simply your "income." Taxable income, on the other hand, is what's left after all your deductions and exemptions. (Pull out your most recent 1040 and you'll see this amount somewhere around line number 40. You'll be able to identify taxable income because it will be labeled "taxable income.") So theoretically you could have an income of a million dollars, but if you have $994,000 worth of exemptions and deductions, you'd still be in the 10 percent tax bracket.

Now let's revisit the term "progressive." Remember, I said that the more you make, the higher rate you pay? Here we see it in action. Look again at the table for single taxpayers. The first $6,000 of taxable income is going to be taxed at 10 percent. So if that's all you made, you'd owe $600, you'd be in the 10 percent tax bracket, and that would be that. But say your taxable income was $25,000. Our table tells us that the first six grand is taxed at 10 percent; then the rest, $19,000, will be taxed at the next highest bracket, which is 15 percent. Our tax bill would be $6,000 x 10% + $19,000 x 15%. Total tax due? $3,450, which is a little less than 14 percent of our $25,000 taxable income. So while we're in the 25 percent tax bracket, we're not paying 25 percent of everything we make in taxes. If our taxable income is $50,000, our total tax bill will be $9,792. We're in the 27 percent tax bracket, and we're paying a little less than 20 percent of our total taxable income in taxes.

I'm sorry to drag you through Tax Accounting 101, but I want you to understand what tax brackets are and what they're not. What they are is a picture of how your *incremental* income (your income after it crosses a certain threshold) is going to be taxed. What they're not is a picture of how your total taxable income is going to be taxed.

There are many ways that you can use information about what tax bracket you're in to potentially lower the amount of tax you pay. For example, suppose you're single and it's December 27. You've got a $1,000 profit in a mutual fund and you're thinking of selling. Should you sell it now or wait till January 1? Based on how much money you've made this year and the amount of deductions you expect to have (information instantly available from your personal finance software program), you determine that your taxable income this year is going to be $28,400. This is exactly where the 27 percent tax bracket begins, which means that if you add to your income by making an additional $1,000, you're going to owe $270 in taxes on that $1,000. If, however, you expect that next year you'll only make $25,000, you could sell the mutual fund after January 1 and pay only an additional $150, since $1,000 on top of $25,000 still leaves you well within the 15 percent bracket. So waiting a few days will save you $120, not to mention postponing the tax bill for an entire year.

This is one way that tax brackets can help you save tax dollars. Another is in an area we've already discussed: buying investments that offer tax-free income. Tax-free interest is obviously worth a lot more to someone in the 38.6 percent federal tax bracket than to someone in the 10 percent bracket. You can't compare tax-free investments with their taxable cousins until you know what tax bracket you're in.

I don't know about you, but I'm now officially sick of talking tax brackets. It's high time we talked timing.

Keep in mind that the vast majority of us are not only calendar-year taxpayers, we're also cash-basis taxpayers. This means that income becomes taxable when you receive it and allowable expenses become deductions when you pay them. As you'll soon see, this is a key ingredient when it comes to reducing income, increasing deductions, and shrinking tax bills.

Let's focus on reducing taxable income first, since this is the factor that presents the fewest options and therefore takes the least effort to understand.

If you're an employee, you don't have to spend a lot of time on your employment income, because you have virtually no control over when you receive it. If your employer writes you a check on

December 30, it's still reportable income for that year, even if you wait till January 1 to cash the check. While you may not have actually received your cash until the next year, it was theoretically receivable in the current year, so not cashing checks won't reduce your taxable income. But suppose you have a year-end bonus coming to you? If you can persuade your boss to cut that check after January 1, you will have effectively postponed the taxes due on that income for an entire year. The only problem with this approach is that convincing your boss to delay a check won't be easy, since your taxable income is your company's deductible expense. So if your company is also on a calendar tax year, postponing your income means postponing its write-off. An idea it probably won't squeal with delight over.

Those of us who are self-employed often have more flexibility when it comes to the timing of our income (which, by the way, is one of many good reasons to be self-employed). If you're a consultant, you can choose to send the invoice for work you did on December 30 out on January 1. Even if your customer pays you instantly (as if, right?), you've still moved that income to the next tax year. Congratulations: You're an income-shifting tax planner!

While your pay is most likely your largest source of income, it's probably not your only source. You could be getting gifts, borrowing money, collecting interest, selling stuff, winning money from gambling or contests, getting alimony, receiving child support, collecting Social Security (or other retirement income), or getting rent checks from real estate. How does each of these sources of cash affect your tax picture?

GETTING GIFTS

When you get money as a gift, you've got nothing to report to the IRS. Gifts aren't taxable income. So, if you can arrange it, my advice would be to receive all your money this way. In addition, this method of paying the bills will also significantly reduce the time you now spend working for a living. In my experience, however, the only people who consistently manage to receive significant portions of their income this way resemble Mae West (wink,

wink). But if you do find a way to accomplish this without the Mae West approach, please forward this information to me ASAP.

BORROWING MONEY

Borrowing money also results in no requirement to report taxable income, because borrowed money is only yours temporarily, and is therefore not considered income for tax purposes. Despite this tax advantage, however, I would stringently advise against this method of making ends meet.

COLLECTING INTEREST

Interest income is just like your salary: totally taxable in the year it is either received or receivable. So when it comes to being able to shift your taxable interest around to try to influence the amount you're reporting in any given year, good luck. In this respect, interest is basically like your salary: You have no control over when it's paid. The only possible exception is the interest from a debt that's owed to you in the form of a personal or real estate loan. Then you might be able to exert some influence on the person who owes you the interest by pleading with or coercing him to pay it in a fashion that would move the interest from one tax year to another. But by and large, your interest income isn't much more flexible timing-wise than your salary. Unless this interest comes from a tax-advantaged source.

The main source of tax-advantaged interest we've already discussed: tax-free interest from various types of government bonds. You'll recall that interest arising from state or local government bonds (say, municipal bonds) is normally federally tax exempt. Interest from federal obligations (such as Treasury bonds) is exempt from state and local taxes. And the interest from bonds issued within the state where you live (local municipal bonds) is the best deal of all, because this can be completely tax-free: federal, state, and local. But as you'll also recall, the problem with these sources of tax-free interest is that the tax advantages are usually offset by lower interest rates, so what you gain by not paying taxes on these sources of interest you lose by not getting as much interest to begin with. Since that's not always true, however, you should periodically check the rates available on tax-free bonds and mutual funds, especially if you live in high-tax states like New York or California. And as we just discovered in our discussion about tax brackets, you should also see what your tax bracket is. Once armed with this information, you're ready for a quick computation. Remember the formula? Taxable rate times reciprocal of tax bracket equals equivalent tax-free rate. Here's an example:

> **Taxable Rate** (for example, the rate available on a medium-term bond fund) **= 5%**
> **Reciprocal of Tax Bracket** (if I'm in a 30% tax bracket, the reciprocal is 1 – 0.3) **= 0.7%**
> **Equivalent Tax-Free Rate: 5% x 0.7% = 3.5%**

Result? We'll have to find a tax-free rate of more than 3.5 percent to be better off than earning 5 percent in a taxable investment. This will probably prove difficult to do in investments of similar risk, but it's still worth scoping out every now and then, especially since it's so easy to do. In fact, I'll do it right now, time myself, and see how long it takes.

The following exercise took one minute and nineteen seconds:

- *Step 1:* I went to Vanguard's Web site at vanguard.com.
- *Step 2:* I went to a listing of all Vanguard's funds, organized by fund type.
- *Step 3:* I scrolled down to the list of intermediate-term bond funds.
- *Step 4:* I noted that the Vanguard Intermediate-Term Bond Index Fund had a current yield of 4.57 percent, while the Vanguard Intermediate-Term Tax-Exempt Fund had a current yield of 3.2 percent.
- *Step 5:* I looked at the tax tables to see what tax bracket I'm in. Since I'm a joint filer and my taxable income is slightly more than $114,650, but woefully less than $174,700, I'm in the 30 percent tax bracket. I multiplied 4.57 percent by 0.7. The answer: 3.199 percent.

Wow! Who'd a thunk it? The after-tax return of these two funds is virtually identical. So if I'm investing in the Vanguard Intermediate-

Term Bond Index Fund, there's no reason to switch because I won't come out ahead after taxes. But it doesn't hurt to check every now and then, especially since it took me less than ninety seconds to do it. Now I can move on with confidence.

Another tax-advantaged source of interest is the money you collect in tax-deferred accounts. Prime example of this type of account? Your 401(k), IRA, or other retirement account. You don't report money you make in these accounts. While you will pay taxes on any money you withdraw, investing in these types of accounts is cool because you don't pay the taxes now, nor do you deal with any time-consuming paperwork reporting interest you receive or profits you make. That's why we like these types of accounts. Yes, we'll have to pay taxes in the long term. But in the long term we're all dead.

SELLING STUFF

What about when you get money as a result of selling stuff? Whenever you sell anything, the government wants a share of the profit you make. It may offer you a tax deduction, however, for money you lose. This is where we learn about what are called "capital gains" and "capital losses."

When it comes to profits, Uncle Sam wants a share of anything you make, period. When it comes to getting a deduction on losses, however, you're only allowed to deduct losses from stuff that you bought for investment. In other words, you don't get to deduct the bath you took on the sale of the family car, but you're supposed to pay taxes on the profit you made by buying a painting at a yard sale for five bucks and selling it to an art museum for a thousand. Doesn't seem fair, does it? Well, if you're willing to risk the wrath of Uncle Sam, be a tax cheat and forget to report the profit on your painting. As long as the museum doesn't tell, perhaps nobody will know and your profit will be tax-free. But if the transaction is being reported, you'd better 'fess up.

Interesting side note: Not reporting gains is how some people find themselves behind bars. Drug dealers often go to prison simply because they live high on the hog but don't file tax returns revealing where the money is coming from. These guys are buying low, selling high (pun intended), and not reporting it. Moral of the story? If you've got a lot of undeclared profits, you might want to avoid luxury living.

Most of us, however, will never face the dilemma of whether to report our gains or other sources of income because we don't have a choice. They're reported for us.

Every January, mailboxes across America fill up with tax forms called 1099s. These 1099s are all about potential sources of income being reported to the IRS by whoever paid it. Consider them a warning from everyone who's sent you a check that they're about to tell the IRS about it. This way, when you file your taxes, you'll be sure to tell the IRS about it, too. (This is another way the IRS catches tax cheats. It simply compares the 1099 forms it gets from money payers with the tax returns it gets from money receivers. If the amounts don't gibe, they write a not-so-polite letter to the taxpayer asking why.)

If you get a form in the mail marked simply "1099," it's normally a record of money you were paid the previous year for work you performed. A 1099-INT is a statement of interest you received. A 1099-DIV is a statement of dividends you got. A 1099-R is a report of a distribution from a retirement plan. And the one we're most concerned with here, a 1099-B, is a report of securities you sold. So if you get a 1099-B, you sold something and you've got to tell the IRS what it was, when you bought it, what you paid for it, and how much profit or loss you realized from the transaction.

As we've already discussed, interest you earn and profits you make in tax-deferred accounts like your 401(k) don't have to be reported. So one way of avoiding 1099-Bs is to confine your investing to tax-deferred accounts. But we've already decided that we're going to be investing in the stock market outside of our retirement accounts. And since we certainly will be aiming to make money, let's see how these things are taxed.

As you know, when you make a profit by selling something, you're expected to share the wealth. If the gain was from something you owned for one year or less, it's considered a short-term gain; if you held on for more than a year, it's a long-term gain. Why does it matter? Because long-term gains are taxed at lower rates. It's also important to note that gains and losses realized during the year are netted against each other before you're taxed on them. Then the result is taxed as either profit or loss, long term or short term.

If this sounds confusing, that's because it is. Nonetheless, you're going to be making profits and losses, which means you should understand how they're taxed. So let's go over this in a bit more detail.

First, here's how gains are taxed based on how long you own the asset:

- **Short-term gains:** These are taxed like any other income you receive during the year.
- **Long-term gains:** If your normal tax rate is lower than 20 percent, you pay 10 percent. If your normal tax rate is higher than 20 percent, you pay 20 percent.

I'll briefly explain the process of netting out your short- and long-term gains, then tell you why it matters.

Say you get a 1099-B in the mail that reveals a bunch of gains and losses, both short and long term. Step 1 is to net your short-term gains and short-term losses. Step 2 is to net your long-term gains and long-term losses. Step 3 is to net the results of both to arrive at a bottom line, which will be either short term or long term. Here's an example.

Short-term gains for the year:	$4,000
Short-term losses for the year:	$5,000
Long-term gains for the year:	$8,000
Long-term losses for the year:	$5,000

- *Step 1:* Netting your short-term stuff leaves you with a $1,000 short-term loss.
- *Step 2:* Netting your long-term stuff leaves you with a $3,000 long-term gain.
- *Step 3:* Netting long-term and short-term stuff leaves you with a $2,000 long-term gain.

So there we have it: a $2,000 net long-term gain. Since it's long term, it will be taxed at a maximum rate of 20 percent.[55] But what if we'd ended up with a net loss? We could use it as a deduction against our income—but not more than $3,000 in any one year. In other words, while gains are fully taxable in the year you receive them, you can only deduct $3,000 of losses in the year you suffer them at least against income. Losses above $3,000 aren't gone forever, however. You get to store them indefinitely until they're used up. So losses in excess of $3,000 this year can be used next year or the year after or however long it takes to use them to offset either gains you make or income you receive. This is called a loss carryover.

Once you understand how gains and losses are characterized as short term and long term, how they're netted against one another, how they're taxed, and how losses are carried over to subsequent years, you're in a much better position to plan. For example, if I can wait a few days to convert a gain from short to long term, I'd normally want to. If I've got a $5,000 loss carryover from last year, that means I can take $5,000 worth of gains this year without having to worry about paying taxes on them. Granted, this isn't the simplest of stuff, especially when you start considering all the exceptions. (You can download Publication 544 from irs.gov to see what I mean.) But it's not really rocket science, so it doesn't hurt to brush up on the basics now and again.

GAMBLING WINNINGS

Winning money by gambling is just like making it any other way. In other words, difficult to do and totally taxable. The money you lose gambling, however, is only deductible against what you've won. So if you're a net loser for the year, you're out of luck both figuratively and literally. If you're a net winner for the year, hopefully you've kept track of your gambling losses to partially offset

[55] The thing that makes taxes so complicated is that there are virtually no rules without exceptions. In this case, the maximum rate for long-term gains is indeed 20 percent, unless it's a gain arising from the sale of collectibles or a couple of other unlikely categories of transactions. Then the maximum rate could be 28 percent.

that income. If you haven't, drive out to the track and grab a bunch of losing tickets off the floor.

ALIMONY

Alimony is generally income for tax purposes and therefore taxable. A bummer if you're receiving it, but righteous if you're paying it, because alimony payments are deductible—providing you meet the list of requirements found in Form 504, viewable at irs.gov.

CHILD SUPPORT

Child support, also covered by Form 504, isn't taxable income to the one getting it or deductible to the one paying it.

The deductibility of alimony and nondeductibility of child support could be of monster importance if there's a divorce in your future. If you're going to be faced with a big property settlement and/or child support payments, you're better off as the payer of this stuff if it's repackaged as alimony, since alimony is pretty much the only divorce-related money you'll pay that's deductible. (Attorney's fees generally aren't.) And making it deductible could ultimately save you 30 percent or more in income taxes. Of course, the amount you'll pay in child support is often statutory, so it may be impossible to have it designated as alimony. In addition, the money you're saving on taxes by paying alimony is money your ex-spouse is losing, since he has to declare it as income and pay taxes on it. But think of the possibilities: You pay the ex-husband alimony, knowing that the schmuck will never report it as income. Let a couple of years go by . . . call the IRS with an anonymous tip . . . what fun!

COLLECTING SOCIAL SECURITY

Used to be that Social Security retirement wasn't taxable income. Then Congress decided that if your income was high, you should be taxed on at least part of your Social Security benefits. What's considered high income? As of the 2002 tax year, it was $32,000 for joint taxpayers. And that income includes half the Social Security benefits you received and all the interest income you received, whether or not it came from otherwise tax-free sources like municipal bonds. If your taxable income exceeds $32,000 ($25,000 if you're single), you could pay taxes on half your Social Security retirement, survivor, and disability benefits . . . perhaps on even more than half. But since there's not much you can do about it, and your tax preparation software will figure it all out for you, there's no reason to dwell on it. That's just the way it is. If you feel like dwelling on it anyway, however, download Form 915 from irs.gov and dwell away.

GETTING RENT CHECKS

Rental income is fully taxable. However, rental income can be offset by deductible rental expenses: see chapter 17, "Real Estate."

INCOME SUMMARY

Now that we've covered the most likely sources of income you'll be receiving, a pattern should be starting to develop. Basically, when it comes to taxes, pretty much every dime you ever see is taxable. To create tax deductions by losing or otherwise parting with money, on the other hand, often requires you to jump through hoops. Surprised?

Income Tax Deductions

You'll recall from the beginning of this chapter that tax planning is all about timing: in other words, exactly when you're forced to report money that's taxable and exactly when you're able to report money that's deductible. You've just learned that most of the money you make is taxable, and that you're pretty much forced to report it when it's receivable. Now it's time to learn that most of the money you spend isn't deductible. But at least you have the flexibility to deduct allowable expenses in the year you pay them, which as you'll soon see can be useful.

Before we continue, let's be clear about what deductions are. A deduction represents money you've spent that ultimately serves to reduce your taxable income, which in turn reduces the amount of tax you owe. As such, deductions are highly desirable. But how can you tell which checks you write will qualify as deductions? Here's a good rule of thumb: If the money you're spending is putting a smile on your face, it's probably not deductible.

Think I'm kidding? Take a look at the form you'll use to report your itemized deductions, the infamous 1040 Schedule A. Here's what you'll find. First category of qualified deductions: medical and dental expenses. Next category: taxes paid. Then interest. Then gifts to charity. Then casualty and theft losses. Finally, job-related expenses.

Real barrel of monkeys, right?

Fact is, with the exception of gifts to qualified charities, the only checks you write that end up helping you deduction-wise are checks you have to write, not checks you want to write. But wait . . . it gets worse. Because even when you write these checks, you may still not end up with any deductions. Why? First, because the government figures that almost everyone will have some deductible expenses, so they allow us all a standard deduction. For married couples filing a joint return, that amount is around eight grand. For single people, around five. So unless you spent more than that on allowable deductions, there's no point in keeping track of them. (At least not for federal tax purposes. If you pay state income taxes, these deductions may still be useful.) Second, even if you have a lot of deductions, Uncle Sam won't let you take them if you make too much money. What's too much money? If your adjusted gross income (total income minus a few things like IRA contributions, moving expenses, interest paid on student loans, and alimony; you can see the complete list of adjustments at the bottom of the first page of a 1040 form) is in the neighborhood of $150,000 for joint filers, you start losing your deductions. Another way that Uncle Sam sticks a fork in rich folks.

All that being said, you should still keep an eye out for deductions, because despite their scarcity, they're still better than a sharp stick in the eye. Let's go back to our list from 1040 Schedule A and have a closer look.

MEDICAL AND DENTAL EXPENSES

If you get to deduct much in the way of medical and dental expenses, odds are that you have one foot in the grave and the other on a banana peel. That's because only those expenses that exceed 7.5 percent of your adjusted gross income are deductible. So if you've got an adjusted gross income of $50,000, you'll need to spend more than $3,750 on unreimbursed medical expenses before you see your first dollar of deduction.

Now that we know this, what can we do with this information to improve our situation? Well, here's where timing comes in. Imagine that it's mid-December. We're watching football, and during commercials we're going over what's happened this year money-wise and what's coming up next year. Hmmm . . . due to an unusual year-end bonus this year, looks like the adjusted gross is going to be around fifty-five grand instead of the usual fifty. That's got us scrounging for some extra deductions. Can we find some help in the medical expense category? Let's see. We know that we're going to need more than 7.5 percent of adjusted gross to get any help. Seven and a half percent of $55,000 is $4,125. Okay, let's see what we've spent. We open our personal finance program and have a look. Our health insurance costs around $250 a month, and that's deductible, so there's $3,000 right off the bat. In addition, because we don't have a lot of bells and whistles on our health policy, we're also out of pocket for copayments, a couple of prescriptions, contact lenses, teeth cleaning . . . it adds up to about $700. In addition, mileage to and from doctor and dentist is deductible: We get to write off 13 cents for every medical-related mile driven. Still, unless we're willing to claim that we drove a thousand miles to see the doctor and fifteen hundred to see the dentist, we're not going to make it over the $4,125 threshold. Oh well . . . but wait! Son Billy is going to need braces next year. Wife Betty is thinking of laser surgery for her eyes. What if we prepaid part of Billy's orthodontic treatments now and gave Betty a gift certificate for eye surgery for Christmas? When we pile these expenses on top of everything else, we're going to generate a deduction after all. (This applies only to people whose health plan isn't employer sponsored. Plus, you can't deduct expenses for services that, according to the IRS, will occur "substantially" beyond year-end.) Never mind that these deductible medical treatments haven't occurred yet. If we pay for them this year, they're deductible this year. We've harnessed the power of timing to offset part of our unexpected, albeit most welcome, year-end bonus.

Feel strangely compelled to find out more about the deductibility of medical expenses? Then you may have a mental problem. But at least the treatment for it is probably deductible, and while waiting for an appointment with a qualified professional you can indulge your bizarre compulsion free by logging onto irs.gov and downloading Publication 502, "Medical and Dental Expenses."

TAXES

You don't get to deduct the federal taxes that have been withheld all year from your paychecks, but you do the money withheld for state income taxes. You also get to deduct real estate taxes you've paid. Here again, we have an opportunity to time our payment and therefore reduce our tax liability if we so choose. Because there's nothing that prevents us from whipping out the checkbook and prepaying part of our property taxes for next year. Except, perhaps, the balance in our checking account.

INTEREST

As you probably know, pretty much the only interest you get to deduct is that on your mortgage. (About the only other deductible interest is investment interest, meaning interest on margin loans. And it's kind of like gambling losses: deductible only to the extent that you've got investment interest income.) But here again, we're presented with an opportunity to time our deduction. Because we can make our January payment in December, capturing that extra interest deduction this year instead of next.

GIFTS TO CHARITY

Don't forget money you give to your church. And don't forget to deduct mileage you incurred while engaging in charitable activity. You can write off 14 cents per mile. (This doesn't mean, however, you should hit the Goodwill box outside Disney World. The cost of out-of-town travel isn't normally deductible.)

You don't get to deduct political contributions, or the value of the time you donate. If you donate stuff instead of money, you get to deduct its fair market value at the time you donated it. And you get to specify its value. (In the Middle Ages, people believed that it was possible to turn lead into gold. Turns out they were right: happens every December at the Salvation Army!)

CASUALTY AND THEFT LOSSES

This deduction arises when you get burgled, lend money to a friend, or otherwise get ripped off. It also applies to your insurance deductible if you have a wreck or otherwise suffer a loss. Too bad your total losses have to exceed 10 percent of your adjusted gross before you get to deduct them. So you have to be a real loser to get any deduction here. In any case, there's not much you can do to plan around, or time, this particular deduction.

(Note: Casualty losses are a perfect example of how the government can appear to lower your taxes while actually raising them. It used to be that casualty losses didn't have a 10-percent-of-adjusted-gross-income limitation. Likewise, the threshold for medical expenses used to be 5 percent instead of 7.5 percent. But these are the types of changes that can be made without citizens really noticing. So when it's time to make headlines, the politicians lower tax rates, then simply go in and fiddle around with deductions like these to keep those lower rates from costing too much.)

JOB EXPENSES AND MOST OTHER MISCELLANEOUS EXPENSES

Here you get to write off money you spent related to your job, along with some other stuff. However, if the total of these things is less than 2 percent of your adjusted gross income, you're toast.

Want to try to beat the 2 percent threshold? The work-related expenses you're looking for include things like tools, uniforms, protective equipment, subscriptions to professional journals, dues to professional organizations . . . anything work related that your employer doesn't pay or reimburse you for.

Far and away the most common income tax question I've been asked over the years is the following: "I only wear suits to work. That makes them deductible, right?"

Nice try, but no dice. Uniforms, yes. Suits, no. While you may only wear your suits to work, you could theoretically wear them elsewhere. Rule of thumb? If you want to deduct your work clothes, make sure your name is sewn on the outside.

You might also get to deduct some work-related educational expenses, but this is a potential minefield, so be careful. To be deductible, the education you're getting has to either be required by your employer (or the law) or serve to increase your job skills. But if it qualifies you for another job, or is required to meet the educational requirements of your current job, it's not deductible. For example, say you're a teacher with a degree in education, but your employer requires you to take a college course every other year. Fine . . . your tuition is deductible. But if you end up graduating from medical school as a result, these costs may not be deductible after all. Your employer required you to take courses, but you chose courses that qualified you for an entirely different job. No deduction.

If this sounds complicated, it just shows you're paying attention, because of course it is.

Despite being a bit on the confusing side, employee-related expenses are an area where you might increase your deductions by timing your cash outlays. Just make sure the purchases meet the requirements. If you're interested, or are having trouble sleeping, the handbook is called Publication 508, and it's waiting for you at irs.gov.

Once you've educated yourself on educational expenses, in the same box of Schedule A you'll find miscellaneous expenses. This category of potential write-offs appears encouraging, but it's not as flexible as it sounds. You can write off the cost of tax preparation, including the cost of the software you bought and the cost of filing electronically. You can also write off the cost of your safe deposit box (whoopee!) as well as a few other expenses too rare to bother mentioning. Besides, your tax preparation software will find out if you have them anyway.

OTHER MISCELLANEOUS EXPENSES

This is where you get to deduct your gambling losses, but only to the extent of winnings you've reported. It's also the place to deduct other common expenses we all wonder about, such as amortizable bond premium on bonds acquired before October 23, 1986.

In other words, this isn't the mother lode for additional deductions.

SELF-EMPLOYMENT

As you can see from our cursory glimpse at the itemized deductions found on Schedule A, expenses that easily convert into tax write-offs are as common as nuns in Vegas. So where are all the tax loopholes we read so much about? Well, many are found along the path to self-employment. Actually, "loopholes" is a pretty strong word . . . "advantages" is probably better terminology.

Businesses get to deduct everything they spend to create a profit: the parts they use to make their products, the machines they buy to assemble them, the wages they pay to their employees, and the building that houses it all. So if you want to create loads of tax deductions, be a business. And that doesn't mean you have to be General Motors. You're witnessing a business in action right now: I'm in the business of writing this book. That makes my computer a tax deduction, along with the electricity that powers it. So are my desk, my chair, my phone, my paper clips, my files, my Internet access, yada, yada, yada. Everything remotely related to producing the tidal waves of income I'm going to be making with this book is deductible. If I had an office, I could write off the rent, but since I'm working at home, what I could do instead is depreciate a portion of my house.

So owning your own business is a huge generator of tax deductions, with the consequence to the IRS of creating irritatingly low tax bills. Which is why they're constantly on the lookout for abuse in this area. So while it's great to generate tax deductions with a home-based business, be sure you ultimately have some income to offset them. In other words, a business that doesn't make money isn't a business: It's a hobby. And hobby expenses aren't deductible.

Bottom line? If you work at home, whether full time or part time, make your business businesslike. Keep your accounting as separate as possible. Likewise with your workspace. (My office is used only as my office . . . it doesn't double as a den.) If you have only one computer and want to fully deduct its cost, don't think you'll convince the IRS that you use it strictly for business. They won't bite. But when properly governed and fairly reported, self-employment is wonderful in terms of both personal freedom and tax deductions.

DEDUCTION SUMMARY

As I mentioned earlier, when you examine federal income taxes, you find that Uncle Sam's definition of taxable income is exceedingly liberal, while his definition of allowable deductions is exceedingly strict. This is, of course, no surprise. But as a cash-basis taxpayer, you can still influence the outcome by using timing to help you batch deductions, thereby postponing liability, or shifting them from a year where they don't do as much good to one where they do. Since it's one of the only tools you have, might as well use it.

Alternative Minimum Tax

Before we conclude, I'll mention one more thing, simply because you may hear about it every now and then and wonder what it means. It's called the alternative minimum tax. You won't have to actually become conversant with this parallel system of collecting income tax, because if it applies to you, your tax preparation software will know what to do. But it's still kind of interesting.

By now you're familiar with how certain actions can change the outcome of your tax story. For example, you already know that the interest from municipal bonds isn't taxable, and pretty soon you'll also learn that real estate can radically reduce your tax liability.

Now imagine that you're really, really rich . . . say you've got a billion dollars. You put the entire billion into 5 percent municipal bonds from your home state. Result? You're now earning $50,000,000 every year totally tax-free. This would make you very happy, but it would make people who earn $75,000 a year and surrender $10,000 of it as income tax a bit miffed. This is why Uncle Sam came along in 1969 with something called the alternative minimum tax, or AMT. The AMT is a totally separate way of computing your tax liability, designed specifically to ensure that rich folks don't get to exploit tax loopholes to the extent that they don't pay anything. The way it essentially works is to have you compute your tax liability under the regular set of rules and again under AMT rules. Then you pay whichever bill is higher. There's no distinct set of warning whistles that would alert you to the possibility of an AMT liability, but in general people with high tax breaks in certain key areas should be aware of the possibility. These key areas are: personal exemptions, state and local taxes, interest on second mortgages, medical expenses, miscellaneous itemized deductions, long-term capital gains, and incentive stock options.

Again, don't worry too much about AMT. First because there's not much you can do about it anyway. Second because your tax preparation software has already studied the subject and is waiting to help.

Conclusion: An Important Note Regarding Minutiae

Aren't you glad this subject is almost over? I can't stand talking about income taxes, much less writing about them.

Even though I was trying to paint in broad strokes, taxes are so comically detailed that I was forced to introduce a bunch of boring details in this chapter. I hope you don't think for a second that you're supposed to remember all, or even part of it. Only a savant could, and only an insane savant would want to. I've been a CPA for more than twenty years and I just relearned practically everything you just read for the millionth time as I was writing it. And every single thing I wrote I found in a few seconds simply by plugging a few search terms into the IRS Web site. Why the heck would I want to attempt to memorize it?

The purpose of this chapter was simply to demystify what's happening in Federal Income Tax Land. In other words, think of what you just read as an overview of how the internal combustion engine works, not a manual on how to rebuild one. In the age before computers, income taxes were the forte of bespectacled magicians known as tax accountants. Like the Wizards of Wall Street in Investment Land, they promised much and charged much. And we had no choice but to pay what they were asking. But that was then. The formerly insurmountable hurdle of six thousand pages of tax law is gone now. Now it's a ten-minute walk in the park with your computer and a $20 tax preparation program that automatically imports the necessary information from your personal finance software and transfers it to your tax return. Like its human counterpart, your software asks you questions to make sure you've taken all the deductions to which you're entitled and claimed all the income you should. It prints a copy of your return for your records, then files it electronically for you. It even asks if you'd like to do a little tax planning for next year. If you understand the basics so you set yourself up properly, know where to go to learn more, and have yourself organized so all the information is in place, what's left for you to do? Hmmm . . . did I hear someone say "Jerry Springer"?

16

Insurance

Money doesn't talk, it swears.

—Bob Dylan

Here's the thing with insurance: If you buy enough to insulate yourself from financial inconvenience rather than financial calamity, you'll create a financial calamity trying to pay for all your insurance. Which is the only financial calamity left in the United States that can't be insured against. I'm sure they're working on it.

When you start keeping track of your expenses, one of the first things you'll notice is the amount of money you're spending on the plethora of policies designed to keep you from the poorhouse in the event of accident, illness, or injury. If you find that about 8 percent of all the money you get your hands on is being handed to an insurance company, congratulations: You're an average American.

Like collecting hate mail? Then do what I do . . . go on TV and suggest ways to save money by eliminating stupid insurance policies. For example, I've done stories several times explaining that insuring the life of a child is a bad idea, because unless your child is a major breadwinner, you're not likely to suffer financially in the event of her death. (Please note the word "financially" in that sentence. My hate-mail collection is quite adequate already, thank you.) And since preventing financial hardship is the purpose of insurance, you would think that telling people not to insure their kids would seem pretty logical, right? Well, trust me: It doesn't seem at all smart to some life insurance agents. Whenever I do this story, or one like it, it's all aboard the hate-mail train. A typical response from an interested viewer might look something like this:

> DEAR BONEHEAD-IDIOT-POSING-AS-A-CONSUMER-REPORTER,
>
> I watched your story this morning on WXXX's news and wanted to tell you how much I hate your guts. You suggested that insuring the life of a small child was a waste of money. This is wrong, and the fact that I make 90 percent of my money by collecting commissions on the sales of similar policies in no way taints my objectivity.
>
> If you had the common sense that God gave a doughnut you'd know that insuring the life of a small child is a great financial strategy. Because if the child develops a health problem later in life, at that point it will be too late to get any life insurance, and she'll be totally screwed. So buying as much life insurance as humanly possible at the earliest possible age should be mandatory for everyone.
>
> I once had a client who bought life insurance on his son at birth and continued to pay the paltry premiums month after month, year after year. At age sixteen, the child suddenly developed Tourette's syndrome, rendering him uninsurable. The permanent policy that I had sold the family at birth was therefore the only policy he would ever be able to get. I would quote from the letter of gratitude he sent me, but due to his condition I'm afraid it's a bit obscene.
>
> In any case, if you continue to suggest that insuring the lives of small children is a bad idea, I wholeheartedly hope that your life insurance is paid up. Because I'll hunt you down like the dog you are and kill you without batting an eye.
>
> Warmest regards,
>
> VICTOR VIEWER

Here is my standard response to letters like this:

DEAR VICTOR,

Thanks so much for taking a few brief minutes away from ripping off members of an unsuspecting public to chastise me on the subject of insuring the lives of children. I hesitate to engage in this battle of wits, however, since you're apparently unarmed.

While it's true that sometimes children do develop health issues that make them uninsurable, the fact is that the cost of insuring against this statistically unlikely scenario outweighs the potential benefit, particularly when compared against other savings alternatives.

Let me respond to your example with one of my own. Every week, someone wins millions in a lottery or with the pull of a slot machine handle. But this doesn't make lotteries or slot machines desirable investments. Why? Because the odds of hitting the lottery are less than the odds of being abducted by an alien. So the lottery will always be a stupid investment, despite the fact that someone wins every single week. The same is true with your example: The fact that one kid grows up uninsurable doesn't make the investment, or you for that matter, any less stupid.

In short, Victor, if we surgically removed your brain and stuffed it up the butt of a bumblebee, it would bounce around like a BB in a boxcar.

Thanks for watching *Money Talks*!

Warmest regards,
STACY JOHNSON

While this exchange was imaginary (I refrain from saying what I feel like saying when corresponding with caustic viewers), suffice it to say that at least some insurance agents don't like the idea of people buying less insurance. Why would they? Their consternation makes sense. What doesn't make sense is basing your insurance-buying decisions on the advice from a person who directly benefits from its sale. And yet that's precisely what you do when you call an insurance agent and ask him what kind and how much insurance to buy. Stop doing this to the extent possible by learning the minimum necessary to understand what you're buying, then buying the minimum necessary to stave off catastrophe, not inconvenience. And while you're at it, streamline the entire process to further your goal of becoming a flawless controller of your finances.

Let's take each category of insurance one at a time. As we do this, I'll tell you a few things to look for and tell you how to organize and shop for each. But before we do this, you need to understand the logic that underlies my minimizing my insurance purchases. It's simply that insurance is not only a boring thing to buy . . . but also not a great use of money. Slot machines typically pay out from 80 to 90 cents of every dollar they take in. But with some types of insurance, like credit life, insurance companies sometimes pay out less than 50 cents of every dollar they take in.[56] Granted, there are more expenses associated with maintaining insurance policies than slot machines. But the point remains that buying more insurance than you absolutely need will divert money from better spots, which doesn't include slot machines but does include your savings. This is not to say that you should abandon insurance entirely; in many situations you definitely do need it. But never a penny more than what it will take to fend off catastrophe, not inconvenience.

Car Insurance

Let's start our view of insurance with a look at the automotive variety.

If you've organized your finances and have everything on your computer, you know how much you're spending on your car insurance. Now it's time to create a spreadsheet so you can see what you're paying for. Pull out your car policy and write down the pertinent information: what's covered, deductibles, phone numbers, policy due dates, and so on. Having this information in one place

[56] Benefits paid out versus premiums paid in is what's known as a loss ratio. According to the Center for Economic Justice, historical loss ratios for group life insurance are around 90 percent. For group health insurance, it's a bit more than 75 percent. For private passenger automobile insurance, just under 70 percent. And for credit life insurance, around 42 percent. For more information, go to www.cej-online.org.

will not only give you a glimpse at the big picture but make shopping for better rates a snap as well. It will also make you feel in control. As I said in chapter 14, on organization, I use Microsoft Excel for my insurance spreadsheets, but you can use just about any program that will allow you to write stuff down and keep it straight.

As an example, here's my spreadsheet for the car I drive:

380 SEL

Company	Wrecks-r-us
Phone	800-wreckus
Policy Number	XXX XX XX
Annual Amount	$655.74
Dates Due	10/1, 4/1

Coverages	**Amount**	**Cost**	**Notes**
Liability (Part A)			
Injury Each Person	$100,000		Maximum payment to each person I maim or kill.
Injury Each Accident	$300,000	$256	Maximum payment for each accident. 300/500 injury: add $123.
Property Each Accident	$50,000	$120	Maximum payment for property I destroy. 100 property: add $8 yr.
Personal Injury (Part B)			
	$10,000	$92	$2,000 deductible. No loss of work coverage. Required. 10K is all that's offered in FL.
Uninsured Motorist (Part C)			
Bodily Injury Each Person	$100,000		As above, but if some uninsured fool does the damage. This covers anyone in my vehicle.
Bodily Injury Each Accident	$300,000	$188	You can't get property for UM. This can be raised, lowered, rejected.
		$656	

Before we look at what's here, let's look at what's not. Notice that there's no comprehensive or collision coverage on my car. Comprehensive and collision, a very expensive portion of any car insurance policy, is what would pay for damage to my car if I screw up and my car is injured as a result. It also would pay if my car gets stolen, vandalized, or otherwise damaged. Why is this important coverage missing from my spreadsheet? Because I don't have any. When it comes to my mistakes with my car, I'm self-insured. How can I take this seemingly foolish risk? Because my car is a 1982 model, and despite the fact that it's solid, dependable, cool to drive, leather-lined, and equipped with a great sound system, it's only worth about three grand. So worst-case scenario, I'm out three grand to replace it. And that's a risk I'm willing to take, because comp and collision coverage would add hundreds to my bill every year. In other words, the cost–benefit ratio isn't there. One rule of thumb when it comes to comp and collision states that if your premiums exceed 10 percent of the value of the car, consider dropping the coverage. I considered. I dropped.

Had I taken the path of the vast majority of my peers, I would have spent twenty-five or thirty grand on a car. Then I wouldn't have been able to make this decision, because self-insuring a car that expensive would have been too risky. And if I had to borrow to buy my expensive car, I'd have to have comp and collision because my lender would make me. See how sometimes less is more? Less car to insure, less time spent shopping coverage, less time spent working to pay for insurance, more time to watch Jerry Springer. Even so, if I did choose to have comp and collision, I'd certainly have as high a deductible as I could afford: at least $1,000. That's what I mean about covering against catastrophe instead of inconvenience. While losing a grand wouldn't be a pleasant experience, it wouldn't send me to McDonald's for a second job, either. It's never ceased to amaze me that so many people have $250 or $500 deductibles on their various insurance policies, yet would never think of filing a claim for less than a grand because they'd be (justifiably) afraid of a rate hike. This is the epitome of nuts, because you're paying premiums that insure against financial inconvenience, but acting in a way that only insures against financial catastrophe. If you're willing to lose $1,000 if you screw up, then raise your deductible and save 10 to 20 percent on your bill.

One more note regarding comprehensive before we move on. If you're in a situation similar to mine—that is, you self-insure your own car and do away with comprehensive and collision—don't forget this when you rent a car. Because if you don't have comp and collision on your car at home, you won't have it on cars you rent, either. This means that if you're not given such coverage free as a perk on a credit card (call to make sure), you may have to voluntarily submit to one of the greatest rip-offs of the modern age: buying car insurance at a rental-car counter. If you don't get it and total your rental, you could be on the hook for a much more expensive car than you're used to self-insuring at home.

Okay, let's look at the rest of my spreadsheet. The liability portion of my policy is coverage for damage I do to other people and their stuff. This is required by state law, and would otherwise be required by common sense anyway. As you can see, I can screw up to the tune of $100,000 per person and $300,000 per event, with a fifty-grand limit on property. For my personal situation, this is probably not enough—for a couple of reasons. First, I live in an area where a lot of people drive cars that are worth more than fifty grand. Second, depending on the day of the week and what the stock market is doing, I'm worth more than $300,000. So I could be assuming the risk that I'll have to part with a lot of money if I screw up. Not good. Here's where I needed to see how much additional liability would cost, then plug it into the cost–benefit equation and decide what to do. I learned that the next level of coverage for injuring other people is 300/500, meaning $300,000 per person, $500,000 per accident. Should I choose to go this route, my note indicates that would add $123 per year to my bill. The next level of property coverage is $100,000. My note says I could increase my coverage in this category for only $8 per year.

The next part of my policy is personal injury protection. This is insurance that covers me and my passengers if we're hurt in an accident. This coverage is required where I live, but I'm buying only

$10,000 worth and I've got a $2,000 deductible. Sound crazy? Well, keep in mind that no matter how I'm injured—plane, train, or automobile—I've got medical insurance that will pay for my reassembly. I don't carry passengers often, but those I do carry also tend to have health insurance. If the accident is my fault, my passengers will be covered by my liability and/or their health insurance. And as I said, I'll be covered by my own health insurance. If the accident isn't my fault, all of us will be covered by the other driver's liability insurance and/or our health insurance. If the other driver doesn't have insurance, then my uninsured motorist coverage will pay the medical bills for all of us. So this coverage wouldn't appear to do me any good, which is why I don't have much of it. Notice, however, how much it costs. Ninety bucks a year: 14 percent of my total insurance bill for this car. And since I have a $2,000 deductible, I'm only getting what amounts to $8,000 worth of coverage. In the meantime, my cost for $300,000 of liability coverage is only $256. Why is personal injury protection so expensive? That's exactly what I asked my friendly insurance company. They proceeded to recite a bunch of gobbly-gook that essentially meant that this payment would be made immediately, rather than having to first establish liability. It also covers lost wages. But since this still doesn't explain why it costs so much relative to my other coverages, I assume that the premium is high because they make more money that way.

The last thing on my policy is uninsured motorist coverage. As the name implies, uninsured motorist coverage pays for the damage caused by people careening around without liability insurance. Uninsured motorist coverage is not required in my state, but it may make sense to have because in addition to all the fancy cars I see around here, there are also many that appear to be held together with baling wire. It wouldn't be a shock to learn that a driver with a plastic bag for a rear window neglected to pay his insurance bill. In any case, unless I specify otherwise in writing, my insurer will provide this coverage in the same amount as my liability. What it doesn't offer, however, is uninsured motorist coverage for property. So if an uninsured motorist totals my car, there won't be any insurance to pay for it. (If I had comp and collision, that would pay, but as I've said, I don't.) Therefore, when it comes to my car, the only justice I'll receive in an accident with an uninsured motorist is from the pistol I keep in my glove compartment.

Now we've gone over my insurance bill for one of my two cars. While I'm sure you found it riveting, much of it will be meaningless to you unless you drive a car like mine, have the same driving record I have, and live where I live. So what was the point of explaining it to you? So you'd see how I manage my car insurance and how you should. Perhaps you think that I knew all this stuff about liability, collision, personal injury protection, and uninsured motorist coverage because I'm a money expert. Wrong. I know this stuff because I called the toll-free number on my insurance policy, sat on the phone with some hapless customer service representative until I understood what I was paying for, and made notes. I went over each and every line of my insurance bill and made him explain it to me, over and over again until I understood it. Then, just to make sure, I repeated back what I thought I'd understood until my explanation matched his. When he didn't know something (like why personal injury protection coverage costs so much), I kept questioning until he was forced to acknowledge his ignorance. Then, when I was sure I totally understood everything, I put him on hold while I made the notes you see on my spreadsheet. (While dealing with insurance is boring, making my insurance company wait was one of the most satisfying things I've ever done.)

Before you pick up the phone to do this, however, be aware of a couple of potential flies in the ointment. First, when you ask questions about your policy, your customer service representative will attempt to refer you back to your policy for answers. While you should have your policy at hand for ready reference, and verify what you're told by finding it in your policy, your policy is a place to form questions, not answer them. It's about as understandable as the income tax code. So be prepared for this blatant attempt at a brush-off and refuse to fall for it. If my insurance company wanted me to be able to find answers to my questions by looking at my policies, it should have written them in plain English. In addition, don't be surprised if the customer service representative you deal with gives you the wrong answer. He's used to people calling with questions about where to send their check, not asking what the heck they're paying for. So while you're on the phone with the representative, look in your actual policy and make sure what you think you're reading matches what you think he's saying. If it doesn't, challenge him. I've found reps' explanations to be incorrect about a third of the time.

Once I'd understood everything about this policy, including how much I'd spend to increase coverages and how much I'd save to reduce them, I was in the position of being able to decide how to customize my policy to meet my personal needs. For example, I could increase my liability so I'd be better protected in the event I messed up. And I could find the money to do that by dropping uninsured motorist coverage if I so desired. Why would I drop uninsured motorist? Remember that if I'm injured in an accident caused by an uninsured motorist, I won't be left lying on the pavement because I have health insurance. And since the uninsured motorist isn't going to pay for damage to my car anyway, why do I have it? As of the moment I cut and pasted this spreadsheet to this book, I hadn't yet decided what to do. But I may decide to drop this coverage, increase my liability to $300,000 per person/$500,000 per accident/$100,000 for property, and still save $57 every year. (Dropping uninsured motorist saves me $188 per year. The additional liability for people costs $123, and for property, $8. $188 – $123 – $8 = $57.)

In addition to being able to make my coverage match my needs, having the facts at hand also allows me to shop this policy easily and virtually instantly. Let's go through this exercise together. First, through the magic of computers, I add a few columns to my spreadsheet to accommodate quotes from other companies:

Company		Wrecks-r-us	Esurance	Hartford	Liberty Mutual	Geico	Progressive
Contact			insure.com	insure.com	insure.com	geico.com	progressive.com
Coverages	Amount						
Liability (Part A)							$596
Injury each person	$100,000						
Injury each accident	$300,000	$256				$429	
Property each accident	$50,000	$120				$184	
Personal Injury (Part B)							
	$10,000	$92				$263	$222
Uninsured motorist (Part C)							
Injury each person	$100,000						
Injury each accident	$300,000	$188				$214	$374
Total		**$656**	**$798**	**$787**	**$863**	**$1,090**	**$1,192**
Date reviewed		12/02	12/02	12/02	12/02	12/02	12/02

The first three companies were chosen for me by an insurance shopping Web site, quotesmith.com. At the top of its home page, Quotesmith implies that it's going to shop my policy among hundreds of companies in order to find me the best deal. Specifically, the heading says: "300 Companies. Buy from the company of your choice." This, sadly, is incorrect, at least in the case of my personal auto coverage, because it actually only shopped my policy with five companies: Allamerica, Kemper, Liberty Mutual, Hartford, and Esurance. (I found this out by calling Quotesmith. I also found out that there are several other Web sites that may appear to be different, but actually are additional Quotesmith labels. Among others, they include insure.com, insurance.com, and comparisonmarket.com.) After shopping my policy with these five companies, it then presented what were presumably the three lowest-priced policies, which are the first three listed on my spreadsheet: Esurance, Hartford, and Liberty Mutual.

In order to shop my policy online, I had to input a lot of information, but pretty much everything I needed I had either in my head or on my spreadsheet. Inputting the required information took exactly ten minutes and forty-two seconds—coincidentally, the approximate amount of time spent in commercial breaks during your typical half-hour sitcom.

About thirty seconds after submitting my info, I got back the results you see on my spreadsheet. Hartford was cheapest of the three at $787 per year, and Liberty Mutual was most at $863. Which means none was as low as what I'm already paying. The prices weren't broken down for me by category; I got only the total. But that's fine, because that's all I'm really interested in anyway. Had prices been low enough to entice me to switch companies, I'd have called the companies and had them reveal details.

I could have stopped here, because all I was really trying to determine was that my current insurer is not ripping me off, and these results would indicate that it's not. But I went on to get quotes from Geico and Progressive just to make sure. I chose Geico because it has historically been a low-cost insurer. Plus, its commercials feature a reptile and I like the idea of supporting companies that don't discriminate against the cold-blooded. I chose Progressive because it insures my Harley, and does it at a much lower price than my current insurer would. Plus, its TV ads claim that it has the best online service, and that if it can't provide me with the best quote, it'll cheerfully furnish the names of companies that will.

It took seven minutes and thirty-one seconds to input the information necessary to get an online quote from Geico. Apparently lizards aren't the only thing cold-blooded at Geico, however, because its quote was a chilling $1,100 a year. And look how much it's charging for that $8,000 worth of personal injury protection . . . $263 a year! And I thought my current company's $92 was a rip.

Progressive's Web site got me a quote in seven minutes and fifteen seconds. Alas, this company, too, was comically out of the ballpark:

nearly $1,200 a year. In addition, despite what it promises in its commercials, it also didn't furnish me with quotes from other competing companies. Its explanation for this was that my car is too old. What that has to do with anything will have to remain a mystery, however, because I wasn't interested enough to call and challenge the company on it.

Okay, now that we've shopped my car policy together, what have we learned? We've learned how to organize insurance so that we can quickly understand what we have, what we need, and how to find competing prices. We've learned that we can visit with seven insurance companies (five through Quotesmith, plus Geico and Progressive) online in about twenty-five minutes total. And most pertinent, at least to me, we've learned that while it may appear I'm paying too much to insure my 1982 Mercedes, I'm actually getting a relatively good deal. This makes me feel like I have both hands on the wheel.

Just for the record, you may think based on my high rates that I have a horrible driving history. Not so. My driving record is spotless. But as anyone who lives in South Florida can attest, this is one of the most expensive spots on the planet to insure a car. Probably because actively participating in accidents is a curiously popular pastime here.

I'm not going to define every imaginable term that you might encounter when it comes to car insurance. As I've said before, the only terms that matter are those pertinent to *your* policy. And the only time you need to know these terms is when you're first discovering what you're personally paying for and making your own notes to translate these terms into a language you understand. Writing down every possible variation that occurs in every state in every situation is a job for authors who have a compelling need to write either long books or multiple books. If you want to understand everything that can possibly happen with car insurance, take a couple of courses on the subject. But if all you want is to understand *your* insurance, someone at the other end of an 800 number somewhere is waiting for your call. Create a spreadsheet, make some notes, shop some prices, and you're done for a year or two. If you want to read more and/or understand various types of insurance, you don't need to go to a bookstore. Just go to the Insurance Information Institute's Web site at www.iii.org. This organization is supported by the insurance industry, so it is perhaps not entirely objective. It does, however, provide decent information when it comes to the basics.

Homeowner's or Renter's Insurance

Let's look at my personal spreadsheet for my homeowner's insurance and talk about a few salient points:

Homeowner's Insurance

Company	Homework Inc.
Phone	800-XXX-XXXX
Policy Number	XXX XX XX
Total Amount	$792.93

	Amount	Notes
Deductible	$1,000	
Dwelling	$199,000	This will gradually increase every year, along with premiums. You can alter it.
Personal property	$149,250	This is set by the insurance company, based on dwelling. You can't alter it.
Loss of use	$39,800	Hotels, food, etc., while home is repaired.
Liability	$1,000,000	If someone is injured, you have to be liable for this to pay.
Medical payments	$1,000	This pays if someone is injured, no matter who's liable.
Extra cost coverages	*Cost*	
Home protector	$33.72	Additional coverage: 25% more than the coverage amount. So on top of $199,000 you have an additional $49,750 of coverage. Total coverage: $248,750. Page 10.

	Amount	Notes
Business occupancy	$58.10	Normally you have only $2,500 of coverage for business property. This eliminates the business exclusion and increases the amount to whatever the personal property limit is on the policy. It also raises the liability limit to that on the policy. (Otherwise you wouldn't have any for business.) Plus, you have $10,000 coverage on property away from home. Otherwise you'd have $250. Page 12.
Building ordinance	$67.43	Required coverage in Florida, unless you decline in writing. If you have to build to new codes, this covers the additional cost.
Jewelry	$16.00	Covered by regular homeowner's policy, except for theft or loss. You're paying $16/year, but that will only give coverage of $3,000 total and only $1,000 per item. Regular deductible applies. If you want to insure something for more than $1,000, you need a personal property rider. For a $4,000 ring, you'd pay $84/year.
Personal computers	$8.00	This lowers the deductible on computers to $100 from $1,000, and adds additional perils coverage. (Like you spill coffee on it.)
Replacement cost	$60.69	This gives replacement value on personal property.
Personal injury liability	$22.00	Coverage for slander, libel. Page 21.
Total extra coverages	**$265.94**	

When you make a spreadsheet for your home insurance, one of the first things you'll note is how much your home is insured for. (This won't apply to renter's insurance, since it provides only liability and contents coverage. If your apartment goes up in smoke, the building is the landlord's problem.) When I made this spreadsheet, mine was insured for $199,000. Why the odd amount? It wasn't this amount when the policy started, but it adjusts automatically every year to theoretically account for inflation. This also automatically increases my premium, and if I don't want it to occur, I have to call the company to prevent it. (You can see that I've made a note indicating I can alter it.) When it comes to your insurance, you obviously want to make sure you've got enough coverage to rebuild your home, but you don't need to insure for the total purchase price of your home. Why? Because it's unlikely your yard will burn down. Home lots in South Florida are very expensive, especially those bordering water. So although I paid more than two hundred grand for my house and the lot it sits on, I'm only concerned with insuring my house. Let's face it: No matter how intense the hurricane, my yard is unlikely to blow away.

The key words when you're talking home insurance are "replacement cost." The key words to avoid are "cash value." In the event of a total loss, replacement coverage replaces your home and stuff with a new home and new stuff. Cash value only provides you with a check for the depreciated value of your home and stuff. And if you've been to a yard sale recently, you know that replacing your stuff would cost a lot more than its current market value. So if you'd rather replace your stuff at a mall instead of at a yard sale, you need to have a guaranteed replacement policy. Furthermore, you need to understand exactly what your company means when it uses the word "replacement." For example, when it comes to rebuilding your home, will your insurer really replace your home exactly as it is right now with a new one? Maybe not, even if you have replacement coverage. Say you have your home insured for $150,000 with guaranteed replacement, but rebuilding it exactly like it is would cost $250,000. It burns down. In the old days, many insurance companies would have written a check for $250,000. More likely today, however, your insurer will limit its replacement to 125 percent of your insurance amount, and it may only do this at extra cost. As you see in my notes under "extra cost coverages," I have what's called "home protector." For an extra $33.72 a year, I'm getting this extra 25 percent replacement coverage, which means that my house is effectively insured for $248,750. If it costs more than $248,750 to replace my house, too bad; I won't get more.

This 125-percent-of-value limit keeps the insurance company from getting nailed if you deliberately underinsure your home. Keep this in mind not only when you buy or shop your home insurance, but also when you make additions or improvements to your home.

What about the stuff in your house? Look at the "personal property" section of my spreadsheet. I've got $149,250 worth of contents coverage, which is about $100,000 more than I need. Too bad . . . my company requires contents to be insured for 75 percent of the home's value, so I can't try to save money by lowering this amount. Ditto with "loss of use." It's set at 20 percent of my home's value. So if I have to stay in a hotel while my home is repaired, take me to the Hyatt.

I have a million dollars' worth of liability, which is a lot more than I have on my car. So if I cause a car wreck, I hope it happens in my driveway.

My last standard coverage is "medical payments." As you see from my notes, this provides a grand to anyone injured in my house without having to first establish liability. This is kind of like the personal injury protection I have in my car policy.

There you have my standard coverages, for which I would pay about $500 a year. But as you can plainly see at the top of my spreadsheet, I'm actually paying close to $800. That's because I'm paying for $265 of extra coverage. Where's this money going?

The first thing we've already discussed: $34 for 25 percent more-than-stated-value replacement cost. The next extra I have because I work from home. If you do likewise, carefully read my notes. Without this coverage, I'd only have $2,500 worth of coverage for business-related stuff ($250 of coverage for business-related stuff away from home) and no business-related liability. So if you work from your house, beware. If the UPS guy trips on your front steps delivering a business package, you could be in trouble. Likewise if you leave your laptop in an airport restroom.

Next we have "building ordinance," which means that if my house has to be rebuilt, any increased costs due to building code changes are covered over and above the insurance amount. If $67 seems like a rip-off for this tiny bit of extra coverage, that's because it probably is. Building code changes are common here in Florida, however.

Now let's move on to "jewelry." A few years ago, I did a news story about how the government forced airlines to double the amount they'd pay on lost luggage from $1,250 to $2,500 per person. Victory for the consumer? More like the airline industry teaming up with Uncle Sam to take you for a ride. That's because exclusions make it virtually impossible to collect anywhere near $2,500. For example, most airlines refuse to compensate you for lost jewelry, cameras, books, photos, business documents, money, and electronic equipment. In addition, most will pay only the depreciated value of what's left, not its replacement cost. Bottom line? About the only thing that's covered in your luggage is clothes, and suitcases big enough to hold $2,500 worth of used clothing won't fit on the plane.

This story came to mind as I reviewed my jewelry coverage. I'm paying an extra $16 every year to insure my wife's jewelry. Even if I didn't pay the extra money, Gina's jewelry would be covered if it melted in a fire, but not if it were stolen or lost. So that's what I'm paying extra for: stolen or lost jewelry. But the amount is no big deal: a maximum of $3,000 of extra coverage, with a limit of $1,000 per item. When I pointed out the limits of this policy to my friendly customer service representative, he responded by attempting to upsell me to a personal property rider, which is precisely what I thought I was already paying for. You can see I made a note indicating how much such a rider would cost for a $4,000 ring.

The next item is "personal computers." For an extra $8 a year, my deductible for personal computers is lowered from $1,000 to $100, and I add perils coverage. What is "perils coverage"? This covers me if I destroy my computer myself by doing something stupid like spilling coffee on it.

Next we have "replacement cost." This does the same thing for my stuff as "home protector" does for my house. It gives me replacement coverage.

The final item is "personal injury liability," which adds slander and libel to my list of things covered by my standard liability. This allows me to confidently say nasty things about people, either verbally or in writing. Of all the insurance I buy, this is probably the greatest bargain.

There you have it . . . my homeowner's insurance. As with my car insurance, I'm now able to make accurate assessments of what I have and whether it's worth paying for or not. Again, keep in mind that I don't have insurance to prevent inconvenience; I have it to protect against catastrophe. Am I paying for anything that doesn't fall into that category? Yes, but not much. If Gina lost her jewelry, that wouldn't put us in the poorhouse, so I can do without this coverage, especially since it sucks anyway. And I can invest in a nonspill coffee cup rather than personal computer coverage.

What about my deductible? As you can see, it's already high by most yardsticks: $1,000. The highest deductible offered by my company is $2,000. Going this route would save me about $100 a year. I could also lower my liability to $500,000 and save $20 a year.

Shopping your homeowner's insurance isn't much different from shopping car insurance. Grab your spreadsheet, wait for a commercial during whatever show you're watching, and go for it. You can use the same Web sites I gave you for shopping your car coverage. Here are some additional ones: allquotesinsurance.com, netquote.com, and insweb.com. Want more? Do a search for "homeowner's insurance." You'll get about half a million additional possibilities.

One last thing: As you may recall from chapter 14, "Getting Organized," don't forget to make it as easy as possible to collect on your insurance policies. Take a videotape of your possessions, dictate what you're recording and the prices you paid, and store it away from your house. Having adequate insurance won't do you any good if you either can't remember what you had or can't prove it.

Now that we've talked about replacing what you have, let's get a little more personal. Let's talk about replacing you.

Life Insurance

If nobody is going to suffer financially by your death, you can skip this section because you don't need life insurance. If you have it, you're wasting money unless you expect your situation to imminently change, or simply want to impress someone by leaving a sack of money at your death. If someone could possibly suffer catastrophically by your untimely demise, however, keep reading.

Life insurance is least expensive when you're young and therefore less likely to die. It's most expensive when you're old and therefore getting closer to your final reward. And this is the way it should be, because most people only need insurance when they're young. Why? Because that's when they're raising a family and incurring debts, which is when the untimely death of a breadwinner could result in financial catastrophe. When you're older, it's likely that either your kids are self-sufficient or you've moved away so they can't find you. Your home is paid for and you have money in the bank. Your death has been reduced from a financial catastrophe to an excuse for your remaining friends to get together and have a drink.

While the above should be obvious, most people don't buy insurance this way. They don't have enough when they're young and most vulnerable, and they have too much when they're old and don't need it anymore.

There are two basic kinds of life insurance: permanent and term. As the names imply, permanent lasts until you die, and term covers you only for a specified term. While permanent may sound better because it's ultimately bound to pay, it's also tons more expensive. And since you shouldn't need insurance when you're older, term is the best bet for most people. For example, you use a term policy to insure yourself from the age of thirty to age fifty while you raise the kids, pay off the mortgage, and build your savings. At age fifty, your premiums would start getting out of sight, but that's cool because your need for insurance is practically gone. You've reached the point of being self-insured. And your life is also easier, because you've one less bill to pay, one less file folder filling up, and one less thing between you and the couch.

The type of term insurance you'll want to get for this scenario is either twenty-year annual renewable or twenty-year guaranteed premium. Annual renewable guarantees that you'll be able to maintain your coverage every year for twenty years without taking any more physical exams, although the premiums may go up as you age. Guaranteed premium not only guarantees that you'll be able to maintain your coverage without new physicals, but also promises that your rates won't rise over that time period. Of course, these bells and whistles come at a price. Twenty-year annual renewable is more expensive than ten-year annual renewable, which in turn has higher monthly premiums than five-year annual renewable, and so forth. And if you want to lock in the rate you're paying, you'll find that guaranteed premium costs more than annual renewable. So you'll have to compare prices, balance risk and reward, and decide what's best for you. For example, you may decide that while twenty-year annual renewable would cover you for the time required, it's so much more expensive than ten-year annual renewable that you're going to take a chance with the ten-year and hope you're still in good shape when you have to take your next physical ten years from now.

No matter what kind of term insurance you end up with, don't neglect to read the fine print. Because while guaranteed premium promises a guaranteed premium, sometimes these policies allow premiums to rise anyway. In short, sometimes guaranteed premium doesn't guarantee premium. Welcome to the wonderful, wacky world of insurance.

There is, of course, a risk to the strategy of insuring your life for a ten-, twenty-, or thirty-year period: the risk that the term ends and you haven't met your financial goals. You hit fifty only to find that those kids who aren't in jail are living at home, you've still got two mortgages, and you have no money in the bank. You're graying at the temples, yet your untimely death would still have a negative financial impact on your family. You still want life insurance, and now it's getting expensive or, worse yet, you've developed health problems that have rendered you uninsurable. You're between the dog and the fire hydrant.

If you're young and believe the risk of this scenario to be high, my first advice is not to have a family. But if you're genetically predisposed to procreate and insist on having insurance till death releases you from this mortal coil, you might be tempted to look into permanent insurance. If so, please read the following paragraphs so this train of thought won't leave the station.

Permanent insurance (also known by names like cash value, whole life, universal life, and variable life) is basically a savings account combined with a life insurance policy. Insurance agents love to sell permanent insurance because the commissions can be huge: as high as the entire first year's premium. And since permanent insurance premiums can easily be many times higher than comparable term insurance premiums, agents are powerfully motivated to stuff this type of insurance down your throat. They'll point out that permanent insurance offers you a forced savings plan, a guaranteed payoff, a tax-deferred savings account, and the ability to access your savings tax-free later in life via policy loans. Then to seal the deal, they'll display written projections that "prove" you'll end up with more money than Michael Jordan.

Rather than refuting each of these arguments individually, I'll just say three sentences that will deal with all of them. Sentence 1: The benefits you'll get from permanent life insurance are not justified by the additional cost. Sentence 2: The commissions and expenses in these policies make them a horrible choice compared to buying term insurance and investing the difference. Sentence 3: The only possible exception to Sentence 1 and Sentence 2 is rich people.

Bottom line? Unless you're rich, buy term. Period.

Now let's make quick work of the one exception . . . rich people. The current (as of 2004) laws governing estate taxes say that when you die, your estate will owe taxes if you're worth more than a million and a half bucks. Your whole estate isn't taxed . . . just the amount that exceeds the $1.5 million threshold. And this exclusion increases to $2 million in 2006, $3.5 million in 2009—and in 2010, estate taxes are history. (If, that is, legislation now on the books remains intact. If Congress doesn't do anything to extend or make permanent the elimination of estate taxes, the exclusion amount will automatically revert to $1 million.) So if you're rich, you might consider a permanent life insurance policy as part of an overall estate plan, especially if your estate would include things you wouldn't want sold to pay estate taxes. We'll touch briefly on this subject again in chapter 18, "Estate Planning."

So this vastly overrated, oversold, and ridiculously expensive form of insurance, found almost everywhere, really belongs almost nowhere.

When life insurance shopping time rolls around, you can get quick quotes from insurance Web sites. As with car coverage, you can go to sites that offer consolidated quotes (in other words, sites that represent more than one insurance company) or you can go to individual company Web sites. A few ideas for insurance shopping sites include selectquote.com, quotesmith.com, einsurance.com, insweb.com, and term4sale.com. Individual companies you might check out could be USAA (usaa.com), Ameritas (ameritas.com), and General Electric (gefn.com/insurance). If you're really bored, you can find plenty of other places to look by using a search engine and looking up "life insurance." When I put that term into Google (my preferred search engine), it returned nearly four million hits, so there's no shortage of places to shop online. But my goal when I'm shopping is primarily just to make sure that what I'm buying now is a decent deal, and the sites mentioned above are fine for that. If I'm actually going to start writing checks to replace or add coverages, then I might do a more thorough search.

Checking out life insurance prices online won't take as long as shopping for other types of insurance, because you don't have to put in nearly as much information to get a quote. You can easily shop twenty companies in five minutes. But if you're actually going to act based on what you find online, don't stop there. Before you buy any life insurance, check with your employer to see what it has to offer, as well as any professional associations you may belong to or be eligible for. Your home insurer may warrant a call, and your credit union could be another cheap source. And don't buy more than you need. Remember the mantra: Protect against catastrophe, not inconvenience. As with asset allocation models, there are tons of Web sites, magazines, and salespeople that will provide advice and mysterious calculators to "help" you determine how much life insurance you need, but most of these sources make more money when you buy more insurance. Result? They can't be trusted. You decide what you need . . . and it's not that hard to do. Simply figure out what bills you'd want paid off and/or how much income you'd want replaced in the event of your death, and buy that much insurance.

I did a news story a couple of years ago featuring a life insurance calculator from insweb.com. I input fictional information, like how much I had in savings ($25,000), how much I owed on credit cards ($10,000), my mortgage balance ($150,000), how much I'd need for burial ($10,000), how much income I wanted replaced and for how long ($36,000 per year for five years), how many kids I had heading to college (one), when she'd start (eight years in the future), and how much college costs now ($10,000 per year) . . . that sort of thing. When I plugged in these hypotheticals, the bottom line was a recommendation of $453,000 worth of life insurance. Then I went back and filled in the blanks again from a "catastrophe" prospective rather than an "inconvenience" one. I still paid off all the debts, including the mortgage, but I replaced my income for only one year instead of five . . . if my widow can't find another provider by then, she can go back to work. And I nixed the money for the kid's college . . . hey, she can go to a cheaper school, get financial aid, or study for a change and earn a scholarship. Result this time? I needed only $162,000 in life insurance: about a third of my first result. And if this was all I bought, my family members wouldn't be devastated. They'd have no bills, they'd own the house free and clear, I'd be buried (in grand style, I might add), and my wife would continue to receive my former income for an entire year. Worse things could happen.

You should have seen the hate mail I got from insurance agents after that story aired!

Another thing that the insurance calculator I used in this story conveniently forgot to take into account was benefits my wife and kid could receive under Social Security. While we think of Social Security as a forced retirement plan, in some cases it also acts as a forced life insurance plan as well, because sometimes it pays survivor benefits. They won't make your surviving spouse rich, but they're better than a sharp stick in the eye and should be considered. In general, Social Security will pay benefits to your survivor once retirement age is reached (sixty-five to sixty-seven depending on date of birth), or if you leave your surviving spouse with kids younger than sixteen years old. Kids under eighteen (up to nineteen if they're still in school) can also receive benefits, and even your parents can get benefits as a result of your death if they're dependent on you (in other words, if you provide for more than half of their support) and are at least sixty-two.

Bottom line? If you've got minor children, your death will probably enable your survivors to get some money from Social Security. If you don't have kids, the only checks your spouse will receive won't arrive until retirement. Sound like a rip-off? Well, Uncle Sam obviously feels the same way I do: that the purpose of insurance is to mitigate catastrophe, not inconvenience. In other words, you need life insurance most when there are mouths to feed that can't feed themselves. In this respect, Social Security does come through, at least somewhat.

Here's where you need to go to figure out whether you and yours are eligible to receive Social Security survivor benefits, and how much those benefits might be: www.ssa.gov.planners. As with determining how much you'll receive when you retire, there are calculators there that will tell you how much your survivors will get if you die tomorrow. You can arrive at an instant estimate in a few seconds, or input more detailed information and get a more detailed estimate. I used the quick calculator, input a $50,000 income and an age of forty, and here's what the calculator said: If I die tomorrow, my kid will get about $1,000 a month, and so will my surviving spouse who cares for that kid. When my spouse reaches retirement age, she'll get about $1,400 a month. Like I said, better than a sharp stick in the eye, and certainly something any decent "needs" calculator like the one at insweb.com should have taken into account.

So deciding how much life insurance you need isn't a huge deal. Just think about what would happen in the event of your death. See what you'd get from Social Security. Then buy just enough insurance to stave off catastrophe. As your savings grow and your debt shrinks, reduce your coverage accordingly. And don't take your eye off the goal: to become self-insured. As soon as you get there, you'll save a ton of time by eliminating the need to shop for and keep track of this expensive and annoying reminder of your mortality.

A word of caution: In the days immediately following canceling your life insurance, the odds of dropping dead increase, since Murphy's Law suggests this would be the worst possible time to stop breathing. So be extra careful. On the other hand, dropping your life insurance could also serve to increase your longevity if your spouse wants to get you out of the way. So if you've got a spouse who's lost that loving feeling, don't forget to mention that benefits from your untimely demise are no longer forthcoming.

What if you've already succumbed to sales pressure and have a permanent insurance policy in place? If you're tempted to cash it in and replace it with less expensive term insurance, good. But be careful. First, there are normally huge surrender penalties in the first three to ten years you have these policies. Second, there may be bad news tax-wise as well. As I said, one of the selling points of these policies is that the savings portion of your policy accumulates tax-deferred. In other words, you don't pay taxes on the interest until you take it out. And that's what you're about to do when you surrender a policy. The penalties for doing this before you reach retirement age are identical to cashing in your IRA early: If you're younger than fifty-nine and a half, you'll pay a 10 percent penalty. And no matter what age you are, you'll have to pay taxes on the interest you've earned. The only way around the early-surrender penalties and paying taxes on the accumulated interest is to exchange your existing life insurance policy for another, less expensive insurance product like a no-load annuity. (Remember those? We talked about them in "Stupid Investment Tricks II.") Swapping insurance products is called a 1035 exchange (named for the applicable section of our tax code), and it has to be done with the appropriate dotting of i's and crossing of t's. If you decide to go this route, do it right. The insurance company you're thinking of switching to will be more than happy to tell you what's required and help you through the process.

If you're replacing your life insurance (or any other type of insurance, for that matter) *don't ever drop your existing coverage* until you're absolutely sure that the new coverage you're replacing it with is *in place* and fully operational. This may seem obvious, but believe or not, many people have made this mistake. They get so excited about getting rid of their old life insurance that they drop the existing coverage before their new policy is issued and in force. Then they take a physical exam for their new insurance only to discover that they have a previously unknown health condition that makes them uninsurable. Then they're in trouble. Then they sue me for bad advice. Then I'm in trouble because I don't have insurance for that.

Health Insurance

Health insurance is like the liability insurance you carry on your car, and the property insurance you carry on your house. It's a must-have, no matter what your situation is. That's because if misfortune occurs and you don't have any protection, your immediate family members will be forced to deplete their own resources and your friends will be forced to have bake sales to raise money for you. Or worse, you may find that you don't have any friends and your family never really liked you that much. In other words, health insurance is superimportant. Which is what makes the difficulty of finding and paying for it a national disgrace.

You already have at least one health insurance policy, paid for by your tax dollars. It's called Medicare. Unfortunately, however, it doesn't do you any good until you turn age sixty-five, and in order to get maximum bang for minimum buck, you have to have been paying into the system for ten years prior to that time. If you haven't, you can still participate, but it will cost more. You can learn about Medicare by going to Uncle Sam's Web site on the subject at www.medicare.gov, or calling 800-MEDICARE. But to decrease your time reading and increase your time watching TV, I'll give you the down and dirty right here, right now.

Medicare comes in two parts. Simply put, part A pays hospital bills, part B pays for doctor visits. Part A doesn't cost anything provided you're fully eligible as a result of paying in for ten years. Part B costs a little less than $60 a month. (This, as well as all the numbers you're about to read, is for calendar year 2003. If you're reading this book after 2003, get the new, undoubtedly higher numbers from medicare.gov.)

Medicare is a good place to start when looking at health insurance, not only because it will probably ultimately affect you, but because it will acquaint you with a few important terms while you're waiting. The first term you'll learn when it's time to join the ranks of those covered by Medicare is "coinsurance," which can also be called "copayment." When you see these words, you know you're about to be paying part of your own bill. In the case of Medicare part A (hospitalization), you're fully insured for the first 60 days you're in the hospital, but from Day 61 to Day 90, you'll be responsible for $210 each and every day: That's your coinsurance amount. Can't crawl out the front door by then? From Day 91 to Day 150, you'll be coinsuring to the tune of $420 per day. Can't get anyone to unplug you by Day 150? Then head off to a nursing home. Medicare part A gives you the first 20 days free; then you're coinsuring $105 a day from Day 21 to Day 100.

Medicare part A will also reintroduce you to a term you're familiar with from other types of insurance: "deductible." The deductible for part A is $840 per year, which means that this is what you'll take from your wallet before Uncle Sam opens his.

Medicare part B also has a deductible: $100 per year. Part B doesn't have coinsurance, however, so that's all you'll be out for doctor visits. Except, of course, for things that Medicare doesn't cover at all. Which introduces us to our next fundamental health insurance term: "exclusions."

The hospitalization part of Medicare pays for a semiprivate room, not a private room. It doesn't pay for private-duty nursing, nor does it pay for a telephone or a television in your room, among other things. Medicare part B (the outpatient part) doesn't pay for prescription drugs, routine dental care, or ambulance transportation to a doctor's office, among other things.

So now we've learned a little more about Medicare, but we've also learned some terms to watch out for when we shop for any kind of health insurance. These terms are important because not only will they help us understand what we're buying, but they'll help us keep our costs lower, too. Because the higher the coinsurance or copayment, the lower the cost. The higher the deductible, the lower the cost. The more exclusions we're willing to live with, the lower the cost. And here's one more term to know: "lifetime benefit." As the name implies, this is the maximum your health care plan will pay over your lifetime. The lower this number, the lower the cost. Medicare doesn't have any cap on the amount of lifetime assistance you can receive, but private insurance normally does. When you're trying to lower your costs by shopping lifetime benefits, however, don't get carried away. You need a lot of zeros: A million bucks is the minimum lifetime benefit you should consider.

If your health insurance is covered or partially covered by your employer, congratulations: This is one of the main benefits of working for somebody else. But even if someone else is paying part of the bill, you should still understand your coverages and your options, which means you should still look through your policy for deductibles, exclusions, and lifetime benefits. You should also know how much the policy will cost if you strike out on your own and decide to continue with your current coverage. (Federal law requires that your employer allow you to continue your current health insurance for up to eighteen months after leaving your employer. You have to pay for the policy yourself, but at least you know you'll be covered. This law is known as COBRA. And as the name implies, you'll feel snakebit when you find out how much it costs to continue coverage!)

Whether you're a faithful employee or totally on your own, there are three basic types of health insurance available, categorized by what doctors you get to see. Ranging from highest to lowest cost, you've got traditional insurance, PPOs, and HMOs.

Traditional insurance is probably the kind the Cleavers used in *Leave It to Beaver*. It's also about as common as black-and-white TV. This type of coverage lets you go to any doctor you want; it will pay all or part of the bill. If you get this type of coverage, expect to pay bigger premiums and endure a higher deductible and/or higher copayments. Golly, Wally!

PPOs and HMOs both restrict which doctors you can go to. To make a long story short, HMOs are generally more restrictive and also cost less in terms of premiums, deductibles, and copayments.

Just to stay consistent, I'll now reveal what kind of health insurance I use personally to give you at least one example of balancing risk and reward when it comes to this category of insurance. I'm self-employed, which means nobody helps me defray my cost of coverage. I also live in Florida, which is not only a ridiculously expensive state in which to insure houses and cars, but also a high-cost state for health insurance.

In order to tell you about my health insurance plan, I don't have to open a bunch of folders or dig through my desk. I just open my insurance spreadsheet and the particulars are all laid out for me. I've got the name of the insurance company, a link to an online guide to the doctors in my plan, the phone number and Web address of my insurance company . . . you get the idea.

I have a PPO plan with a $5,000 annual deductible. This is high, but I have a special savings account with $5,000 in it specifically to defray medical expenses and meet this high deductible. This gives me much lower monthly premiums than I would otherwise have; my savings account is earning interest, and if a medical disaster strikes, I'll be taken care of. The cost for this coverage for my wife and me is about $400 a month. (In Ohio, where I used to live, the same coverage was about half that price.) After I meet the deductible, I have no copayment. My maximum lifetime benefit is $3 million. My policy has lots of exclusions, including mental health care (that drives me crazy), dental care (takes the bite out of the premiums), and breast augmentation (bummer, man!).

Why do I have such a high deductible? You already know . . . to keep my costs down. But remember, the reason I have medical insurance is to cover my wife and me in the event of a financially catastrophic illness, not to reimburse me for having my teeth cleaned. Still, what's right for me isn't necessarily what's right for you. I'm a healthy, forty-seven-year-old guy with a healthy, astoundingly flawless wife and no kids. I rarely go to the doctor. And as I said, I'm comfortable insuring myself for the small stuff. If the person I just described isn't you, then the coverage I just described might not be right for you, either. That's your decision. Just make it an informed one.

(Note: If you like the sound of the coverage I have, and you're self-employed, check out MSAs. "MSA" stands for "medical savings account," a special plan that gives you deductions for your insurance premiums, tax deferral for the interest on your savings account, and tax-free withdrawals from the account to pay medical expenses. The only drawback to MSA plans is that not many insurance companies are set up to deal with them, which limits your ability to shop. To learn more about MSAs, you can do a Web search for "medical savings accounts." I also found a decent article at insure.com.)

If you're an employee, you don't have to worry about shopping your health insurance because you probably don't get a whole bunch of choices. Your employer has done the shopping for you. If you're self-employed and do have to shop coverage, you can go to some of the same sites I mentioned for life insurances, like quotesmith.com, einsurance.com, and insweb.com. This only takes a few minutes. You should also check with any professional associations to which you belong (or could belong) as well as giant carriers like Blue Cross, Blue Shield (bcbs.com). And by the way, if you're between jobs or just recently graduated from college, these sites can also hook you up with temporary health insurance. Don't forget Murphy's Law!

Disability Insurance

Need your income to stay afloat? Then you may need disability insurance. As with all insurance, this is again all about balancing costs and benefits. The odds of your becoming disabled are remote, but maybe not as remote as you think. According the Social Security Web site, a twenty-year-old worker has a 30 percent chance of becoming disabled before he reaches retirement age. Of course, the odds of a coal miner or professional wrestler becoming disabled are certainly higher than a desk worker's. In any case, how devastating disability would be to your life depends on what would happen if you no longer had a paycheck. For most of us, no picnic.

The first step in disability is to find out if your employer is already furnishing you with it. If the answer is yes, however, you don't get to skip this section because you still need to understand your coverage.

The next step in determining what would happen if you were unable to work is to check on the insurance you're already paying for: Social Security disability. Basically, you'll qualify if you've been paying into Social Security for the last ten years, but you can see the exact requirements by going to ssa.gov. To see how much you'd get, stay on the site and use one of its handy calculators. I plugged in a forty-year-old with $50,000 of income and came up with $1,400 a month. Your spouse and/or kids could also be eligible to get a check based on your disability, but no matter what your situation is, your whole family combined can't get more than 180 percent of what you're personally eligible for.

Uncle Sam is pretty strict when it comes to determining what "disability" means. For Social Security purposes, it generally means you're unable to work at all for at least a year. So if whatever's keeping you from working is expected to go away within a year, you're not going to get a dime. Ditto if you're capable of working in any capacity . . . not just at your current job.

Workers' compensation is another potential source of income in the event of your disability, but it applies only if you're injured or otherwise become disabled while at work. Otherwise, no help.

Okay, now you've scoped out the benefits you're already paying for, and you don't have what you need in the event you become disabled. What now? You either assume the risk, or you buy disability coverage. Here's what to look for.

Obviously, the first thing you need to find is a big enough check to keep on keeping on if you become disabled. Keep in mind that if you're paying your own disability insurance premiums, your benefits will be tax-free. (If your employer is paying for your policy, the benefits will be taxable.) So even if you need every penny of take-home pay you're currently earning, you still only need to replace the take-home pay, not your pretax income.

The next thing you'll need to think about is duration, or how long the policy will pay. Think you'll have enough money to take care of yourself by the time you're fifty? Then buy a policy that coincides with this birthday. If the only day you plan on missing work is the day you die of old age, you'll need a longer policy. And you'll pay more for having it.

How a policy defines "disability" is another factor that will radically affect the price. For example, if I suddenly became unable to speak, I couldn't make a living in TV news. I'd be disabled by my definition, but not by Social Security's, because as far as it's concerned I could still work in some capacity. A policy that pays off if you can't do your current job is called an own-occupation policy, and these are a lot more expensive than those that mean completely-unable-to-work-in-any-capacity when they use the term "disabled."

When we were talking about term life insurance, we discussed guaranteed renewable policies, and this also applies to disability. To refresh your memory, guaranteed renewable means that the insurance company can't force you to take periodic physicals, then drop you if your health is deteriorating. Are noncancelable policies more expensive? Take a wild guess.

You can make your car and home insurance cheaper by raising your deductible. You can make your disability insurance cheaper by raising your waiting period. The waiting period is the time between when you become disabled and when you get your first check. (With Social Security, this period is one year.) If you've got a healthy savings account, you can afford a longer waiting period, which will substantially lower your premiums.

These are the biggies, but there are a few other things to know about disability policies, like future insurability (lets you increase coverage without starting over with a new policy . . . handy if you think your pay and/or financial obligations will increase), and whether your benefits will include adjustments for inflation. But the key to disability is the same as for any kind of insurance. Don't buy more than you need, reduce it as your ability to self-insure increases, and shop it like mad. Get it through your employer, a professional association, or one of the online shopping sites we've already covered.

Conclusion

Well, we've finally reached the end of the line on the topic of insurance. Aren't you glad? I am. But before we move on, a couple of last thoughts.

First, what you've read in this chapter is largely a reflection of my personal tastes—and these tastes may not match yours. That's perfectly okay. If you feel the need to have insurance that guarantees you'll never lose a dime, fine. Just recognize that there's a cost for this peace of mind, and it's likely to be a high one. This doesn't make it wrong. But at least now you have the tools to decide on the right mix of risk and potential reward for you.

Second, my job as a consumer reporter has taught me that despite reassuring advertising phrases that I'm "in good hands," or that my company is "like a good neighbor," the truth is often different. The insurance industry has thrived for hundreds of years on the belief that insurance is necessary for financial survival. We're raised to think that only a crazy person would do without as much insurance as he can afford in every category in which it's offered. It's true that we do need insurance for things we can't afford to replace, like other people's stuff, our health, and our future earnings. But just because something is necessary doesn't mean that more is by definition better.

Most insurance is overbought for one simple reason: It's oversold. What insurance should be is simply an efficient method of spreading the risk in the event of disaster: a way to pool our collective resources so you can help me recover from a hurricane in Fort Lauderdale and I can help you if a tornado touches down in your neighborhood. And the middleman who holds our money for us, the insurance company, deserves to be paid for this service. But in my opinion insurance has evolved, in some cases at least, into something less altruistic and more sinister. People are routinely sold more than they need because the people providing the advice are commissioned. Companies increase their bottom lines by seeking to exclude less profitable policyholders (in other words, those likely to file claims) and dragging their feet when it's time to write a check to those that remain. We're made to feel fortunate to even have the ability to buy some types of coverages, which makes us less likely to question the cost. The terms and conditions are so complex we throw up our hands and hope for the best.

Since we're probably not going to change the existing system, let's do what we can to make sure we're not victims of it. In days gone by, this would have entailed a ton of time, since learning about insurance required books, and shopping it required extensive legwork. But that was then. The Internet-enabled money manager knows how to find fast facts and how to shop policies in no more time than it takes for a commercial break.

17

Real Estate

When a fellow says, "It ain't the money but the principle of the thing," it's the money.

—Kim Hubbard

There are only a handful of ways that most people achieve financial freedom. Either they inherit (my personal favorite), they marry someone wealthy (fine method, providing you either genuinely like your spouse or have a knack for long-term role playing), they own a business, they invest in stocks over long periods of time, or they own real estate over long periods of time.

There's nothing much you can do to control when or if you inherit. Not many of us will be lucky enough to find money and love in the same place. While the odds of achieving financial freedom through self-employment aren't nil, it's hardly a certainty, either. So that leaves us with stocks and real estate held over long periods of time. In fact, even if you fall into one of the first three categories, you might as well toss a few stocks and real estate investments into the mix while you're at it. Gotta do something during commercial breaks, right?

We've already covered investing in stocks over long periods of time. Nothing to it . . . subtract your age from 100 and throw that percentage of your available investment dollars at an S&P 500 index fund. Investing in real estate is a bit more complicated—which, as I'll explain, is both a good thing and a bad thing.

Remember when we talked about owner and loaner investments? Real estate, like stocks, is obviously an owner investment. But real estate has one huge advantage over stocks. It's called leverage.

"Leverage" is a fancy term to describe what amounts to buying something with someone else's money. If you buy a $100,000 house by putting down $5,000 and borrowing $95,000, you're 95 percent leveraged. If the house goes up by five percent the first year, it's worth $5,000 more, and you've achieved a 100 percent return on your $5,000 investment. Very cool. Of course, if the house goes down by $5,000, you've suffered a 100 percent loss. Very uncool. But that's the way it is in the land of leverage.

Theoretically, stocks also offer leverage. That's because you can borrow up to 50 percent of the value of the stocks or mutual funds you buy. (Leverage in real estate is achieved with a mortgage loan. Leverage in the stock market is done with a margin loan.) But the leverage available in the stock market isn't nearly as attractive as real estate leverage. First, you can't borrow as much: 50 percent is max. More important, if the stock or fund you're leveraging happens to temporarily fall by a significant amount, you'll be asked to pony up more money. If you can't come up with the money, your stock will be sold and your paper loss will then become quite real. Not a pretty picture.

Interesting historical note: When a brokerage firm puts the bite on you for additional money, this is what's known as a margin call. In 1929, rules then in effect allowed investors to borrow up to 90 percent of the price of the stock instead of today's 50 percent, meaning people were a lot more highly leveraged. When the stock market began to fall, brokerage firms began to issue margin calls. Investors who couldn't meet these calls had their stocks sold, which caused the market to fall further, which in turn caused more margin calls, which sparked more selling, and so on. This vicious circle culminated in the crash of 1929, followed shortly thereafter by the Great Depression. It was the inability to meet margin calls—

the process of converting paper losses into real losses—that helped so many hapless investors take a flying leap in that infamous stock market crash.

There . . . now you have something to bore your friends with at your next gathering!

Back to the subject at hand. Over time, real estate and stocks have achieved about the same return: Both have rewarded their investors with a few percentage points more than the inflation rate. But partly because of leverage and partly because of inefficiencies in markets, real estate can sometimes do even better than stocks.

What do I mean by "inefficiencies in markets"? Well, think about the stock market. One of the reasons that an unmanaged stock index fund will often outperform a managed stock mutual fund is that the stock market is highly efficient. The term "highly efficient" means that stock prices react virtually instantly to whatever news affects them, because there are so many informed investors paying attention. In other words, there are thousands of Ivy League MBAs buying and selling at the same time based on the same information. Unless they're willing to break the law by accessing inside information, nobody's going to know more than anybody else and everybody's going to have the ability to react instantly to whatever information there is. Therefore, unless you can see something that nobody else sees, which you probably can't, or have information that nobody else has, which you probably don't, over time you can't expect to do better than anybody else, which you probably won't. This is why there's no point in becoming an expert or paying for one. The stock market is so efficient (and because of technology becoming more so all the time) that the price of stocks accurately reflects their true value at any given moment. And if everything's priced at its true value, it's impossible to find bargains. In short, professional investors can't beat the market because professional investors *are* the market.

Now consider real estate. About eight years ago, my friend Fred called me from Tucson to tell me that he was on his way to a land auction being held by the University of Arizona. The property being sold was two acres of commercially zoned land located in a rapidly growing area of the city. The minimum bid was $300,000. When Fred arrived, despite the fact that the auction had been publicized in the newspaper, with the exception of the auctioneer he was all alone. The auction started, he bid the minimum and left a few minutes later with the land. Within a week, he was contacted by a real estate broker who said he had a buyer for a part of the parcel who was willing to pay $500,000. Other calls from additional interested parties followed shortly thereafter.

To make a short story shorter, Fred had to pay for some engineering and other stuff for the land, but he ended up selling it about eighteen months later for a little more than a million dollars.

This true story could never have occurred in the stock market, simply because of the vast number of people paying attention. There's nothing affecting stocks that will ever go unnoticed the way that this Tucson land bargain went unnoticed. Why didn't the people who apparently wanted the land show up to bid against Fred that day? Maybe they missed the article in the paper announcing the sale. Maybe they had a conflicting appointment. Who knows? The only certainty is that the lack of informed investors that day was an information inefficiency that Fred ultimately exploited to the tune of about $700,000. I say "information inefficiency" because while it may appear that it was a lack of buyers that allowed him to steal that land, it really wasn't. It was the fact that the information about the potential bargain wasn't efficiently distributed. In other words, if everyone in town knew that a million-dollar chunk of land could be had for $300,000, it would have been standing room only at that auction.

The efficient and instantaneous distribution of information affecting stock prices is what makes it standing room only at pretty much all of the thousands of stock auctions taking place on Wall Street every trading day.

Price is another potential market inefficiency when it comes to real estate. Again, consider stocks. Stocks are repriced every second of every trading session. There's never a scintilla of doubt as to what a share of stock is worth at any given time. Why? Because the price you're seeing represents what a real, live buyer is willing to pay for your shares at that very moment. That's efficient. But real estate? The only way to find out what real estate is worth is to hire an appraiser, wait a week, and get a price. But this price is still just theoretical, because there's no buyer standing there willing to pay it. That's inefficient.

Price inefficiency could potentially benefit real estate investors in a couple of important ways. First, with the exception of the day it's originally appraised and the day it's sold, your lender will never really know the value of the real estate covering its loan. This is what prevents margin calls from happening in real estate. In other words, imagine borrowing $95,000 to buy a $100,000 house. Now imagine that the value of this house is printed in the paper every day. One day, the value falls to $80,000. Think the lender wouldn't be nudging you for more money? Think it wouldn't be threatening to foreclose and sell the property if you couldn't come up with it? If the law allowed it to, bet your life on it. So the lack of price efficiency inherent in real estate keeps leverage providers in the dark, which in turn prevents them from demanding more collateral from you, which in turn prevents your paper losses from becoming real ones, which in turn keeps you from jumping out of a window.

An even greater benefit to price inefficiency is that sometimes the owner of the property is just as much in the dark as to value as the lender is. If the true value of a piece of land or a building was displayed in the paper every day, it would be kind of hard to approach the owner with a lower offer, wouldn't it? Happily, however, real estate prices aren't posted. So if you're willing to do enough homework (pun intended) to know what homes are worth in your neighborhood, it's quite possible that you can approach an owner with an offer that he considers fair but that you know to be a bargain. Hats off to inefficiency!

Okay . . . so let's stop here and digest something interesting when comparing stocks and real estate as potential investments. When it comes to investing money, both are good ownership investments. Over long periods of time, both have returned about the same, beating long-term inflation rates by a few percentage points. But when you're about to invest your time and energy, you're much better off with an investment that allows you to exploit inefficiencies to your advantage. As I've just explained, you can invest all the time in the world and still find no inefficiencies to exploit in the stock market. So don't use your valuable time trying: Buy an unmanaged stock index fund instead. Then invest the time you're saving there into real estate, a field where your time could result in finding inefficiencies, exploiting them, and outperforming the average return. Doesn't that make sense?

The first real estate investment you want to make is, of course, your home. You probably know people who have become wealthy simply by trading up from house to house over the years and thereby developing enough equity (the difference between the value of the house and the amount owed on it) to be considered rich. Nothing wrong with that, except perhaps the fact that you ultimately have to move out of your home in order to live off your profits. Another good thing about investing in a personal residence is that a large part of the money you're investing is what's called in Accounting Land a "sunk cost." In other words, it's money you'd have to spend no matter what you do. You've got to put a roof over your head anyway . . . might as well pay off a building at the same time, especially if you're planning on staying put, and the city where you're planting your roots is growing, a condition normally resulting in rising home values.

Whether you're investing in shelter for yourself or in rental property, real estate offers unique income tax advantages that can potentially turn a decent investment into a huge winner. For example, when it comes to your primary residence, you don't have to pay income taxes on your profits. The only conditions are that the home was your primary residence for at least two of the last five years, and that you don't profit by too much: $500,000 is the maximum profit that goes untaxed on each transaction. (That's for joint returns. If you're single, try not to make more than $250,000 at a whack.) This is a double-edged sword, however; you also don't get to deduct losses on the sale of your home. And this only applies to your personal residence, not rental real estate, unless you kick the renters out and live there for two years before you sell it.

Tax advantage number two: You get to deduct the interest on the loans you use to leverage your real estate. We've already discussed this in other sections, but as a reminder, if you're paying 6 percent interest on a mortgage loan and are in a 30 percent combined state and federal income tax bracket, the 6 percent you're paying is essentially reduced by the 30 percent you're saving on taxes, making your effective rate not 6 percent, but 4.2 percent (100 – 30% = 70%; 70% of 6% = 4.2%). So if your home is increasing by more than 4.2 percent per year, your leveraged bet is paying off.

Rental property offers yet another tax advantage that really rocks. To understand it, you'll have to come to grips with a new term or two, but trust me, it's worth it. For example, depreciation. "Depreciation" refers to the gradual wasting away of basically everything on the planet, including you. You age, and as you do, you wear out, you lose your usefulness, and finally it's time for a long dirt-nap. But don't feel alone. This is also true of your car, your furniture, your house, and pretty much everything else made out of atoms. That's just the way it is.

While Uncle Sam can't do anything to keep your stuff from wearing out, he can lighten your load a bit by giving you tax breaks as it happens. But the IRS is only willing to give you a break on expenses you incur in the process of earning income. You may recall from chapter 15, on taxes, that certain expenses are deductible from your income for tax purposes, and that when you're running a business, virtually everything you spend there is tax-deductible, because everything you're spending is related to generating income. So when you buy paper, the cost is tax deductible. And when you buy a printer to put the paper in, that's a write-off, too. But there's a difference between the paper and the printer when it comes to how much of the cost you can write off on your taxes every year. Paper is going to be used up quickly, while a printer should theoretically last for years. So while you get to deduct the cost of the paper when you buy it, you're supposed to deduct the cost of the printer over its useful life. In tax terminology, things you would normally use up within one year are called "ordinary expenses," while things that last longer than this are called "capital expenses." The amount of write-off you get for capital expenses is its depreciation for that year.

Example: Say you spend $1,000 on paper. You get to take a $1,000 deduction on your taxes that year. This is true even if you buy the paper on December 31, because although there's no way you can use up $1,000 worth of paper in one day, paper is still an ordinary expense for tax purposes, because it's not made to last a long time. So you get to write it off in the year you buy it. In other words, it's fully depreciated instantly. Now say you spend $1,000 on a printer. A printer should last three years, so you only get to write off one-third of the cost of the printer in the year you buy it. Your deduction for depreciation is one-third of $1,000, or $333. The next year you get to write off another $333, and $334 the final year. (If your printer should break in the second year and become garbage, you get to finish writing it off in that year rather than waiting for Year 3.)

The government gives you deductions because it recognizes that when you're in business, you need to buy materials to create the product or service that ends up as taxable profits. And it wouldn't be fair to tax the profits without allowing you to deduct the expenses incurred in creating them. Plus, in the long run Uncle Sam still wins. Because the money you're saving on taxes by writing off depreciation every year could theoretically be saved, set aside, and used to help offset the price of a new printer when the old one wears out. Being able to replenish your business assets keeps your business alive, which keeps your profits alive, which keeps your tax bill alive, which keeps Uncle Sam alive. Make sense?[57]

[57] If you understood this explanation, you're now in a position to understand some of the accounting scandals that rocked Wall Street a couple of years ago. Remember WorldCom and the billions of dollars of accounting irregularities that helped send the company into bankruptcy? What the WorldCom folks were doing is taking ordinary expenses, like paper,

Now that you've endured a tedious explanation of depreciation write-offs, let's see what the heck this has to do with real estate.

If you buy yourself a house to live in, you're not buying a business asset, because the house is being used for shelter, not profit. So while you may get to write off the interest on your mortgage loan, you're not going to get tax deductions on the house itself. But if you're buying a rental house, that's a business asset. Now you have to report the rents you take in as income, but you get to write off expenses incurred to generate this income: the interest on the mortgage loan, the paint, the utilities, the ads . . . anything having to do with the business of maintaining and renting the house . . . including the house itself. The costs of the interest, utilities, and fix-up supplies are all ordinary expenses, deductible in the year you spend the money. The house itself, however, is a capital expense that you depreciate over its useful life, taking proportionate deductions every year. So if you pay $100,000 for a house, and the house should last twenty years, every year you get to write off one-twentieth of the cost, or $5,000.

Being able to depreciate and deduct the cost of a house in this fashion is the best thing since sliced bread. Why? Because you're generating depreciation deductions on an asset that isn't going down in value . . . in fact, it's probably going up in value. You know how many things that you can write off that are actually going up in value? Not a printer . . . you'll be lucky if that lasts three years. Not a car . . . it drops in value 20 percent the day you take it home. In fact, real estate is practically the only thing you'll ever buy that generates a deductible "paper loss" that in real life is more likely a profit than a loss. Call it a loophole if you'd like, but I call it pretty darn cool.

This free lunch isn't completely free, because the depreciation you write off every year while you own your house will increase the

---

and classifying them as capital expenses, like printers. In other words, they were spreading expenses over several years when they should have been taken in one year. Result? Less expense this year equals more profits this year. This is what is known in tax lingo as "fraud." And the fact that their auditors supposedly didn't notice this blatant manipulation is what most people call either "turning a blind eye" or "total incompetence."

taxable profit when you finally sell it. To continue our example above, say we own our $100,000 house for ten years. During this time, we've written off half its value, or $50,000. This means that for tax purposes, we only have $50,000 left in the house because we've already written off half. Our depreciated basis (in other words, our cost) for tax purposes is $50,000. Now we sell the house for $150,000. If we hadn't been depreciating it, we'd have a $50,000 profit: $150,000 less the $100,000 we paid. But because our investment has been reduced by $50,000 worth of depreciation, we now have a gain of $100,000: $150,000 less the $50,000 basis remaining on our books. While this does help Uncle Sam recoup some of the breaks he's given us, we're still ahead of the game for several reasons. First, we got to save tax money every year and we didn't have to "repay" the write-offs until the house sold. And we could have postponed that indefinitely if we'd wanted to. (Remember, in the long term, we're all dead. And if you leave your rental house to someone in your will, he gets to start the depreciation process all over again based on the house's value at the time of your death.) Second, if you own something for longer than a year, gains are taxed at a lower rate than ordinary income. Twenty percent is the most you'll pay, rather than the 30 percent or more that you'd pay on ordinary income. Third, you can delay paying taxes on the gain entirely by trading your house for another one instead of selling it. This is called a 1031 exchange, and it postpones the gain by transferring your depreciated value to the new building.

Okay, so now you see how a house can be more than a shelter; it can be a tax shelter. In fact, courtesy of the paper losses provided through depreciation, it would theoretically be possible to reduce your taxable income to zero. Ever hear people complain that so-and-so-rich-guy makes all kinds of money but pays very little in income taxes? This is one way he could have been accomplishing this laudable goal. I use the word "theoretically" in the above sentence, however, because the alternative minimum tax (discussed in chapter 15, on income taxes) pretty much assures that you'll pay some tax no matter how many deductions you're able to generate.

The income tax advantages alone would be enough to convince most people to invest in real estate. But there are other advantages as well. Rents normally rise with inflation. In fact, as you'll recall from chapter 12, on inflation, rents are a primary component of the consumer price index. So if you use income property as a source for retirement income, your rents will rise as your cost of staying alive rises. And, of course, you hope that the value of the property itself is at least keeping up with inflation and maybe even beating it.

All in all, real estate is a pretty decent investment. If, of course, you buy it right and manage it well.

How do you get big bang for your real estate buck? Before you think about buying real estate, make sure you're doing it in the right place. Many people believe that real estate never goes down in value. They're wrong. While there's never been a nationwide meltdown in real estate prices, there have been plenty of temporary setbacks. In one of my news stories, I mentioned several examples, including 20-percent-plus declines in home values that happened in the not-too-distant past in Los Angeles, Houston, and New York. These all occurred due to location-specific, job-related issues. Los Angeles lost a ton of defense industry jobs between 1989 and 1996, which made housing prices bomb. When oil prices plunged in the mid-1980s, the oil industry cut jobs and the housing market was nonc too slick in Houston. New York real estate crashed along with stocks in 1987. In each of these cities, the problem was job losses. And in each city, it took the better part of a decade for those who bought at the top to recoup their investment.

These examples tell us that job growth is the main thing when it comes to housing prices. Real estate goes up in value because the supply is finite relative to potential demand. So before you invest in any real estate, make sure the city you're living in is growing, and that the growth is expected to continue. Of course, growth won't happen in a straight line; there will always be recessions when growth slows, no matter where you live. But make sure the long-term trend is up when it comes to jobs and population.

In addition, remember that unexpected things will happen, so make sure that your real estate investments, like your stock investments, are long term. If you can't do the time, don't spend a dime. As with stocks, five years should be the minimum you're planning to own real estate. Planning on living somewhere for three years, and think you're going to be an absentee landlord when you move on? Think again. It may be possible, but not advisable. Managing real estate isn't rocket science, but it's a lot easier and less expensive if you're close to your property. In addition, it's pretty hard to sell without an agent if you're far away, and as I'll explain, selling without an agent is something you'll want to do.

Finally, try not to overpay for your real estate. How can you know if you're overpaying? We've already discovered that because of the price inefficiencies inherent in real estate, it's tough to know what property is worth. Even if you have it professionally appraised, odds are good that the appraisal won't be all that accurate. So how do you gauge it? If you're dealing with rental real estate, especially multiunit apartments, the trick is to think of the property as an investment (which is exactly what it is) and see how much it's going to pay relative to other investments. For example, say you're looking at a $100,000 duplex that will rent for a total of $1,000 a month. If you owned it free and clear, and didn't have to pay for maintenance, utilities, taxes and insurance, you'd be making 12 percent on your money ($12,000 ÷ $100,000 = 12%), not including the appreciation you'd hopefully be getting. But unless you're lucky enough to find tenants who are going to pay your utilities, taxes, insurance, and maintenance, as well as doing all the labor involved, this estimate won't be realistic. So think about the time you'll take to deal with your rental. Consider that you probably won't stay rented 100 percent of the time. Conservatively factor in all the costs, including labor, and then do the math again. You'll probably find that even if you value your time at zero, by the time you subtract a vacancy factor and the checks you'll be writing, your net income will shrink to a number more like $5,000 to $7,000. If so, that's okay . . . 5 to 7 percent is nothing to sneeze at. Plus, the deductible money you've spent and the depreciation write-off you'll get will make a large part of that $7,000 essentially tax-free. And then there's the icing on the cake: Your property will hopefully be going up in value, and even if it doesn't, your rents should increase over time. When you compare this duplex to other types of investments, is it a good deal? Is it better than you'd get from stocks, bonds, or other stuff? This is how you'll know if you're making a smart move. Many of the things you'll be using in your estimates will be uncertain, because life is uncertain. Nobody can predict when the local rental market will tank, when a pipe is going to break, or when a roof is going to give out. Nor can you know for sure at what rate your property will appreciate. All you can do is look at enough property, talk to enough knowledgeable people, and study your local economy enough to make informed guesses. Which is pretty much the same thing the "experts" do when they're trying to figure out where the stock market is heading. The more legwork you do, the more informed your guesses will be.

What about a house to live in? How do you know that's a good deal? From a strictly financial perspective, you can do pretty much the same thing you would with rental property. Just see what houses like the one you're considering are renting for and do the math just as you would for a rental property. Compare that hypothetical return to other investments, and see how the math works for you. You'll probably find that single-family houses won't provide the cash return of multiunit rental property. This is because rentals are priced as investments and houses are priced according to pride of ownership. In other words, the housing market isn't driven by financial returns; it's primarily driven by spouses who say, "This is the house I want, and if you expect further conjugal visits, you'd better come up with the money to buy it." So here's a little formula to determine the fair value of an owner-occupied house: Divide the monthly cost of owning the home by its theoretical monthly rent. If this number is more than 1.3, you could be paying too much. For example, say the monthly cost of your mortgage, taxes, insurance, and maintenance is $1,000. You do a little research and figure the house could rent for $800 a month; $1,000 ÷ $800 = 1.25. This is less than 1.3, so you're in the ballpark.

What if your house falls way outside this number? What if your cost is $2,000 a month and the market rent is only $500? When plugged into our formula, that would give us an answer of 2.0. While this does represent a red flag, it doesn't necessitate your backing out of the deal. Remember, we're talking rule of thumb here. Odds are good that you are indeed paying too much, but it's also quite possible that houses are appreciating especially rapidly in the area. It's also possible that having this particular house at this particular moment is more important than getting a screaming deal, and conjugal visits are high on your list of things to do. But using this rule of thumb, or one like it, will help you separate the financial part of your housing transaction from the emotional part. So will looking at enough property to make you conversant with the local market.

Now I'm going to devote a little time to Realtors, since this is a group of people you're likely to encounter anytime you're considering buying or selling any type of real estate.

Here's a cut-and-paste line from a story I did back in 1998: "Buying and selling houses isn't brain surgery, but you'd never know it by the price. The average surgeon's fee for brain tumor removal is $2,266. Which means you could have six brain tumors removed for the same price you'll pay to sell a $200,000 house."

When it comes to real estate agents, there's no question they can add value to a real estate transaction by helping find property when you're a buyer and buyers for your property when you're a seller. They can help you become knowledgeable about which neighborhoods are best and let you know when new properties come on the market. They can drive you around and show you specific property. And when you finally enter into a transaction, they can stay on top of the paperwork for you.

The problem is that they charge too much money for these simple services. Learning the market, finding buyers or sellers, and doing the required paperwork isn't brain surgery and shouldn't be priced like it. In addition, because they work on commission, the advice you get from an agent is often tainted. Would you trust a brain surgeon who worked on commission?

Realtors are quick to point out that since sellers are the ones who pay real estate commissions, buyers get all the benefits of their services without any cost. As you know if you're ever sold a house through a Realtor, however, this is hogwash. When you're selling a house by listing it with a Realtor, what's the first thing you do? You compute how much you'll be paying your agent and do everything possible to add this amount to the price of your home. And if you're successful, who's paying the commission? The buyer.

Another problem you face when buying through Realtors is that they'll only show you property that's been listed through another Realtor, because that's the only way they'll get paid. Which means you won't see every available property in a given neighborhood, because you won't see the ones being sold by owners. In addition, because agents attempt to inflate the seller's profit (and their commission) by pricing the property at the maximum realistic selling price, the odds of finding a bargain through a Realtor are thus radically diminished.

So whether you're buying or selling, if you can avoid using a real estate agent, do so. Sometimes you can't, like when you're new in town and need to find a place immediately. (It would probably be better to rent for a while until you learn the local market, but sometimes you just don't want to wait, and only a masochist would relish the idea of moving twice.) Another situation where you may be forced to use a Realtor is when you're a seller in a hurry and therefore don't have the extra time to market a property yourself. Whatever the situation, if you have to use an agent, fine. Just don't expect your best deals to happen this way. If you're buying, you're unlikely to end up with a radically underpriced property. If you're selling, you might end up disappointed at the amount of money you pay for the amount of value you receive.

Bottom line? When you're buying real estate, learn your specific market inside and out. Whenever possible, deal directly with a seller, hopefully one who doesn't know as much as you do. When you're selling real estate, avoid paying thousands of dollars and sell it yourself.

How do you learn your local real estate market? This involves a simple three-step process:

- *Step 1:* Look in the newspaper and/or the Internet for the type of property you're interested in. See what things are selling for in different parts of town.
- *Step 2:* Visit enough property (both listed with agents and for-sale-by-owner . . . known as FSBO) until you get a feel for how things are priced. It won't take as long as you think. While you're doing this, you're going to meet lots of people who know a lot more than you do about whatever kind of property you're interested in. Question these people incessantly until they either get a restraining order against you or you know as much as they do.
- *Step 3:* While following Steps 1 and 2, get financing arranged so you can jump on a bargain the instant you're finally in a position to recognize one when you trip over it. In other words, get whatever cash you intend to bring to the table lined up, and get preapproved for whatever money you intend to borrow.

One of the reasons people think a Realtor is necessary is that the knowledge required to put together a contract, put a deal in escrow, and properly execute the closing documents is over their heads. This is absolutely true. What they don't realize, however, is that these technical details are also over the heads of most Realtors. The people who know how to dot the i's and cross the t's are not found at the Realtor's office; they're working at a title and/or escrow company. So if you're going it alone, it makes sense to call one of these people early on in the process. Simply explain that you're planning on either buying direct from an owner or selling by yourself and would appreciate their assistance. You'll be amazed at all the friendly, free help you'll get in exchange for using them when you're ready to do a deal. They'll often furnish you with free documents (like a fill-in-the-blanks contract) and free advice. It's these people who are the administrative brains behind real estate deals, and they work extremely inexpensively, especially when compared to the outrageous fees that real estate agents charge.

When it comes to selling property without the assistance of an agent, the idea is basically the same as the process of becoming a knowledgeable buyer. In other words, you'll obviously have to learn the local market in order to know where to price your property. Once you've done this, then it just becomes a matter of attracting buyers. How do you do it? You talk to your buddy at the title or escrow company to get your paperwork together. You study newspaper or Internet ads that attract your attention, and shamelessly copy wording and technique when you place your own. You visit open houses being held by Realtors and observe their sales methods—things like brochures and clever sales lines—then craft your own. You put a sign in your yard. You screen prospective buyers by asking them if they're preapproved for a loan, as well as other questions that will separate the serious buyers from the looky-loos. (You'll be amazed at the number of annoying people who want to see your property but have no intention of buying it. You know . . . jerks exactly like you were when you were learning the market.) And when your ducks are all in a row, you'll sell your property yourself and save enough by doing so to pay for a good used car.

The steps I've listed here are the forest when it comes to real estate. You'll want to learn the trees as well. Since it doesn't directly relate to being a flawless manager of family finances, however, I'm going to stop here. Especially since, as you might imagine, there's plenty of information already out there on the subject, from investing in rental property to selling your own house. You can find it on the Web, you can find it at the library, and you can find it by talking to anyone both knowledgeable and willing to stand still. So if you have the urge to learn about real estate, I heartily encourage you to act on it. Fortunes are made this way, and it's not that complicated. When it comes to creating wealth, protecting against inflation, and providing a retirement income, real estate is as good an investment as any. It certainly takes more time than simply investing in an S&P index fund, but because of the market inefficiencies discussed earlier, those willing to invest the time often find themselves rewarded for their efforts.

Although I was a stockbroker for more than twelve years, I've made a lot more money in real estate than I ever did in stocks.

Before we leave the topic of real estate entirely, however, let's go over one more thing: finding the right mortgage. This advice will serve you well whether you're shopping for a first home or refinancing your existing one for the fourteenth time.

Obviously rate is the most important thing to look for when you're mortgage shopping. To check out current rates, you can go to bankrate.com and see a listing of lenders who are willing to lend mortgage money where you live. (The lenders could be across town or across the country.) This list can then be sorted by interest rate, APR (annual percentage rate), or other factors. Another Web site that offers mortgage rates by location is www.hsh.com. There are others, of course. Plug the phrase "mortgage rates" into a search engine and you'll come up with nearly two million hits. But if you go elsewhere, be careful that you're getting objective information. The vast majority of mortgage Web sites feature only companies that pay to be represented, which makes them as useful as screen doors on a submarine.

If mortgage shopping simply meant finding the lowest rate, there would be nothing to it. Unfortunately, however, there's more than rate to consider, because mortgages come with fees attached. Fees are more often than not imposed in inverse proportion to the amount of knowledge you bring to the table. Please bring some.

The first thing to remember about the fees associated with a mortgage is that nearly all of them are negotiable and many of them are garbage; that is, they exist simply to fatten the lender's profit margin. To get an idea of the fees you might pay to refinance, you could go back and look at the fees you paid when you first took out your loan. Only this time you'll make a spreadsheet that will help you compare apples to apples so that when this situation arises again, you won't be starting from square one.

Here's what my mortgage comparison spreadsheet looks like:

Mortgage Comparison Worksheet

Company	**Mortgage Depot**	**Debt-R-Us**	**Bigger Is Better Inc.**	**Obscene Mortgage**	**Screw You Finance Company**
Number	888-12depot	800-debtrus	800-DoubleD	800-XXX-XXXX	888-screwyou
Contact	Perry Points	Larry Lizard	Barbara Boob	Sam Sham	Richey Fees
Rate	5.0	5.0	5.0	5.0	5.0
Fees					
Points	0	0	0		0
Origination	0	0	0		0
Credit report	$10.50		$10.00		$20.00
Tax service fee	$80.00	$78.00	$95.00		$59.00
Underwriting fees			$200.00	$375.00	$445.00
Processing fees			$300.00	$350.00	$295.00
Broker fee					$1,800.00
Express mail		$50.00			
Appraisal fee	$275.00		$250.00	$275.00	
Document preparation			$195.00		
Application fee	$375.00	$325.00			
Pest/roof inspection					
Courier fee			$20.00		
Flood certification	$19.50	$11.00		$21.00	
TLG review & certification					
Total	**$760.00**	**$464.00**	**$1,070.00**	**$1,021.00**	**$2,619.00**

This is my actual mortgage comparison worksheet, which I cut and pasted from an Excel spreadsheet that I keep stored on my computer. I've used it twice before, and I include it here virtually unaltered with the exception of the names and phone numbers. Don't think, however, that I changed them to protect the innocent, because there are no innocent mortgage lenders.

Let's go through the mortgage shopping process together to see how we can use this tool.

The process of surfing to bankrate.com, pulling up a mortgage lender list, and sorting it by annual percentage rate for my city took forty seconds. (Prior to the Internet, if such a list were even possible at all, it would've taken many hours to do.) We sorted the bankrate list by lowest APR, which, as explained above, stands for "annual percentage rate."

The difference between "interest rate" and "annual percentage rate" is that the APR is the interest rate after you add in a couple of lender fees, like discount points and/or origination fees. For example, if you're paying 5 percent interest but the loan costs $10,000 in points, you're actually paying a lot more than 5 percent interest. The APR includes that ten grand. Hence the APR will always be higher than the interest rate. Unfortunately, however, the APR never includes *all* the lender fees, which is why we have to call the lenders individually to find out what their fees are. Still, starting with lowest APRs will help us isolate potential candidates.

Okay. We've found four companies that promise a 5 percent APR. We simply cut and pasted their names and phone numbers from the Bankrate list to our spreadsheet. In addition, we also included our existing lender, if we have one, for two reasons: It might lower its fees to keep our business, and since it already knows how wonderfully responsible we are, it might cut us some slack when it comes to paperwork. (This obviously would only apply if we're refinancing or had some former relationship with a lender. If we were starting from scratch, we'd find all five lenders from the Bankrate site or other sources.)

Now it's time to use our spreadsheet to separate the wheat from the chaff. This we do by calling all of our lowest-APR companies and asking them about their fees. (Maybe we'll call one lender during every commercial break.) When we call these companies, we'll ask simple and direct questions about their fees. But we won't get simple answers. Instead, our potential lenders will attempt to confuse us by talking about title transfer fees, prepaid interest, and anything else they can throw at us that has nothing whatsoever to do with the questions we're asking. They'll deny some of the fees they'll ultimately end up charging and outright lie about the amount of others. We expect this. Our only hope of keeping them somewhat honest is to take control of the conversation by asking them not to interrupt us as we recite the list of fees on our spreadsheet. Then, to make sure we've covered all the bases, we'll ask them if we've left anything out. When they've told us what we've left out (we'll be making notes of these fees so we'll be better informed for the next company we call), we'll ask them again if that's truly all there is. When we've got it down, we'll thank them for their time, get their name, and move on until our spreadsheet is filled in.

If you ignore this advice and let the mortgage salesperson control the conversation, trust me, you'll hang up with no idea whatsoever what that particular lender will cost you. But it will certainly cost you more than you think.

Keep in mind that the spreadsheet I've included here is mine, which means it's been used in Florida. If you live in another state, you might have a list of fees that's different in a few respects, or maybe many respects. But as you start getting information on fees, you'll soon be up to speed on what fees apply in your area.

As you're dealing with mortgage lenders and mortgage brokers, your greatest tool is competition, and you'll use it often. As you get responses to your fee questions, you'll be saying things like, "You charge a document preparation fee of $195? Bummer, man. I've called three other companies that don't charge anything!" This is how you'll reduce and/or eliminate fees. (In fact, you should even attempt this tactic with the interest rate.) More important, should you decide to go forward with your loan, you'll refer back to the amounts you've been told and are placing on your spreadsheet. You'll be amazed at how the fees you were quoted have magically increased and multiplied.

To repeat: Most of the fees associated with the mortgage process are negotiable. This especially includes fees that the mortgage salesperson specifically tells you are never, ever negotiable. Dealing with a mortgage salesperson is exactly like dealing with a car salesperson. The game is called "baffling with BS." Their goal is to try to steer you into a commitment as quickly as possible with as little explanation as possible, load you up with as many charges as possible, and get on to the next loan as soon as possible. Your goal is to stop, look, and listen. To understand every single fee you're paying from document preparation to express courier charges, and eliminate as many as possible. Please note that these goals are diametrically opposed. So go into the hunt expecting conflict. Here's an example of something that's happened to me, and will surely happen to you as well.

ME: That's all your fees? You don't charge for express mail?

THEM: Well, yes, but that's only fifty bucks. That's nothing.

ME: Oh, great! I'm glad you think that $50 is nothing. I'll mark it as zero on my spreadsheet and you can pay it.

You get my drift . . . expect these people to be a pain in the butt. If they're not, you'll be pleasantly surprised. If they are, you'll be prepared.

If things are looking fairly good on the mortgage front, and it looks like a loan is in the offing, we can take the next step in the process: finding out how much a title company will charge to insure our title and act as middleman in closing the loan. Since these are local companies, here we search the yellow pages instead of the Internet. One of the companies could be the one we used when we last bought real estate. Or if we're virgins, they can be selected pretty much at random. (We can also ask our loan officer for recommendations, or perhaps ask a more experienced friend.) I have another section of my mortgage comparison worksheet for this:

Title Company Fees

Company	Untitled Title	Titlerama	Titles Unlimited
Number	XXX-XXXX	XXX-XXXX	XXX-XXXX
Contact	Terry Title	Tommy Title	Tilly Title
Title insurance owners	$1,053	$1,053	$1,053
Simultaneous issue	$12	$18	
Title endorsements	$173	$255	$203
Title exam	$100	$150	$125
Title closing fee	$50	$250	$100
Title search	$220	$235	$185
Total	**$1,608**	**$1,961**	**$1,666**

Since title company fees aren't normally as high or as variable as the fees charged by mortgage companies, I go to only three instead of five as I did with potential lenders. Notice that the biggest expense, "title insurance owner," is the same for all three companies. This is because the rate is set by law, at least where I live. (And by the way, when I was told this, I called the state department of real estate and verified it.) The other fees, however, are totally negotiable, so we do what we can to reduce or eliminate them by pitting one company against another. (Depending on where you live, you may use a lawyer instead of a title company for this part of the loan process. Doesn't matter. The principle is the same: Find out what the fees are and shop them.)

Once you've decided on a mortgage lender and a title or escrow company, you're nearly there. But now's when a lot of games begin, so don't put away your spreadsheet just yet. After you've agreed to do your loan, your lender will send you a good-faith estimate, which you're normally required to sign and send back, acknowledging that you know what you're doing and how much you'll be paying. The good-faith estimate includes pretty much everything it's told you regarding interest rate and fees. Here's your first opportunity to see if it's trying to slip something in. Compare the numbers on the good-faith estimate to the numbers on your spreadsheet. If there are differences, call your lender and ask the folks there why. If you've been doing a good job of hammering them about fees, they may screen your call. But don't worry: Eventually they'll return it.

You'll probably find that your good-faith estimate is an accurate portrayal of what you've been told. The real test comes when you get your settlement statement. You might not see this statement until you actually sit down to sign the papers, but usually it will arrive from fifteen minutes to two days before the final closing. Get it as early as you can, because your settlement statement is where the chum meets the sharks. In other words, it's the final tally of who owes what to whom, and is thus where we often find buried fees.

When I bought a house in Cincinnati a few years back, the title company faxed my settlement statement to my home just half an hour before our appointed time to close. In fact, the sellers of the property were already waiting at the title company when my lender faxed it, and that was a fifteen-minute drive. Needless to say, Gina was a bit antsy to get on the road. I wasn't. I went over my settlement statement, checking each fee against my spreadsheet entries. And guess what! I found a $450 loan origination fee buried in there that I'd never seen before. I called my loan salesman and asked him about it. He said something like, "Oh that? It's standard. It's required on all our loans." I replied, "Well, you never told me about that fee." He said, "Oh, sure I did, Mr. Johnson! Like I said, that's a mandatory fee. I'm not allowed to do loans without it, so I must have told you about it."

"Look," I said. "I may have been born in the morning, but not this morning. This fee isn't on my good-faith estimate, nor did you ever disclose it verbally or in writing. So it's this simple: Either you fax me a piece of paper with my signature on it that discloses this fee, or you take it the hell off my settlement statement."

"But Mr. Johnson! Aren't you closing soon? You don't want to lose the house, do you? We can work it out later. And after all . . . it's only $450."

"Exactly," I responded. "It's only $450. You don't want to lose the loan, do you? And I'll bet you don't want me to sue you, either. So I'd suggest you move your ass and get the fee removed. You can work out the details with your boss later."

That's a true story. The closing was late, but it happened, sans the $450 fee. How many people do you think would have even noticed this fee, much less raised a stink about it? Not many. Most people are so happy that someone's willing to lend them a couple of hundred thousand dollars that they'd probably hand over their firstborn child, much less raise hell about hidden fees. But that's not how I am, and that's not how you are. That's why when we close real estate loans, we go over every single blank that's been filled in. We recompute the accrued interest. We figure out how property taxes are paid and what's going into our impound account. (This is the account where they accumulate the money you'll owe for taxes and insurance if your mortgage company is paying these for you.) We don't leave anything up to chance, and we ask however many questions are necessary of all parties involved until we know exactly what we're paying for.

Now perhaps the remark I made at the beginning of this section makes sense. "Fees are more often than not assessed in inverse proportion to thc amount of knowledge you bring to the table. Please bring some."

18

Estate Planning

I've got all the money I'll ever need,
if I die by four o'clock.
—Henny Youngman

Since the only things in life that are certain are death and taxes, no self-respecting book on personal finance can afford to avoid these topics. We've talked taxes. Now it's time to deal with death.

Ornithologists (people who study birds) have known for years that ducks are completely unaware of ghosts. This is why when it comes to planning for your death, it's important to get your ducks in a row while you're still alive. But rather than call this process something distasteful like "death planning," the financial community has adopted a much more pleasant term: "estate planning." This way we can at least feel wealthy and sophisticated while facing the fact that ultimately we're all dead ducks.

When it comes to planning for the great beyond, you've got three main goals. First, you want to leave an easy-to-follow paper trail for those you leave behind, so they can spend all their time remembering you rather than trying to remember where you kept the savings accounts and life insurance policies. Second, you want to reduce the cost and hassle of transferring your money and things to your heirs, a process known as probate. Finally, you want to keep the tax collectors at bay. Let's hit these things one at a time.

Leaving a Proper Paper Trail

In my former life as a stockbroker, I met many widows whose husbands had died unexpectedly and left them without the organizational skills or fundamental knowledge necessary to carry on. This is unnecessary, and it's cruel. Leave your significant other in this position and you're taking a person who's already upset, then piling on additional stress by forcing him to learn everything from scratch with little reliable help. Ignorance and stress combine to form confusion, and confusion is the mother of mistake. Next thing you know, your ghost is watching a securities salesperson sitting in your favorite chair advising the bereaved on high-commission, no-return investment strategies. Not a pretty picture, and one that's easily avoided by simply being organized and bringing pertinent people into the loop.

My father has what he calls a "death book." Nothing fancy: just a three-ring binder that has a brief handwritten summary of where everything is, from T-bills to funeral plots. He's even written out his own obituary, along with a general description of what his funeral should look like. The reason I know about this book is that a while back he made me sit down and go through it, then he told me where he keeps it. While I think he could have chosen a catchier title, his idea is a good one. Simplify, organize, share the information. Imagine that you dropped dead this moment. Would your spouse know where the important papers are? Could he find your life insurance contract? Does he know how to apply for Social Security survivor benefits? Does he have access to ready cash? Does he know whether you want to be buried, cremated, or just left by the curb? Do you have a will so it's clear who gets what? Will your browser history reveal that you spent your last minutes visiting porn sites?

If you've been following some of the organizational tips in this book, you're already vastly ahead of the game when it comes to some of the answers. Your investments are as simple as they can be. Your accounts are as few as possible. Your files contain only what's necessary. So providing your survivors know where to look, they can quickly figure out what's what and then focus on your disgusting Web-surfing habits.

Eliminating Probate

If you're lucky enough to have perfect timing, you'll spend your last dollar as you draw your last breath. Sometimes, however, either by accident or design, we leave money or possessions behind. In some ancient societies, worldly goods were buried with the deceased so they'd be able to use them in the next world. But in modern America, they're given to people who can get greater use out of them.

If you're single, absent a legally executed document to the contrary, upon your death everything you have will go to your parents. If that's what you want, fine, but do you really think Mom will fully appreciate your *Penthouse* collection? If your parents aren't alive, all your stuff will go to your closest living relative. If the state can't find one, they'll keep it for themselves. Talk about a group of people that won't appreciate vintage *Penthouse*!

This is why pretty much everyone should have a will. Yes, even twenty-five-year-olds.

A will is nothing more than a legal piece of paper that typically does the following:

- Names a person who will assume the responsibility for following the will's instructions. This person is called an executor or sometimes a personal representative.
- Tells the executor who's supposed to get what.
- Names the person who will assume custody of any minor children left behind. This person is called the guardian.
- Reveals other miscellaneous details, like how your earthly vessel is to be disposed of.

Wills are easy to come by. In most states, you can literally write one on a napkin, sign it, have it witnessed, and you've got yourself a legal document. (A handwritten will is called a holographic will.) But since it's easy to do it the right way, leave your napkin in your lap.

In precomputer days, having a will meant going to a lawyer and parting with a bunch of money. And while this option is certainly still available, these days most folks should just get a simple software package and zip one out at home in no time. One place you can buy a software package for will making is www.nolo.com. (Also a good source for just about any kind of legal information, including estate planning.) Kiplinger (www.kiplinger.com) will also sell you software called WillPower for around thirty bucks. Quicken's (www.quicken.com) version is called Quicken Lawyer 2003 Wills and is also priced at around thirty bucks. If that's too expensive, Broderbund (www.broderbund.com) will sell you software for $10, or www.legaldocs.com lets you to prepare your will online and print it out for fifteen bucks. So you can see that having something priceless doesn't have to be pricey. (By the way, these same sources also offer software that will print forms and offer assistance on lots of other legal topics, like leases, loans, powers of attorney, and bills of sale. But if you're facing a criminal proceeding, always go for the personal touch. I would stringently advise against letting software represent you when you're facing twenty-five to life.)

Provided your will is legal and its instructions are, too (no, your will can't dictate your body be stuffed and propped up on your favorite barstool), everything you requested in your will should be promptly performed by your executor upon your demise. And that would be that, except for one problem. Who's going to make sure that your executor executes? Since our society believes that your last wishes are important, and lots of money is often involved, a system was created to make sure there's no hanky-panky. The system is called probate. Probate happens in probate court, where the state, through a judge, verifies that your will is authentic, grants authority to your executor to do his job, instructs your executor to find and inventory your belongings, orders the applicable debts and taxes to be paid, legally appoints the guardian you named, makes sure potential heirs are properly notified, and, if all is in order, assists the executor in handing out the booty.

It's a good thing that the state makes sure your last wishes are followed, but the bad part is that the process of probate can be cumbersome and expensive. And as with most legal proceedings, it may also take time and require the assistance of a lawyer. This, of course, will be of no consequence to you since you're by definition beyond frustration. But it won't make life any easier, or cheaper, for your heirs or the executor of your estate. So it would behoove them if you found ways to bypass the expense and red tape of probate. How much probate costs and how long it takes vary wildly depending on which state you die in and how big your estate is, but it can certainly cost hundreds, even thousands of dollars and take months, even years to complete.

Before you worry too much about probate, however, it's important to note that a lot of your money may not have to be probated. A retirement account is an example; so is an insurance policy. You can identify an account that misses probate by looking for the word "beneficiary" when you set it up. A beneficiary is so named because he benefits from someone else's largesse. When you set up a retirement account, you name a beneficiary. Likewise when you set up a life insurance policy. That's why these things don't have to be probated: You've already said what you want to happen when you die, so the court doesn't have to read your will and oversee the transfer.

Another tool you can use to bypass probate is to hold title to possessions in such a way that probate isn't necessary. This is possible with things that have your name legally attached to them—things like investments, your car, your house, your boat, your motorcycle, and any other toys you were dying to own and then die owning. If these things are titled in your name and that of your significant other, followed by the words "joint tenancy with rights of survivorship," probate won't be necessary because you've already stated who has the right to them if he survives you. All he'll have to do is flash a death certificate as proof you've passed and he owns the item. No probate, no judge, no delay, no expense.

Obviously, since joint tenancy gives the joint owner a partial ownership interest the instant it's titled that way, it's best reserved for spouses or extremely significant others. In other words, if you put me on your yacht title as a joint tenant, you're giving me half of it right now and all of it when you die. While this is a desirable outcome whenever dealing with me, it may not be for other people in your life. What then? If you're dealing with a bank account, there's another way that might work. It's called a payable-on-death, often cleverly shortened to POD.

You can go to just about any bank, savings and loan, or credit union, sign a simple form, and have your savings titled with your name and somebody else's payable-on-death. That designation will do exactly what it says: pass the full value of the account to the person you've named upon your death. But unlike the case of joint tenancy, you've given him nothing while you're still alive, and you're free to change your mind whenever you want.

You also may be able to use a similar technique with brokerage or mutual fund accounts. It's just like payable-on-death but called transfer-on-death, or TOD. Not all states or brokerages allow this, however, so you'll need to check with your investment firm.

While joint tenancy, POD, and TOD can be handy in certain situations, they have glaring limitations in others. Since joint tenancy gives half your asset away instantly, this method of ownership is suitable only for people pretty darn serious about their relationship. And POD and TOD accounts will only work with things like bank accounts, stocks, and mutual funds; aren't always available; and often can't be used to transfer assets to people outside the family. How else can we bypass probate?

The most flexible and effective way to avoid probate is to take everything out of your name and give it to an entity that can't die. This is exactly what you're doing when you create a trust. The most common form of trust used to bypass probate is the revocable living trust, so named because you can change your mind if you want to (revocable) and you made the trust when you were alive (some trusts only come alive when you no longer are). Here's how they work. First, you draw up a trust. Next, you transfer everything you own to the trust with you as the trustee. For example, instead of your house being owned by "John Smith," it will now be owned by "John Smith, trustee for John Smith Revocable Living Trust dated July 12, 2004." There you have it: Your house is now owned by something that can't die, but you still control it as much as you ever did. You can sell it, borrow against it, or do whatever you want; the only thing that's changed is the legal title. In addition, the trust names who's supposed to get the house when the trustee is gone: In other words, it names the beneficiaries. And since the beneficiaries are named, there's no probate. Pretty clever, huh? A revocable living trust can even add more flexibility by naming a successor trustee that can't die, like a bank. For example, suppose you and your spouse want to leave half your joint estate to your children and the other half to your grandchildren. Problem is that your kids aren't old enough and/or responsible enough to serve as trustees, and your grandchildren are babies. No problem. You name yourself and your spouse as trustees, and ABC Bank as successor trustee. If the trustees die while the beneficiaries aren't ready to benefit, the successor trustee safeguards the money until they are. As everybody ages and things change, you can modify the trust.

Revocable living trusts also normally contain a will inside them as well, for at least two reasons. First, it takes care of stuff not titled in the name of the trust (if, for example, the trustee forgets to do it). Second, if you want to name a guardian for minor children, a will can but a trust normally can't. So most revocable living trusts will also include a will.

Now we know that revocable living trusts are a good way to bypass probate. There are only two problems with this approach: hassle and cost. Trusts are a hassle because they require you to transfer everything transferable into the name of the trust, which means a new deed for the house, new title for the car, and new ownership for all your mutual fund and bank accounts. And trust paperwork is also more expensive than a will, especially if you go to a lawyer. The reason why this is so, however, is a bit of a mystery.

Both trusts and wills feature common language, called boilerplate. In other words, the vast majority of the wording for both documents is already on your lawyer's hard drive: All he's doing is filling in some blanks. (That's why these things are perfect items to prepare yourself with inexpensive software.) And yet wills drawn up by lawyers normally cost a couple of hundred dollars, while trusts routinely cost a thousand or more. Why do lawyers charge more for trusts than wills when the work to prepare them is about the same? Perhaps because the word "trust" makes it sound more sophisticated and therefore worth more money. But another reason might be because when you do a trust, your lawyer is no longer in a position to make money by probating your estate when you die, so he feels the need to make more money while you're alive. A common pitch from a lawyer for a trust might be, "Hey, Ms. Client. This trust is going to save your heirs thousands in probate fees. So spending $1,200 now is a bargain." What he's neglected to mention is that the several-thousand-dollar probate fee your heirs are saving is made up almost entirely of the lawyer's hourly rate. The lawyer has also understandably neglected to mention that you can do your own trust with the same type of software I just told you about when we were talking wills, available from the same vendors.

Despite having executed a fine "death book," as I write this, my dad still has the house titled in his name alone, without my mom on the deed. And my parents have wills, not trusts. This means that when Dad dies, the house will be probated according to the terms of his will (which of course leaves the house to my mom), and when they're both gone their entire estate will have to be probated. Why hasn't my dad put the house in joint tenancy with rights of survivorship? I don't know. But I do know why my parents haven't gotten a trust: because my parents' lawyer told them that where they live (Georgia), probate is fast, cheap, and simple, and therefore it's not worth paying $1,000 or more for a trust. Which sounds like solid, considerate advice. But I can buy software for $50 or less that will prepare a revocable living trust for my parents and thereby avoid the delay and expense of probate entirely. I surfed the Web and found that the fees to file the required papers in a Georgia probate court are $200. And that's just to file the papers, not fill them in. How much will this thoughtful lawyer charge to fill out the papers and oversee the process? I don't know, but I do know that this lawyer is likely to charge at least $150 an hour for his time. I've never hired lawyers to probate an estate in Georgia, but I have hired them to do many other things, and I have yet to hire one who completed a job for me in fifteen minutes. So I'm thinking the family will benefit by a revocable living trust for my parents. Will it be a hassle to retitle everything in the name of the trust? Sure. But it won't be a picnic to probate the estate, either. And my parents are in a better position to help with the process right now than they will be after their funerals.

Lest you think you need to drop everything and immediately get a living trust, however, let's pause for a moment. While living trusts aren't a ton more complicated or expensive to self-produce than wills, they are a bit more so. So there's no point in getting one unless you need to. Who needs to?

If you're a typical person in good health, you're married, you're younger than sixty, and you're not a multimillionaire, then don't worry about a trust right now. You've got plenty of time to deal with it later. In the unlikely scenario where both you and your spouse die prematurely, your wills will suffice. After you've retired and have more time on your hands, then you can deal with creating a trust and retitling all your assets. If, that is, it's still necessary. Who knows what probate will be like years from now, much less what techniques will then be around to avoid it?

And if you are over sixty (or concerned about someone who is), you still may not need a trust. See what you can accomplish with simple techniques like joint tenancy and POD. If you've got a lot left to deal with, see if you live in a high-cost state when it comes to probate. (You can do this with a Web search. For example, when I was scoping out how to advise my parents, I just did a search for "Georgia probate costs.") If probate's expensive, or you have a lot of assets that you can't otherwise protect, check out a trust.

Bottom line? When it comes to avoiding probate costs, how much effort you expend will be directly related to how old you are, how rich you are, how single you are, and how much hassle and expense probate entails where you live. And even if you find that you should be considering a trust, researching these topics and dealing with them post-Internet will require a small fraction of the time and money it did pre-Internet. Anyone can make it happen during commercial breaks over a few weeks. No biggie.

Avoiding Estate Taxes

Imagine that you work with your parents on a five-hundred-acre family beet farm, handed down through the generations. While the land you're farming only cost your great-grandfather $1 an acre, these days it's worth $20,000 an acre. The land is in your parents' name and they both die, leaving it to you through a revocable living trust. You've successfully bypassed probate and can therefore carry on the family business without missing a beet. Or can you?

Your parents already paid taxes on everything you just inherited. They paid income taxes on the money they made and left you. They paid property taxes every year on the farmhouse and the land. They paid sales taxes on the belongings they bought. So there's nothing you've inherited that hasn't already been taxed in one form or another. You'd therefore logically think that you'd never have to pay taxes again on the same stuff, but you might be very wrong. Because you've now got to worry about estate taxes.

Many years ago Uncle Sam decided that if you were rich enough, your estate should be required to pay taxes. And this can present huge problems for many people. In our example, though our use of a trust allowed us to successfully eliminate probate, our parents left us land that is theoretically currently worth $10 million (500 acres x $20,000 per acre). And while we may be barely scratching a living from this land, to Uncle Sam we're still rich. Your parents' estate is valued at ten million bucks and it owes estate taxes of around four million.

To see how we arrived at this number, first let's see the estate tax table that applies from now till 2010.

Year	2004	2005	2006	2007	2008	2009	2010
Estate exemption	$1.5m	$1.5m	$2 m	$2 m	$2 m	$3.5 m	NA
Maximum tax rate	48%	47%	46%	45%	45%	45%	0%

Assuming your parents die in 2004, the first $1.5 million is exempt from estate taxes, but most of the remaining $8.5 million will be taxed at 48 percent, leaving the estate with close to a $4 million tax bill. What will you do? Beets me. Probably be forced to sell enough land to pay the bill, which will leave you with insufficient land to grow enough beets to make a living. Now you can see why estate taxes have been criticized as a root cause for the disappearance of so many farms, as well as other family businesses.[58]

Let's now leave this sad story and look at the good news to be gleaned from the estate tax tables. As you can see, the amount that is exempted from estate taxes grows from $1.5 million in 2004 to $3.5 million in 2009. And in 2010, estate taxes are zero; they're dead. This is a result of federal legislation enacted in 2001. But unless Congress does something to keep them dead, in 2011 estate taxes come back to life, and with exemptions and rates worse than those now in effect: an exemption of $1 million and a top rate of 55 percent.

From a planning perspective, this tells us several things. First, you've got to be a millionaire for estate taxes to matter at all. Second, if you've got millions of dollars, you'd really be doing your heirs a favor if you'd die sometime during 2010. Third, if you're planning on having a large estate, you might want to familiarize yourself with some techniques to deal with estate taxes.

Because estate taxes affect only millionaires, we're not going to spend a lot of time talking about how to reduce them. Suffice to say that there are techniques available to do so. These include other types of trusts (do a Web search for "AB trusts" or visit Web sites like nolo.com), leaving money to charity, getting money out of

[58] Not everyone agrees that estate taxes are a bad thing. William Gates, father of Bill Gates and head of the largest private charitable foundation on the planet, argues vehemently in favor of estate taxes. He's even written a book on the subject: *Wealth and Our Commonwealth: Why America Should Tax Accumulated Fortunes.*

your estate prior to death by gifting, and using life insurance proceeds to pay estate taxes. (You may recall from our discussion of life insurance that the only people who should consider the use of permanent insurance were rich people. This is precisely why.)

Conclusion

Before the thought of estate planning even entered the mind of a flawless financial manager, he'd already done the most important thing possible in the event of his untimely death. Because the steps he took to simplify and streamline his own life will do the same for the people he's left behind. He has a will, he has a spreadsheet saying where everything is, he's told people who matter where to find the spreadsheet, and he's informed those same people of the logic and mechanics of the investment strategies he's employed. He's taken the simple steps to avoid probate, and if the cost–benefit ratio of a trust indicated that one was advisable, he's spent a few bucks and made one. If his estate was big, he took a little extra time to see what strategies he could employ to reduce the estate taxes that might one day accrue.

As you can see, estate planning doesn't have to be a grave issue.

19

Bringing It All Together

Give me the strength to change the things I can,
the grace to accept the things I cannot,
and a great big bag of money.
—Jack Handey

So what do you say we bring all this stuff together and see exactly how you're going to become a flawless manager of your family's finances? After all, unless you're my mom, my editor, or terrifically bored, you have no other reason to read this book.

This is where we stop talking the talk and start walking the walk. In other words, this is where you manage your financial life in manageable chunks, measured in minutes. And like a speed-reading course, keep in mind that the promise is not only increased velocity, but increased comprehension as well. From this day forward, you're going to get it done fast while understanding a lot more of what you're doing. You're in complete control.

As you learned in chapter 14, "Getting Organized," you'll always be recording everything you spend in your computer's personal finance program. So you'll always know exactly where you are cash-wise, debt-wise, and every-other-wise. But every now and then, you'll want to sit back, stare at the numbers, and make sure you're accomplishing your goals. As with a successful business, you'll want to perform a review. A great time to do this is just before year end . . . say, between Christmas and New Year's. Although you can do your reviewing whenever you'd like (including hopefully right after you first organize your financial information), this particular period is ideal for the following reasons.

- Year end is when we naturally think of getting or staying organized, as well as a time when we're typically thinking about goals.
- If you're going to try to do anything to influence your calendar-year income tax liability, your options narrow considerably after the ball drops in Times Square. So this is a great time to review what's happened this year, what's in store for April 15, and what can be fiddled with to make the year less taxing.
- You can often only make changes to your 401(k) or other retirement account quarterly. So if you're thinking of changing the amount or allocation of contributions, now would be a good time to get ready.
- If you're going to make changes to your employer-sponsored health plan, the beginning of the year is also often the time for that.
- The holidays often present us with a cruel combination of time off and relentless proximity to extended family members, sometimes resulting in stress and disturbingly violent fantasies. "Taking care of some last-minute business" is one of few acceptable excuses for escape. (Picture this: While the rest of your hapless family is trapped watching Uncle Ned and Aunt Agnes's latest vacation video in the den, you're watching a movie in another room, "taking care of some last-minute business" during commercials. This alone is adequate incentive to become your household's minister of finance.)

But no matter when you do it, don't think of a financial review as a trip to the dentist. As you'll soon see, managing your money is going to be lightning fast and totally painless. Plus, since no Novocain is required, you won't drool afterward.

Financial review means nothing more than reviewing what you own, what you owe, where your money's coming from, and where it's going so you can fine-tune in order to reach your goals as quickly as possible. Let's go through the process together and see how it might look.

You start by opening your personal finance program and looking at your asset and liability accounts: what you own and what you owe. Since you've eliminated the accounts you didn't need and used savings to pay off debt, there won't be that many.

Let's have a look at debts. In this task, as in all the tasks you're about to perform, your personal finance program is the foundation for speed and accuracy, because providing you've been entering all your financial transactions, it's poised to spit out all the pertinent details relating to everything you own and everything you owe. In the case of your debts, it presents you with an up-to-the-minute picture of every dime you owe, as well as a comparison of where you are now to where you were last year so you can see whether you're making progress.

Do you have any nonmortgage debt? If so, maybe you should pay it off with savings. Your savings balances have also been updated and are right in front of you, so you can instantly see how much is available. You can also see how much interest you're paying on the debt and how much you're earning on your savings. If you decide you can spare some cash to pay down debt, you can do it by either transferring a lump sum from savings, increasing monthly debt payments so you'll pay it off faster, refinancing it, or using a combination of any or all of these.

Example: You observe that the balance on your car loan is $7,500. This five-year loan was originally $15,000 when you took it out two years and nine months ago. The interest rate is 8 percent, and monthly payments are $300. You look at your money market fund and see that your balance is $15,000, and it's earning 2 percent.

Hmmm . . . it would make sense to pay off this loan entirely, and you have the money to do it. But this money market fund is your safety net—your uncertainties fund. And you've already decided that it needs to have $15,000 in it at all times as a cushion. (Yes, you've ignored my advice about drawing down your savings to pay off debt and instead using debt for emergencies. That's okay . . . my feelings aren't hurt.) So that money is out. But paying off the debt in a lump sum isn't your only option. Maybe you should opt instead to stop adding to the money market fund every month and redirect those resources to the car loan.

Currently, you're automatically having $200 transferred from your paycheck to your money market account. Should you put that extra $200 toward paying off your 8 percent car loan instead of adding to your money market? If you did, you'd be paying $500 on the loan every month instead of $300. Let's see what would happen.

Using the calculator built into your personal finance software (or one readily available elsewhere on the Internet at sites like moneytalks.org or bankrate.com), it only takes a few seconds to compare scenarios. Here's what you discover: If you do nothing, your car loan will run another twenty-seven months, and you'll pay another $700 in interest. If you add $200 to your monthly payments, however, you'll pay off the loan in seventeen months and save about $300 in nondeductible interest. Cool. But you're also giving up the interest that your $200 a month could have been earning. How much is that? Another simple calculator tells you that $200 a month at 2 percent for seventeen months would earn less than $50 in interest, and that's before taxes. Assuming a 30 percent tax bracket, that fifty bucks shrinks to thirty-five. (70% of $50 = $35).

Bottom line? You've found out that paying down debt rather than adding to savings will leave you about $265 better off—$300 interest you won't be paying, minus the $35 you won't be earning.

While the computations to arrive at this bottom line may seem time-consuming and complicated, they were neither. The computerized calculators made it quick and easy. Much more important, you didn't need to do any calculations anyway. Because you certainly don't need a calculator to know that you'd be better off eliminating 8 percent nondeductible interest than earning 2 percent pretax. Learning exactly how much you were saving may have been interesting, but it was purely academic. All you really needed to know was that you had debt and you had the available resources to pay it off faster. Case closed. You could have checked this item off your list in less than a minute without doing any calculations at all.

If we had more nonmortgage debt, like credit cards, we might do a similar exercise. And if we had choices to make about which debt to pay first with our limited resources, we might choose to attack the debt with the fewest payments, the one with the highest interest rate . . . or maybe we'd split our $200 of surplus cash equally among them all. In any case, the point is the same. We see what we're paying, what we're earning, what's available to apply, and we move forward with a strategy.

Another thing we might do while reviewing debt is to think about refinancing a debt or two. Should we borrow against our home to pay off our car, our credit cards, or other debts?

Example: You see that you're paying 6 percent interest on your mortgage. Maybe you should refinance your mortgage, and while you're at it increase it enough to pay off the car loan and the credit cards as well. Or maybe you should just take out a home equity loan, which is also deductible, and available at a 6 percent rate. Since you itemize and are in the 30 percent combined state and federal tax bracket, after taxes a 6 percent mortgage means you're out of pocket 70 percent of 6 percent, or 4.2 percent. Your car loan is certainly higher than that . . . nearly twice as high. Your credit card interest is three times higher. You'd definitely be better off if that debt was included in your mortgage. This took almost no time to figure it out, nor did it require a calculator.

But before you start rolling your debts into a bigger mortgage or taking out an equity loan, you'd better figure out if the debts in question resulted from temporary insanity or permanent insanity. In other words, we know why you have a car loan: because you either couldn't or wouldn't pay cash for a car at that moment in time. But why do you have a balance on your credit cards? Is it because you momentarily ran amok, or because you're continually living beyond your means? If it's the latter—you're spending more than you're making—then using your home equity to pay off your revolving debt is a very temporary, and dangerous, solution, because you'll most likely run out of equity before you run out of things to buy with it. This is the kind of borrowing that, if left untreated, will ultimately leave you living in your car.

Let's assume, however, that your debts are the result of behavior that occurred in the dark days before you seized the reins. Now you live with a spending plan, save money every month, have clearly defined goals, and live below your means. All you want to do is simply dispatch those financial reminders of days gone by as quickly and painlessly as possible.

To learn the details of successfully finding a new mortgage, check out the mortgage shopping section at the end of chapter 17, "Real Estate." (This information addresses a new mortgage, but most of it applies to home equity loans as well. You can shop either type of loan at bankrate.com.) If you do opt for completely refinancing your mortgage, I'm not going to lie to you and say you can complete the entire process during a commercial break or two. But you can see what's available in seconds and you can find the best deal in minutes, so we're not talking monster amounts of time, either.

Okay, we're done with debt, and we have yet to break a sweat. Let's have a quick look at the other side of the balance sheet: savings.

Using a calculator, you subtract your age from 100. Since you're thirty (what do you know . . . we're the same age!), you come up with 70. That means you should have 70 percent of your savings in some type of ownership investment: either stocks or real estate. While the thought of rental real estate is alluring, you've already decided that it's too time-consuming to fool with at this point in your life. Therefore you decide, at least for the time being, to stick to stocks. So you should have 70 percent of your savings in stocks, with the rest equally divided between money market funds and intermediate-term bond funds—15 percent in each.

Now see if reality reflects your strategy: Let's look at your various accounts. You've got a 401(k), and so does the spouse. Within these accounts, you both have S&P 500 index funds, as well as intermediate-term bond funds and money market funds. You also have joint accounts with the same funds outside your retirement accounts. A lot of accounts, but not hard to review because when it comes to asset allocation, you're not all that concerned whether the funds are in a retirement account or not: You just want to see how the whole schmear looks percentage-wise. Nothing to it . . . you've been updating your personal finance software every month, so all your contributions to these various accounts have been recorded and everything's up to date. With the click of a mouse, your personal finance software instantly downloads today's values. Another click and you get a report presenting you with the total current value of all the money you have in stock, bond, and money market funds. This final tally includes all the money you have everywhere, in both retirement accounts and regular accounts. (Again: The details regarding taxes, withdrawals, and so forth, of these accounts are different, but for the sake of this exercise we don't much care because we're just trying to make sure we've got the right overall mix.) Here's the result:

Investment	Amount	Percent
S&P 500 funds	$40,000	35%
Intermediate bond funds	$15,000	13%
Money market funds	$60,000	52%
Total	**$115,000**	**100%**

Hmmm . . . this isn't right. You've got the wrong mix . . . too little in stocks, too much in money market. What will you do? Obviously, you're going to shift some money around. But before you do that, keep in mind that this ideal mix applies to money that you're investing for the long term. In other words, if you know you're going to be buying a car in six months or remodeling a bathroom next month, the money thus earmarked shouldn't be considered. This money doesn't exist for investment purposes because it's already committed. Likewise your uncertainties fund of $15,000: You always have that around. No big purchases planned in the next year? Okay, then all we've got to worry about is the uncertainties fund.

Let's take that fifteen grand out of the mix by pretending it doesn't exist. Now let's have another look.

Investment	Amount	Percent
S&P 500 funds	$40,000	40%
Intermediate bond funds	$15,000	15%
Money market funds	$45,000	45%
Total	**$100,000**	**100%**

Now, let's go forward and decide how to reallocate your savings so they match your ideal mix. We'll add a couple of columns so you can see what you should have, then we'll figure out how to make it happen.

Investment	Amount	Percent	Ideal Amount	Ideal Percent
S&P 500 funds	$40,000	40%	$70,000	70%
Intermediate bond funds	$15,000	15%	$15,000	15%
Money market funds	$45,000	45%	$15,000	15%
Total	**$100,000**	**100%**	**$100,000**	**100%**

Your bond funds are fine . . . no changes needed there. All you need to do is move $30,000 from money market to S&P 500 funds. If the extra cash is outside your retirement plans, you can make this transfer here and now by logging onto your mutual fund company's Web site and completing the change. If the extra cash is your 401(k) plan(s), you'll have to wait until you can make the lump-sum transfer by jumping through whatever hoops your plan requires. As with paying off debts, you could also opt for the slower route by merely changing your contributions to these accounts so that they're more heavily weighted in stocks. In other words . . . let's say you're currently contributing $600 a month to your 401(k) and each contribution is equally divided by investing $200 into your stock account, $200 in bonds, and $200 in money market. You could start putting $600 a month all into the stock account until it approaches the desired percentage. What would make you choose lump sum over gradual? If you've got a gut feeling the stock market is about to shoot skyward, ride along with a lump-sum transfer. If you're feeling squeamish about stocks, do it gradually. If you're feeling neutral, do half and half. Don't sweat it too much: Over the long term, it's probably not going to matter that much anyway.

Asset allocation is now done for this annual review. (Or for this six-month review, or this quarterly review . . . however often you choose to do it.) Although it took a long time to describe this process, it really didn't take much time to do it. Just ten minutes: a few commercial breaks.

But having now allocated your assets, you've got some questions and concerns about the hows and whys of moving money. So before we move on, let's answer them.

Having so little in cash makes me nervous. What if I suddenly decide to buy something expensive, and the stock market has tanked. I'll have to sell out at a bad time. Trouble, right?

Yes, you could potentially be in trouble if at some point you need more cash than you have available in money market funds. And the last thing you want is to allow circumstances to force you to cash out any investment that fluctuates in value, which includes both the S&P 500 index fund and, to a lesser extent, the intermediate-term bond fund. As anyone who's been in the investment business for more than fifteen minutes knows, portfolio performance is always inversely related to your need for cash. In fact, even if your stock or bond investments have increased in value, you still don't want to sell them because unless they're in a retirement account, you'll pay taxes on the gain. This is why you may opt to keep extra cash around. Hey . . . it's your plan, not mine. You decide how much cash you need to have around at all times so that you feel comfortable. Just keep in mind the cost.

The cost of your cash cushion is whatever you're losing by not having that money in stuff that pays more. And this isn't always easy to determine. When the stock market is zooming, the cost is high. When the stock market is falling and money market funds are paying 15 percent, you're way ahead by keeping your powder dry. Historically speaking, however, if you want to know what your cash cushion is costing over the long run, the answer is in the range of 5 to 7 percent per year. Because money market funds traditionally pay about the same rate as inflation, and owner-type investments traditionally pay 5 to 7 percent more. So having an extra $10,000 around "just in case" will cost you about $500 to $700 every year over the long term. Still, that's fine. Just because that's what it's costing doesn't mean you're an idiot—any more than you're an idiot when you pay for insurance. Because that's exactly what a cash cushion is. Just be aware of what it costs, and weigh it against what you're buying: peace of mind.

Bottom line? Asset allocation is designed to make you as much money as possible, but comfort always comes first. There's no return that justifies nail biting.

I see the logic of investing in stocks, and I'm all for it. But my husband is a sniveling wimp. He's saying that any amount in stocks keeps him up at night. What now?

You could get divorced, but you'll probably find that this is more expensive in the long run than reducing your stock percentage. So you should either slip him some Xanax before bedtime or reduce your stock percentage until he feels comfortable, even if this means taking it all the way to zero. As I've said, the subtract-your-age-from-100 formula is a rule of thumb. It's designed to give you a simple starting point, but it's just a starting point. The only right answer is the answer that's right for you. Maybe he'd like some other ownership investment better, like rental real estate.

You say to subtract my age from 100, but there are two of us . . . whose age should I be using?

Use the older person's age, unless you like the outcome better when you use the younger's age instead. Or average your ages. In other words, it's not that big a deal either way. Stop being nitpicky and get on with it already.

In the example above, you had me shifting $30,000 from money market into stocks. That's a big chunk of cash to throw at the stock market all at once, isn't it? And what if I don't have any excess money every month to add to my stock account?
You're right to be concerned about putting so much into stocks all at once. And if you don't want to fool with putting new money into your stock account every month, or don't have any, maybe you should transfer money gradually out of your money market fund instead. That way you're using a dollar cost averaging approach instead and making the transfer over a longer period of time: maybe a year, even two. (Remember dollar cost averaging? It's explained in chapter 9, "The Only Investment System You'll Ever Need.") This makes sense, and it will definitely be a stress reducer. It doesn't have to take additional time away from Jerry Springer, either: Just instruct your mutual fund company to do it for you automatically every month. So now you've got three choices: lump sum, new additions, or dollar cost averaging existing money. You can also combine these approaches. This is a personalized, long-term investment strategy. There's no reason to rush, and in the great scheme of things there's nothing wrong with taking a year or two to reach the right mix. The only instance in which you'll regret the slow approach is if the stock market surges while you've still got money waiting on the sidelines. But nobody can predict what the stock market will do over the next year or two, so don't worry about it; set it and forget it.

What about taxes? Since I don't have to pay taxes on the gains in my retirement plan, at least until I take the money out, wouldn't it be better to put my S&P 500 index fund in my 401(k) and have the money market part of the mix held outside the plan?
One of the beauties of an S&P 500 fund is that since changes to the S&P 500 index are rare, there's not much trading in these funds. And if there's not much trading within the fund, there's not much in the way of gains or losses to report and not much in the way of taxes to pay. In other words, this type of fund isn't going to create tax traumas for you whether or not it's held in a 401(k) or

another tax-advantaged account. Another thing to consider is the taxes you'll be paying on your money market funds and intermediate-term bond funds. As I write this, interest rates on these things are so low they're laughable. But I can also remember a time back in the early 1980s when money market funds were paying 18 percent interest, and the stock market absolutely sucked. In this scenario, you'd be a lot better off tax-wise with your stock funds in regular accounts and your money market shielded from taxes in your 401(k). Bottom line? Don't sweat it either way, but if you can manage it, spread your stocks and other types of investments roughly evenly between retirement and nonretirement accounts. Over the long term, this will require less fiddling around.

Okay, now you've reviewed your debt and allocated your assets, kicked around a few options, made some plans, and fine-tuned your finances. Unless you're doing something intense, like taking out a new mortgage loan, total time spent shouldn't be more than half an hour. Let's move on and do some comparison-shopping and see if we can save some money. During the next commercial break, we'll comparison-shop your insurance policies.

As you know from our discussion regarding organizing and shopping insurance, once you've dissected, understood, and recorded the pertinent prices and details of your policies, shopping your insurance can be extremely quick and virtually painless. (If you don't remember this process, have another look at chapter 16.) The sharper you make your pencil, the more time it will take . . . in other words, if you demand the best possible deal ever struck in the history of humankind, you'll have to shop harder and take more time doing it. But if all you want to do is to see that you're still in the ballpark deal-wise and to remind yourself of how much you're paying for what you're buying, you can do it during commercial breaks: one break for each type of policy you have. And as you review the policies, make sure that the coverage you have still meets your needs. Paid off your mortgage? Spouse recently get a humongous raise? Kid just get drafted by the NBA? Maybe you can reduce or eliminate your life insurance. Getting rich? Maybe you need to increase your automobile liability. Start working from home? Maybe you need to add coverage to your homeowner's policy to protect your business equipment. You get the drift . . . open your personal finance software, put your financial information on the screen, then look at the insurance you've always paid for but now understand. If you need to make changes, make them. If you don't, you're done until the next time you choose to review everything.

Speaking of the next time you review, let's pause and talk about how often you should be reviewing expenses like insurance. A good rule of thumb is every other year. But there are exceptions. As I just said, if your financial situation changes radically, you need to make sure your insurance reflects your needs. Another time I choose to review my insurance coverages is when my bill goes up or my benefits go down. Keep in mind that the lion's share of consumers don't understand exactly what they're paying for when they buy insurance. They're basically content to follow the herd and hope for the best, which makes them vulnerable to rate increases. Therefore, when an insurance company (or a mechanic, doctor, lawyer, plumber, or other potential predator) asks me for money, that's when I comparison-shop. It's a simple reminder to myself and to them that I'm not their next meal.

Bottom line? Review insurance once every other year, or when:

- Your overall personal and/or financial situation changes, because this could alter how much coverage you need.
- The price you're being charged goes up. This is to make sure your insurance company isn't confusing you with someone who would rather write checks than understand why he's writing them.
- The coverages you're receiving are decreased but the price isn't. See the explanation above.

Since we all have a boatload of insurance, what I do is review insurance relating to property (car and home) one year and insurance relating to my body (health and life) the next. This way I never take more than a couple of commercial breaks a year to stay on track.

Okay, so much for insurance. What else can we review? We look at our spending plan every month to make sure we're staying on track, and we seem to be doing fine. But since it's annual review time and Uncle Ned and Aunt Agnes are still out there, let's see what the income taxes are looking like, and then maybe see if we can squeeze a few extra pennies out of the household budget while we're at it.

How will we check out our tax picture? Instantly, that's how. We've already got our personal finance software open: All we have to do is go to the "taxes" tab and select "tax planning." With the click of a mouse, the program imports information from last year's tax preparation program, compares it to the information we've input for this year, and presents us with a list of questions to consider for minimizing our liability. All this happens in less than ten seconds. We go through the questionnaire and come up with some ideas. In addition, now that we understand how taxes work and how it's possible to shift deductions by prepaying expenses, taking losses before year end, and using other timing techniques, we're also able to make a few suggestions of our own. When we're done, a few minutes later, we're now informed regarding what to expect and we're confident we've done whatever's possible to plan the outcome to our greatest advantage. We've also got a great head start on our taxes, and it's not even January yet!

Since we're on a roll, and we can still hear the vacation video droning on, let's hang for a few more minutes and see if we can save a few bucks. We look again at our expense summary for the year, casually glancing at where our money's been going. Here's an interesting item: phone service. We're paying $40 a month for local service. Didn't we hear that there are now options available for local phone service? Wonder if we could do better than Bell? For this search, we don't have to use the Internet; we just have to open the local phone book. There it is . . . on page five of my white pages: a long list of local service providers. Let's call one and see if it can beat the deal we're currently getting from Ma Bell. We log onto Bell's Web site and bring up our latest bill to see what we're paying, then call competitors listed in the phone book and start shopping.

We won't go all the way through this exercise, but if your situation is like mine was, you'll probably end up saving some money by doing it. I saved $40 a month by switching my local service away from BellSouth as a result of doing exactly this. Granted, my local phone bill is probably a lot higher than yours, so it was easier for me to save this kind of dough. (I have three lines because I work at home.) Still, by making a simple spreadsheet and making a few phone calls, I saved nearly $500 a year. When compared to watching commercials, I'd call that time well spent.

What about long distance? Here the Internet can be a huge help. There are lots of long-distance comparison sites, easily found by doing a search for "long distance comparison." (Phonesaver.com, trac.org, and getconnected.com are three I've tried, but this doesn't mean you can't find ones just as good or better.) I went from 6 cents a minute to 3.9 after doing this exercise. Again, I probably use more long distance than the average person, so this was a big deal to me. But no matter how much you use, it's not hard to shop, it's not hard to switch, and if you can save more than 30 percent by doing it, why wouldn't you? Especially when it's so quick and easy.

When shopping for long distance, you're obviously interested in cost per minute, but you're also interested in billing increment. That's how the service prices your calls. Some companies have a one-minute billing increment, which means that if you talk for six seconds, you get billed for a full minute. The company you choose, however, will have six-second billing increments (the lowest I've found) which means that if you talk for six seconds, that's all you'll pay for. You also want to ask about rates for in-state calls, and if there are any monthly service charges or minimums.

So much for local phone service and long distance. We close our price comparison spreadsheet, which now contains information pertinent to local and long-distance phone service, including Web site addresses, phone numbers, and notes, so we'll have a starting point next time we feel the urge to do this. Is there anything else we can do?

Of course, the answer is yes. We can, if we choose, go down our entire list of expense accounts and try to find ways of saving money in any of these categories, or all of them. If our imaginations fail us when it comes to exactly how to save money, we can go to one of the many Web sites dedicated to money-saving tips and seek out ideas. (You've got a bunch of them bookmarked, right?)

Or we can close our program and watch the movie, leaving some of this stuff for another day. Whatever we decide, it's fine. There's no hurry, because whenever the money-saving mood strikes and we feel like fiddling with our finances, a glance at our expense report is all it takes to know exactly where we need to focus. And we know exactly where to look on the Internet for a plethora of ideas on saving in virtually any category. Our money doesn't control us. We control it, so there's no rush.

When it comes to bringing it all together, I hope you now realize that it's a lot easier than you thought it was—and certainly a lot easier than it used to be. Technology has made it possible to do many tasks in seconds that used to take hours, even days. In fact, some tasks now take zero time, because they're virtually automatic. All that was missing is the logic behind the way things work, which I hope you now have. The common sense to understand this logic you've always had.

No matter what your situation, I feel confident that you're now better prepared to tackle your personal world of money, and do it as quickly as possible. More importantly, I hope you'll feel more comfortable about the processes involved, now that you finally understand what you're supposed to be doing and why you're supposed to be doing it. This will result not only in maximum comprehension, but minimum apprehension.

As to speed, how many actual minutes it will take to manage your personal finances, that's impossible to say, because personal situations are infinitely variable. A person who just graduated from college making $25,000 a year is certainly going to spend a lot less time at their computer than a family with four kids in college making $250,000 a year. But what I hope you gained from this chapter, and this book, is the following. First, the knowledge required isn't that big a deal. You can learn it, whether you were an English major, an accounting major, or work in diesel repair. Second, once you do, it won't take much time to stay on top of things, especially once you're organized. And third, and most important: there's nobody out there more qualified to control your investments than you, and there's certainly nobody more interested in the outcome.

CONCLUSION

Your current circumstances are
nothing more than the embodiment of your past beliefs.
So take note of where your thoughts wander ...
that's where you'll likely end up.

—Stacy Johnson

As I conclude, the first and most important thing I have to say regards Jerry Springer. I've made many references to watching Jerry Springer throughout this book, so it's important that I now tell you: I wouldn't watch Jerry Springer if he were standing in my living room. (The thought that I share a genus and species with the people appearing on his show sends chills up my spine.) In fact, I'm not a huge proponent of TV in any form. I refer to "commercial breaks" in so many instances simply because it's a measurement of time our society has become, sadly, all too familiar with.

The smartest thing that I did when I wrote my first book, *Life or Debt,* was to include my e-mail address at the end. This is because I got so many cool e-mails from people who liked it and thought it changed their lives for the better. The value of such comments to my fragile ego cannot be overstated. So I will now repeat this exercise and hope like hell for a similar outcome. It's stacy@moneytalks.org. Groupies, especially, take note.

My news series, *Money Talks,* airs within the local news of some station or another (no particular network affiliation) in about ninety cities nationwide. There are, however, more than two hundred cities with local news, so it's certainly possible that you can't see me where you live. This is a tragedy of indescribable dimension. If you're not seeing me on any of your local newscasts, then either you'll have to move, or I'll have to sell *Money Talks* to some station in your market. Which option is better depends on how much you like where you live, but it will be probably be easier in the long run for me to end up on the air in your market. I'm trying, believe me. Bottom line? If you want to see me on TV, write Gina at answers@moneytalks.org and she'll tell you if it's possible where you live. And if it's not, I'll try to fix that. And if I can't? Then I'm sorry, but you'll have to move.

There: That concludes the commercial portion of this chapter. Now let's get to the reason we gathered here today, which is a conclusion to this book.

Odds are good that we only live once, at least in the body we're currently occupying. So I really hope that you're doing it as well as you possibly can and will continue to do so. The part I'm attempting to play in helping you live well isn't to make you rich. It's to help you find adequate resources to align what you do with who you are. And when I use the word "resources," I refer not only to money, but to time. Because while money is important, its only true value is buying time. That's what *Life or Debt* was about, and that's what this book was also about. Not buying things; buying time. Because when you're lying on your deathbed, as your life passes you by, I doubt very much that you'll be smiling at the things you've had. You'll be smiling at the times you've had.

Hopefully a lot of what I've laid out here will help you feel in control of where your money is going, and enable you to manage it a lot more effectively in a lot less time. If you're successful in freeing up this time, please do me and everyone else on the planet a favor by using it to do what you were put here to do. Maybe it's making people laugh. Maybe it's discovering the cure for cancer. Maybe it's writing a book, or reading one. Maybe it's putting your toes in the sand and thinking profound thoughts. Whatever it is, you're hopefully now equipped to find it faster.

So here's my final advice. When it comes to making money and accumulating physical possessions, don't buy into Madison Avenue's idea of happiness. Because unless you're as shallow as a puddle, you'll never find happiness in a $50,000 car, a $2,000,000 house, or a closet full of clothes. For me happiness is hanging with my wife, making my friends laugh, riding my motorcycle, and reaching out to give objective advice to complete strangers via TV and print. When you find out what it is for you, make exactly enough money to achieve it: not a penny more. Because if you don't, you'll be wasting time that can never be replaced.

INDEX